P9-AZW-627

"Collaboration in the nonprofit world is very complex. You try to collaborate with people who share your values, but who also compete for the same funds and often work with the same constituencies. Yet collaboration is critical because it can create the power necessary for positive social change. Russ Linden's book gives us excellent guidance, useful ideas, and inspiring examples of people who overcame the collaboration obstacles to create exciting change. It is highly recommended for anyone who wants to promote social change in collaboration with others."

—Rachel Licl, Israeli executive director, New Israel Fund

"Russ Linden has written a book that is at once practical and inspiring. Collaboration is learnable, and he shows us how with compelling stories from education, government, industry, and real life. All health care professionals will benefit from Linden's approach and the thoughtful ideas in this important book."

—Dorrie K. Fontaine, Sadie Heath Cabaniss Professor
of Nursing and dean, University of Virginia School
of Nursing, and author, *Critical Care Nursing*

"Collaboration is vital in our networked society and this book offers great insight into the collaborative process. This book is a must-read for anyone interested in better problem solving and decision making."

—Tom Martin, captain, Virginia State Police (retired)

"Hard knocks have taught the big lesson: we need far better collaboration in doing the public's work. Saying it and getting it, however, are two different things. In this imaginative and creative new book, Linden not only nails down the case for stronger collaboration, but he also identifies—in clear and convincing language—the steps leaders need to take to achieve it. That's an invaluable contribution to anyone charged with shaping organizations, big and small."

—Don Kettl, dean, University of Maryland School
of Public Policy, and author, *The Next Government
of the United States*

"Government is increasingly turning to non-hierarchical ways of doing business, often called collaborative networks and boundary-less organizations. Linden has written a practical guide to collaborative leadership, providing policy makers and program managers a clearer understanding and examples showing how to become collaborative leaders who can work across organizational boundaries in ways that achieve broader outcomes."

—Jonathan D. Breul, executive director, IBM Center for The Business of Government, and former senior executive, U.S. Office of Management and Budget

"Linden's book challenges us to re-think how we work and to step outside our comfort zone into new ways of interacting. He gives numerous examples of the synergistic effects of collaboration—leading to new and sometimes unanticipated levels of productivity, efficiency, and innovation. This is a must-read for administrators who strive for success, regardless of setting!"

—Timothy W. Griffith, director, Baltimore County Department of Social Services

"I read Russ Linden's book *Leading Across Boundaries* and found it immediately relevant to my own work. This book is a desktop manual for public sector and nonprofit practitioners who truly want to understand the mechanics of collaboration in a Web 2.0 world and practice it effectively to make a difference."

—Cristine Nardi, executive director, Center for Nonprofit Excellence

"In the mid-90s, as we in Army Intelligence formed the National Ground Intelligence Center, we could have done the job with much less 'broken china' had we applied Linden's collaboration concepts! He provides an exceptionally clear treatment of a complex issue—a comprehensible road map for establishing a collaborative environment. This work is a must read for any mid- to senior-level managers and executives who want to enhance cooperation, information sharing, and overall mission accomplishment among independent organizations."

—Bill Rich, former executive director, National Ground Intelligence Center

Leading Across Boundaries

Creating Collaborative Agencies in a Networked World

Russell M. Linden

JOSSEY-BASS
A Wiley Imprint
www.josseybass.com

This publication is a companion to *Working Across Boundaries:*
Making Collaboration Work in Government and Nonprofit Organizations.

Published by Jossey-Bass
A Wiley Imprint
989 Market Street, San Francisco, CA 94103-1741—www.josseybass.com

Readers should be aware that Internet Web sites offered as citations and/or sources
for further information may have changed or disappeared between the time this was
written and when it is read.

Jossey-Bass books and products are available through most bookstores. To contact
Jossey-Bass directly call our Customer Care Department within the U.S. at 800-956-7739,
outside the U.S. at 317-572-3986, or fax 317-572-4002.

Jossey-Bass also publishes its books in a variety of electronic formats. Some content that
appears in print may not be available in electronic books.

Additional credits are listed on page 319.

Library of Congress Cataloging-in-Publication Data
Linden, Russell Matthew.
    Leading across boundaries: creating collaborative agencies in a networked world /
Russell M. Linden. —1st ed.
        p.   cm.
    Includes bibliographical references and index.
    ISBN 978-0-470-39677-3 (cloth/website)
        1. Interorganizational relations.   2. Organizational change.   3. Corporate
culture.   4. Complex organizations—Management.   5. Business
networks.   6. Strategic alliances (Business)   I. Title.
    HD30.3.L547   2010
    658'.044—dc22
                                                                    2009048366

Printed in the United States of America
FIRST EDITION
HB Printing   10 9 8 7

Contents

Part 1. Creating the Foundations of Collaboration   1

Lessons from Cisco Systems' transformation to a decentralized culture that rewards collaboration, how the Millennial Generation can transform your agency, and how collaborative leaders develop and foster a collaborative mindset to make a difference

Tables, Figures, and Exhibits

Tables

Figures

Exhibits

Major Case Studies

The following table summarizes the major case examples presented in this book.

Case	Chapter	Sector and Issue
Hurricane Katrina	1	*Federal government*. FEMA got all the (terrible) headlines, but Thad Allen and the Coast Guard made a positive difference after Katrina struck.
Alliances for Graduate Education and the Professoriate	2	*Academia*. Nine universities form an alliance to increase the number of minority students in graduate school programs.
Jamestown, New York	5	*Local government*. A strategic planning commission works with the mayor, city council, and key stakeholders to improve economic conditions in an old industrial town.
Interagency Network of Enterprise Assistance Providers	6	*Federal government*. Agencies form a network to share information and improve services to businesses.
Tobacco initiative	7	*Nonprofit sector*. Tobacco farmers and health advocates join forces to improve health and create sustainable options for tobacco communities and families.

Case	Chapter	Sector and Issue
Neighbors for Joint Development in the Galilee	8	*Nonprofit sector (international).* Residents from neighboring Arab and Jewish villages in Israel learn to communicate and work on projects that benefit both municipalities.
Joint Intelligence Virtual Architecture	9	*Federal government.* Intelligence agency analysts form virtual teams to share information and collaborate on common problems (with mixed success).
Financial Management Service	9	*Federal government.* A new leader creates major cultural change in a balkanized agency.
Integrated Air Defense System	9	*Federal government.* Intelligence agency analysts form virtual teams to share information and collaborate on common problems.
Internal Revenue Service	10	*Federal government.* A new manager has to deal with a strong, control-oriented manager in order to restart a failed IT program.
Virginia Retirement System	10	*State government.* An agency head transforms a top-down agency where information hoarding was once the norm.
Buffalo arts organizations	11	*Nonprofit sector.* Three arts organizations co-locate in order to share ideas and information, improve programs, and save money.
Child Advocacy Center	11	*Local government.* Police and social workers co-locate and work in teams to prevent and deal with child sexual abuse.
Fusion centers	11	*All government levels.* Officials from homeland security, intelligence, police, and other units are co-located and share information to help first responders deal with threats.

Case	Chapter	Sector and Issue
Government Management Accountability and Performance	12	*State government.* Washington's governor uses a structured method to hold managers accountable for real outcomes on shared goals and her priorities.
Cisco Systems	14	*Private sector.* Cisco Systems transforms itself from a classic top-down hierarchy to a model of decentralized collaboration for a networked age.

Web Contents

Collaborative Leadership Self-Assessment

Expanded Case Studies

    Financial Management Service (FMS)

    Internal Revenue Service (IRS)

    Fusion Centers: Issues and Critical Success Factors

Simulations on Collaboration

    Friday Night at the ER

    The Search for the Lost Dutchman's Goldmine

Articles

    Abraham Lincoln: Leadership Lessons for Our
      Times (and All Times) (Chapter 5)

    The Power of Resilience (Chapter 5)

    What'll It Cost Me? (Chapter 6)

    Getting Stuck on the Escalator (Chapters 9 and 10)

    When Adults Act like Children (Chapter 10)

    Getting Off the Dance Floor and On the Balcony (Chapter 14)

To Jackie—
For working so hard to support our own collaboration, and for sharing in its many joys

Introduction

Collaboration is vital, difficult, and learnable.

Vital. In today's networked world, the most important work is done through collaboration—working across organizational boundaries. Whether the work involves protecting children from abuse, developing clean sources of energy, providing quality health care, improving our schools, or working with a host of other issues, nonprofit and government agencies are dealing with increasingly complex challenges. Meeting these challenges successfully is vital to our nation's well-being. Yet none of them can be solved by any one agency or skill set: complexity by its very nature requires a variety of perspectives. That is to say, it requires collaboration.

Difficult. Simply put, collaboration is not for the faint of heart. In Chapter One and throughout the book, I'll be discussing a host of collaboration hurdles. Some of them stem from people's psychological wiring (think of the delightful egotists and information hoarders who sometimes make you wonder why you came to work that day). Some are organizational, like the hiring, measurement, recognition, and promotion systems that focus people on individual performance (even though the agency's leaders stress teamwork). And some hurdles are built into the very fabric of our individualistic society.

Learnable. Like chaos theory, which reveals the order beneath seemingly random events, there is an underlying structure to successful collaboration, a framework that helps people work across boundaries. There is nothing mysterious about this framework; one doesn't need advanced training or magical leadership skills to learn it. Indeed, one of my objectives in writing this book is to take the mystery out of collaboration and to help you apply your skills and knowledge effectively to that endeavor. The main requirement is a fierce desire to work in partnership with others on common concerns and common aspirations.

Why I Wrote This Book

I've taught several thousand managers and leaders since the release of my 2002 book *Working Across Boundaries*, a book that takes a broad look at collaboration's challenges and potential. I've learned an enormous amount from these students. Conversations with them have convinced me that the art and craft of collaboration is learnable, and feedback from them has guided me in making some revisions in my collaborative framework. I've also seen a steady decline in the number who ask, "Why should we collaborate?" and an increasing hunger for an answer to the "How do we collaborate?" question. So one reason for this book is to provide a structured, detailed guide to the how of collaboration, and Part Two is devoted to explaining the process and also offers several strategies for overcoming the hurdles.

A second reason for this book is to stretch readers' minds about a number of emerging trends that are changing the way work is done in some agencies. New structures, methods, and systems are showing us powerful ways to foster collaborative cultures. These are detailed in Part Three.

The third, and most important, reason for this book isn't about collaboration per se. Rather, it is to demonstrate that the most important unmet societal needs can only be addressed through collaboration. When we learn of yet another child who has fallen through the social services safety net and been injured or killed by his "caregivers," of a failure to share information among intelligence agencies, or of several nonprofits duplicating each other's programs and refusing to join forces, it makes most of us angry. Which it should. What's needed is to harness that energy and focus it on change. More than anything else, this book is about leadership for change. Collaboration is a means, a critical means, for making our most important changes.

Who Should Read This Book

This book is written for practicing managers and leaders, the people most responsible for our organizations' performance and outcomes. These individuals deal with the challenges of working in a networked world every day, and they have the greatest impact on organizational cultures and direction. They need practical guidance for making collaboration work—tools, strategies, and tips from experienced practitioners. This book offers that and more.

This book is also of value for academics, especially those who teach courses for graduate students, mid-career managers, and executives. Academics and their more advanced students should find special value in this book's many case studies, the conceptual framework offered in Part One, the model for collaborative process in Part Two, and the emerging trends described in Part Three.

Finally, this book is for tomorrow's leaders. Research is showing that many employees in their twenties and thirties are natural collaborators. Sharing information, working in teams, and forming informal networks are talents that are part of their mental software. But how can they use these preferences and skills in agencies that are still configured around hierarchy? How can they add value and fulfill the desire to make a big difference if their managers and leaders don't put them into appropriate leadership roles? The younger members of our agencies can use this book to find insights into these riddles and to take inspiration from the many examples of exciting collaborative projects that started in the middle levels of an agency, not at the top.

Organization of This Book

This book is divided into three parts. Part One, "Creating the Foundations of Collaboration" (Chapters One to Five), makes the case for collaboration, describes the hurdles, and explains my collaboration framework. Chapter One includes examples of critical collaboration failures as well as successes. It describes two major impediments to collaboration and a number of benefits. It also illustrates an ongoing tension in American life—our need for autonomy versus our desire to connect to something larger than ourselves. Effective collaborative leaders find ways to meet these fundamental needs.

Chapter Two is a detailed case study of a federal manager who has helped universities in California and other states develop alliances to increase the number of minority students going to graduate school. This manager used each of the key elements in the collaboration framework, which I begin to describe in Chapter Three. That chapter looks at five of the seven framework elements. Chapter Four focuses on a sixth element in the framework (trusting relationships) and offers a variety of strategies for developing trust in collaborative teams.

Chapter Five describes the final factor in the framework, collaborative leadership. In a sense the entire book is about collaborative leadership, but this chapter spells out the collaborative leader's characteristics and skills. It includes a detailed study of a collaborative leader who helped public and nonprofit groups work together to resuscitate a blue-collar town that has been losing population and jobs for decades.

Part Two (Chapters Six to Ten) focuses on dealing with the process and people issues involved in collaboration. Part One takes a big-picture view of collaboration; Part Two tackles the concrete and specific issues involved. Chapter Six details the processes and steps for getting started. A case study describes an alliance formed by several agencies to better serve their small business clients. Chapter Seven tackles a major process issue: How can collaborative teams create common direction and gain agreement? Many of the insights in this chapter come from the story of an unlikely nonprofit alliance of tobacco growers and health advocates that forged common direction around shared interests, contributing to national breakthroughs in smoking and health.

Chapter Eight addresses the issue of working across different organizational cultures. How can teams work effectively when team members represent organizations with different values, norms, and operating environments? The answer to this question draws on lessons from an Israeli nonprofit that helps Arabs and Jews overcome enormous cultural and political differences to work on significant projects of common interest.

Chapters Nine and Ten address the difficult people and difficult situations involved in collaboration: the people with "silo" mentalities, the "800-pound gorillas" who accumulate power and share nothing, the perfectionists, and others. I'll offer a continuum of options for dealing with such fascinating souls, including the most profoundly difficult people. The case examples discuss the IRS, intelligence agencies, and two financial services agencies.

Part Three, "Developing Sustainable Collaborative Cultures" (Chapters Eleven to Fourteen), considers the future and some intriguing emerging trends. Here I'll describe structures and methods and systems that are changing the ways some public and nonprofit agencies are operating. The ideas in Part Two are especially important for those leading collaborative teams; the ideas in Part Three are critical for leaders who want to grow more collaborative cultures.

Chapter Eleven focuses on a structural change—co-locating different units in the same space in order to share information and staff and to integrate certain operations. The cases present the co-location experiences of nonprofit arts agencies, a child advocacy center, and fusion centers (where personnel from all levels of government, health care, and other areas share information to increase public security). Chapter Twelve offers an in-depth look at a powerful method known by several names: CompStat, CitiStat, and PerformanceStat. This method gives leaders a way to forge collaboration on an organization's top priorities and to hold managers accountable for real results. We'll take a close look at the State of Washington, which is using this methodology to improve the lives of people in the state.

Chapter Thirteen addresses the exciting development of Web-based tools that help people share information and work together. This chapter isn't written for techies; it's for managers and leaders who want to harness Web 2.0 tools to engage people in pursuing their agency's mission and making change in society. We'll look at several examples of formal and informal groups that are using the Web to create new programs, capture employees' innovative ideas, and even save lives.

Finally, Chapter Fourteen looks at the people most able to transform agency cultures—today's leaders and tomorrow's. In particular, it shows how Cisco Systems moved from a top-down structure and "cowboy" culture to a decentralized structure and a culture of information sharing, collaboration, and high performance. It also presents an analysis of the Millennial Generation, the young people now entering the workplace, whose attitudes and preferences seem perfectly suited to working in a networked world. And it ends with guidance for leaders who want to open people's minds to different ways of thinking and acting.

Some Suggestions for Readers

Notice the Book's Major Themes

This book reflects the following themes and assumptions, which I've developed since my study of collaboration began in the mid-1990s.

- There is an underlying structure to most collaborative efforts, made up of seven key ingredients (described in Chapters Three, Four, and Five).

- Most people in Western countries have two fundamental needs that must be met if they are to be effective in the workplace. These needs are (1) to be competent (and respected as such) and (2) to belong, to connect to something larger than themselves.

- These two needs are expressed in four questions that most team members ask (not necessarily out loud):

  1. Do I have something to contribute that is needed, recognized, and used by the team?

  2. Are we working on a project that is important to me and my own organization?

  3. Are we making progress; do we have a reasonable chance for success?

  4. How will this project support or threaten any of my core needs or interests (and those of my home organization)?

- When members of collaborative teams perceive positive answers to these questions, they're much more likely to move from *me* thinking to *we* thinking, the key transition in any team.

- Collaboration is a powerful strategy and set of skills, but it isn't for everyone. It is a *means to an end,* not an end in itself. But for almost all work that has any level of complexity, it is the preferred approach.

- Effective collaboration is about more than a framework, strategies, and new structures. It's also about a *collaborative mindset.* Some of the largest collaboration hurdles reside in the *software of our minds* (to paraphrase the title of a wonderful book by Hofstede and Hofstede, 2005)—

hurdles that stem from our fear of losing control, from our zero-sum assumptions (your gain is my loss), from our desire for individual recognition, and from our need for neat and tidy solutions in a world of messy problems.

• Collaboration does not have to begin with senior leadership action. In fact, the great majority of cases in this book were initiated from the middle of organizations. Senior leadership is vital for creating a collaborative culture, but for most collaborative projects it isn't the overriding factor.

Note These Definitions of Key Terms

A number of words are often used today in discussions of collaboration. Here are my definitions of the key terms. They may also be seen as describing levels of partnering, from least to most.

Cooperating	Sharing information; being polite; "playing well with others."
Coordinating	Joint planning; adjusting to others' actions when implementing plans (but not working on joint projects).
Collaborating	Two or more units or agencies working together on a common project or service. This may also be called *partnership*; I use *partnership* interchangeably with *collaboration*.
Integrating	Fusing functions from several agencies together: for instance, creating one payroll department for several government agencies or one intake unit for a group of nonprofit human service providers.
Merging	Creating one new organization from two or more formerly separate ones: the Department of Homeland Security was created this way.

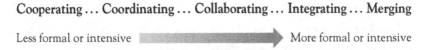

Figure I.1. Collaboration Continuum.

These terms and levels are not mutually exclusive, of course. Each level builds on the previous one(s). This book focuses primarily on collaborating, with some examples of integrating functions. Figure I.1 captures these different terms as a continuum, ranging from less intensive to more intensive.

Make This Book Your Own

I hope this book stimulates your thinking. Even more, I want it to affect your practice of collaboration. So please make this book your own. Scribble notes in the margins; debate the concepts; adapt or add to the various tips and strategies. And I hope you'll use the exercises in this book. Just before Part One, you'll find a Self-Assessment. If you use it before you start the first chapter and use it again after you finish the last chapter, you'll be able to gauge how your thinking may have evolved while reading this book. In addition, on page 90, you'll find an assessment you can take to evaluate your collaborative leadership skills.

Finally, Resource A offers a structured tool for checking the status and progress of your own collaborative projects. You can use it with a collaborative team to compare team members' perceptions of the team's status and to stimulate important conversations about how to move forward.

Why I'm Passionate About Collaboration

In 1957, President Eisenhower appointed the first members of the newly created U.S. Commission on Civil Rights. These six individuals reflected the varying beliefs of the nation at that time, and Ike wondered if they could ever come to agreement. After two

years of meeting they reached an impasse. So one member, Father
Theodore Hesburgh, president of the University of Notre Dame,
brought them to a picturesque retreat site in Wisconsin. During
dinner they discovered that they all loved to fish. Hesburgh saw
an opening. He got a boat and took the group for a fishing trip on
the lake. They fished, they relaxed, and they talked. And in that
setting, they discovered some common ground. The commission
soon issued resolutions that were reflected five years later in the
landmark Civil Rights Act of 1964.

Hesburgh understood some things about collaboration. He
knew that it is *vital*; the nation had to let go of its segregated past
and embrace people of all races. He knew that collaboration is *difficult*. The commission's first two years demonstrated that as commission members frequently saw no way to find common ground.
Yet Hesburgh and his colleagues ultimately also demonstrated
that collaboration is *learnable*. And we are all the better for their
perseverance.

I am passionate about the topic of collaboration because there
is simply no other effective way to address the most pressing issues
facing our communities and nation. In a networked society filled
with complex and interconnected problems—schools filled with
kids who don't learn, a global economy, a reliance on nonrenewable energy sources that pollute and are in part controlled by
countries that support terrorists, ethnic tensions, the outsourcing
of millions of jobs, and global warming, to name a few—working
in partnership with others is no longer just important. It is vital.
Because it is also difficult, my fervent hope is that this book makes
it more learnable.

August 2009

Russell M. Linden
Charlottesville, Virginia
russlinden@earthlink.net

Self-Assessment

I invite you to make this book more useful by responding to as many of the following questions as you find relevant. Respond before you read the book in order to focus your reading. Respond again after you have completed the book so you can gauge how your thinking may have changed.

1. What are the most challenging aspects of collaboration for you? And what are the most challenging for your agency?

2. What are your strengths as a collaborative leader? And what would you like to improve?

3. How do others view your collaborative interests and abilities? And how would you like them to view your interests and abilities?

4. *If you're currently working on a collaborative project*, what would help your collaborative team move from being a set of individuals to having a team identity, that is, from *me* to *we*?

5. What higher purpose do you want this team to achieve?

Part 1

Creating the Foundations
of Collaboration

In the mid-1980s, a basketball coach gave a talk to one of my management classes. He discussed the importance of team chemistry and talked about getting to know his players well and about developing their leadership skills. He actually sought input from his players, sometimes asking for their suggestions during time-outs, and encouraging the players to continually give each other feedback on the court and off.

The most interesting comment he made had to do with a question about the qualities he sought in players: "I look for many things, but none is more important than 'court vision.'" How's that? *Court vision*? "That's what I call it when a player has very wide peripheral vision. When a player looks at one spot on the court but can see what's happening in a 180-degree arc. Players who exercise court vision usually excel."

People who collaborate well also have good court vision. Like successful basketball players and other team athletes, they communicate laterally, look for ways to share ideas, and form relationships well. They tend to be natural networkers, understanding that organizational success relies at least as much on horizontal as hierarchical relationships.

Collaboration is a mindset, a way of seeing and interacting with the world. It is also a discipline. Like all disciplines, it is built on certain principles and practices. What are those practices? What are some examples of those who collaborate well? And how do you develop court vision if it doesn't come naturally?

These are some of the questions we'll address in Part One.

1

The Promise, and Challenge, of Leading in a Networked World

The future is already here; it's just not very evenly distributed.

—*William Gibson*

Something powerful is happening in the United States. Public and nonprofit organizations that have typically worked on their own and created incentives for their employees to do likewise are now creating partnerships and rewarding collaborative behaviors in new and creative ways. Here are some examples.

"The Future Is Already Here . . ."

In the Arts

Nonprofit arts organizations have long struggled for financial support in this country. Too often they have struggled alone. Today some are sharing space, staff, and even information about funders in an effort to improve their bottom lines and programs. More than that, they're finding that co-locating (sharing the same physical space) generates creative ideas for new programs (more on this trend in Chapter Eleven).

In Law Enforcement

Information sharing is always a critical need in the law enforcement community. LInX (Law Enforcement Information Exchange) is a regional law enforcement information-sharing program developed by the Naval Criminal Investigative Service that is meeting that need. LInX helps state and local agencies electronically share law enforcement records and analyze information. Member agencies include state and local police departments, county sheriffs, U.S. Department of Justice agencies like the Federal Bureau of Investigation (FBI) and Drug Enforcement Administration (DEA), U.S. Department of Homeland Security agencies, and criminal investigative service agencies in the armed services.

Participating agencies provide information on crimes, suspects, arrests, and so forth, to a centralized data warehouse. Law enforcement officers can quickly access LInX to gain information from multiple jurisdictions. LInX also helps agencies collaborate on joint investigations. Because of this network, LInX partners no longer have to check multiple databases to pull together information on a suspect or crime. LInX has helped law enforcement officials to find suspects accused of sexual crimes, kidnappings, assaults, and other illegal acts when no other database could provide a "hit." As of 2009, there were more than 500 law enforcement agencies in the LInX program, with approximately 25,000 authorized users sharing data.

In Human Services

In Cedar Rapids, Iowa, the *Patch* approach emphasizes service integration for children and families. Patch (a British term for neighborhood) assigns an interdisciplinary team of nonprofit and public-sector staff to work with families in need in each given neighborhood. The families get to know and trust the staff, who view themselves primarily as part of their team, not as members of separate agencies. Team members exchange information regularly on their shared clients. They also work with the natural helping networks in the neighborhood (churches, clubs, neighbors), some of which become *partners* to the families in need. Perhaps most important, Patch team members take an *integrated* approach, viewing each family as a whole and dealing with the family through its members' own geographical and social networks.

Through the Web

The development of *Web 2.0*, the highly interactive tools that enable consumers to post, edit, and discuss content on the Web, has been breathtaking. Today, people with no special technology skills can determine the contents of news Web sites like digg.com, edit the content of the online encyclopedia Wikipedia, exchange comments on their department leaders' blogs at the Department of Homeland Security, and post videos about innovations on the Coast Guard's YouTube channel.

> *One of the major trends on the Web is creating a sense of community.*

One of the most significant Web trends is the way these new Web tools foster a sense of community among users. When Craig Newmark created craigslist, he wasn't looking for a quick buck. Rather, he wanted to make it easy for people to advertise what they need to buy or sell. And did he ever! Today, craigslist receives 3 billion page views a month. All ads are free (except for businesses posting job listings). Craigslist users frequently refer to it as a community; users interact with each other without direction from someone in charge (there is no one person in charge).

Among Unusual Suspects

And it's not just agencies partnering with like agencies. One of the intriguing trends involves agencies partnering with *unusual suspects*—groups that appear to be unlikely partners. The U.S. Bureau of the Census partners with over 140,000 groups for the decennial census. For example, in partnership with cities like Los Angeles, it trains sanitation, utility, and other city workers to spot people who might be living in the city but wouldn't normally be counted (looking for signs of converted garages, multiple TV antennas, multiple mailboxes, and the like). The result? Over 38,000 nonstandard dwellings were confirmed in LA for its 2000 census, adding significantly to the city's population count.

Among Public and Nonprofit Funders

And many funders, from small private foundations to local United Ways to huge federal agencies, are insisting that grantees must collaborate in order to receive funding. One of the most exciting examples is in the area of biomedical research. "Fed up with the glacial pace at which new discoveries become medical treatments, . . . [some funders] are insisting that the scientists they fund swear off secrecy in favor of collaboration" (Begley, 2004). Gail Johnstone, former director of the Community Foundation for Greater Buffalo, notes the same trend in the nonprofit world. By the start of this century relationships among many nonprofits were "way beyond communication and coordination. There was a widespread culture among nonprofits in which funders were saying, 'collaborate, collaborate, collaborate!'"

". . . It's Just Not Very Evenly Distributed"

These examples point to the good news. Yet even with the explosion of collaboration successes, there continue to be failures and missed opportunities. And that's the bad news. Sometimes it's the tragic news. On April 16, 2007, a mentally unbalanced Virginia Tech student named Seung-Hui Cho killed thirty-two students and faculty before taking his own life. The Virginia Tech Review Panel spent months studying the incident and found that many professors at Tech realized that Cho was in serious trouble and spoke up to senior school officials, yet little was done to deal with his needs and his threat. As the panel concluded: "During Cho's junior year at Virginia Tech, numerous incidents occurred that were clear warnings of mental instability. Although various individuals and departments within the university knew about each of these incidents, the university did not intervene effectively. No one knew all the information and no one connected all the dots" (Virginia Tech Review Panel, 2007, p. 2).

And there were many dots to connect. After Cho was accused of stalking two female students in December 2005, a Virginia special justice declared him mentally ill and a danger to himself, and ordered Cho to get outpatient treatment. He never received the treatment, although he sought help three times at the University's Counseling Center; and nobody at Tech took responsibility to see that he did, although one English professor tried desperately to get him into counseling. The order to seek treatment wasn't entered into the National Instant Criminal Background Check System, and that meant Cho was able to buy the two guns he used in the shooting spree. In one class that Cho attended, most of the roughly thirty other students stopped attending because of Cho's bizarre and sometimes frightening behavior (he was finally removed from the class).

Noting the information silos that existed at Tech, a law professor who met with the Virginia Tech Review Panel said, "There was no single person, office or team that oversaw the whole process for troubled students at Tech. Nobody was in charge."

That last sentence bears repeating: nobody was in charge. As public administration scholar Don Kettl writes, "the intersection of the American constitutional separation-of-powers system with federalism ensures that no one is ever fully responsible for anything" (Kettl, 2009, p. 61).

Dealing with Complex Challenges in a Networked World

If the good news is that there are many exciting examples of collaboration from which to learn and the bad news is that we have a very long way to go, the challenging news is that there is little choice anymore. "The 21st century will be the age of alliances," predicts James Austin (2000, p. 1), who studies nonprofit-corporate partnerships. Goldsmith and Eggers (2004) write that "governance by network represents ... trends that are altering the shape of public sectors worldwide" in their insightful book *Governing by Network* (p. 9). Abramson, Breul, and Kamensky (2006) include networks and partnerships as one of "six trends transforming government."

Why the huge emphasis on collaboration? There are many factors, but perhaps the most significant has to do with the *complexity* of the challenges facing public and nonprofit agencies today. Pick up a newspaper or check your favorite news Web site, chances are you'll be reading about issues that are enormously complex:

- Pandemics
- Global economy
- Narcotic trafficking cartels
- Kids who struggle in school
- *Nonstate actors*, such as Hezbollah and other terrorist groups
- Global warming
- Piracy (!)

These and other problems require multiple skill sets and mindsets. One of the most significant realities of our networked age is this:

The most significant challenges facing our society cannot be addressed by any one organization. They all require collaboration among many organizations.

Hurricane Katrina Reveals the Challenges and Promise of Collaboration

A profound example of complexity requiring collaboration began on Monday morning, August 29, 2005, when Hurricane Katrina hit the Gulf Coast. It was the costliest and one of the five deadliest hurricanes in U.S. history. Billions of people around the world watched in disbelief as the world's superpower seemed astonishingly unable to save the inhabitants of a major city. Close your eyes and no doubt you can still conjure up images of desperate people clinging to the tops of their houses, pleading for help as the waters rose.

Government at all levels failed the people of New Orleans despite the valiant efforts of thousands of people who worked countless hours to save the city and its citizens. Most of the subsequent anger focused on the federal government's emergency management agency, FEMA. Many reasons have been offered for FEMA's dismal performance: it lost its independent status when it was moved to the Department of Homeland Security in 2003; the FEMA director no longer had a cabinet-level position, thus losing direct access to the president; post 9/11 the agency was primarily focused on human threats, not natural ones. Each of these is true, but there's another critical factor.

Michael Brown's main problem was his mindset; he thought his job was to manage FEMA.

In the months after Michael Brown was fired because of FEMA's poor performance during Katrina, he argued that he had managed FEMA well but couldn't control other agencies outside his span of control. Seems reasonable at first glance, no? Actually, Brown's statement reflects a mindset totally inappropriate to his task. As Don

Kettl (2009) has argued, Brown's primary job during the disaster was to *develop partnerships* in order to take care of the storm's victims and get the city running. To borrow the term used by the basketball coach mentioned in the Introduction to this section, Brown lacked court vision. He didn't accept the task of creating an alliance with the other players who had to be involved in the game.

This broader job definition wasn't a radical notion at FEMA. Indeed, one of the many gifts that James Lee Witt brought to FEMA when he led it from 1993 to 2001 was his emphasis on forging partnerships with local communities (for a thorough look at FEMA's use of networks during the 1990s, see Waugh, 2004). Witt's successors stopped emphasizing partnerships. They defined the job as managing a hierarchy, not developing a network of partners. A number of potential partner organizations around the country contacted FEMA to offer assistance after the storm struck. Tragically, many such offers weren't taken.

Katrina is the poster child for all that can go wrong when complex challenges aren't addressed by a collaborative response. Multiple agencies with overlapping jurisdictions quarreled and pointed fingers as people died; an out-of-state manager helping with the cleanup counted at least six New Orleans agencies that had independent police authority. Relationships that should have been well established prior to the storm were weak or nonexistent: a senior emergency management official was stunned to see some members of Governor Blanco's cabinet introducing themselves to each other at a special state cabinet meeting held soon after the storm hit. Lessons learned from training exercises designed to prepare the city for a huge storm were ignored.

Before you throw your arms up, don't despair. There's also a wonderful side to the Katrina story that needs to be emphasized.

Thad Allen—A Different Leader, a Different Mindset

On Friday, September 9, 2005, Thad Allen, an officer of the U.S. Coast Guard, was appointed principal federal official in charge of search, rescue, and recovery efforts during the post-Katrina period, replacing Michael Brown. His no-nonsense demeanor started to create a sense of confidence. Despite extraordinary challenges, Allen and his colleagues were able to slowly start turning things around.

Over the course of the next three weeks, thousands of people were rescued from New Orleans, most of them by the Coast Guard. A sense of order was returned to the city, rescue and recovery efforts were better coordinated, and many of the key political players who'd been pointing fingers at each other just after the storm hit were starting to cooperate. Allen received considerable credit for this improvement. How did he do it?

- One of his first moves was to invite a number of his most trusted colleagues to work with him in New Orleans. Virtually all said yes. Then, Louisiana Governor Kathleen Blanco issued a blistering statement criticizing the federal government for failing to retrieve bodies from New Orleans waters. Allen ignored the White House when it urged him to bash Blanco. Instead, he called her and asked, "Governor, have I done something to give you the impression that I'm interested in anything else but helping the people of Louisiana?" (Kitfield, 2005, p. 1). That call helped soften her criticism and bought a little time.

- Within twenty-four hours of arriving, he and Army lieutenant general Russel Honoré established a planning group that met daily (Honoré was commander of the Katrina Joint Task Force). The two also reported daily to New Orleans Mayor Ray Nagin and Governor Blanco on their goals for the next day. They kept polit- *Allen is a strong believer that "transparency of information breeds self-correcting behavior."* ical leaders informed and involved at every step. Allen told those reporting to him that they were "to treat every citizen they helped as if they were a family member" (Newcomer, 2006, p. 14).

- In both symbolic and substantive ways, Allen acted on one of his favorite sayings: "Transparency of information breeds self-correcting behavior" (Kitfield, 2005, p. 1). He told reporters that he would meet with key rescue officials and other stakeholders, have an open discussion, create a clear direction, and move on out. He opened up the recovery process to the media, inviting the media to become partners in telling the public what was being done to help the residents.

- Allen, who was promoted to Commandant of the Coast Guard in 2006, relied on an approach refined by the Coast Guard over the years: focus on *strategic intent*. Rather than develop detailed plans, he sought agreement with partners on a general direction and major priorities, determined who was responsible for what, gave partners great flexibility, and emphasized constant communications.

- Allen defined his role as coordinating a huge network of agencies. His team leveraged about 130 boats from other organizations. They got local responders to share knowledge of the city with those who came from out of state. They worked closely with a variety of state, local, and federal government agencies and nonprofits that arrived to help.

- Throughout, Allen and his team emphasized open, ongoing communications. He focused on the partners' agreed-upon results, not on policies and procedures. The preexisting relationships with the individuals he brought from the Coast Guard were also critical to dealing with an unprecedented emergency.

Michael Brown and Thad Allen: Hierarchical and Collaborative Mindsets

As painful as Katrina was (and still is), its lessons are powerful for anyone interested in collaboration. Table 1.1 captures the key differences between Brown's and Allen's approaches for dealing with the great storm. My point isn't to portray one as a superhuman hero and the other as totally responsible for inept government responses

Table 1.1. Dealing with Katrina: Comparing the Approaches
of Michael Brown and Thad Allen.

	Michael Brown	Thad Allen
Focus	Manage his agency.	Lead a network.
Key assumptions	Can only use formal authority to accomplish goals.	Can use relationships, influence, the media, and peer pressure to achieve goals.
	Need senior leader support to succeed.	Need strong partnerships pulling in same general direction to succeed.
	Go by the book.	Be flexible, use requirements of the situation to set your course.
Communications	Control the message tightly.	Shine a light on the operations; show the public your work.
Political power	You gain power through access to senior leaders.	You gain power by listening, speaking truth to those with power, making good on the promise, and delivering results.

to a massive disaster. No single person was responsible for either the failures or the successes (of which there were many). The reason for contrasting Brown's and Allen's leadership styles is simply this: their performance during Katrina reflects key differences between the bureaucratic hierarchical approach and the collaborative approach.

Note: For an excellent discussion of the different approaches Allen and Brown used in New Orleans, see Kettl, 2009.

Two Overriding Collaboration Challenges

As collaboration veterans know, there are many hurdles to successful collaboration (see Exhibit 1.1), and most of them were reflected in the Katrina episode. Collaborative leaders like Thad Allen are far more effective at dealing with these challenges than are leaders who think in hierarchical terms. Here I'd like to describe two mega-challenges to collaboration: our organizational structures and systems and our individualistic nature.

Trying to Solve Twenty-First-Century Problems Using Eighteenth-Century Structures

If we get up to 30,000 feet and survey the collaboration landscape, it becomes apparent that one of the biggest hurdles to collaboration lies in the very DNA of our public and nonprofit organizations. To put it simply, we're trying to address complex, twenty-first-century problems using eighteenth- and nineteenth-century organizational structures and systems. These rigid forms are vestiges of another, more stable era. They reflect industrial-era thinking. Goldsmith

---

Exhibit 1.1. Common Collaboration Hurdles.

- Egos
- Turf
- Fear of losing control, autonomy, mission, resources, quality
- Different cultures
- Lack of trust or history of antagonism between the parties
- Lack of resources or competition for resources
- Power imbalances
- No perceived reward for collaboration
- Lack of time
- Different goals among the parties
- Silo mentality
- Concern that exchange between parties won't be reciprocal

---

and Eggers put it well in *Governing by Network* (2004): "Rigid bureaucratic systems that operate with command-and-control procedures, narrow work restrictions, and inward-looking cultures . . . are particularly ill-suited to addressing problems that often transcend organizational boundaries" (p. 7). In addition, for a variety of reasons, the services and information provided by our public and nonprofit agencies are frequently *fragmented.*

That fragmentation enormously complicated the rescue efforts after Katrina hit; thousands of people were working their hearts out to save lives, yet each of their agencies saw only part of the problem. An assistant fire chief from northern Virginia who worked for several weeks in New Orleans reflected that "the government and recovery effort was very fragmented. There was a total disconnect between city, state and federal efforts. . . . The groups working there were independent and didn't endorse a holistic approach to the overall recovery effort." Public and nonprofit agencies often have difficulty trying to take a holistic approach to their challenges. There are many reasons why this is so (see Figure 1.1).

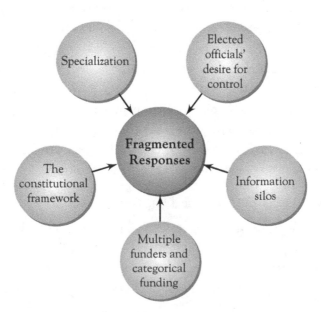

Figure 1.1. Causes of Our Fragmented Organizational Responses.

The Constitutional Framework

The framers of the U.S. Constitution had one overriding purpose: to prevent tyranny, either of another king or of any one arm of government. Their main strat-

The framers' strategy of separating power has prevented tyranny but has also made it incredibly hard to solve complex challenges.

egy was *separation*; three separate branches of federal government, separate powers through checks and balances, and a further division of power between the federal government and the states. It was a brilliant solution. It suited our inherent distrust of government. There's just one problem: dividing power into so many slices makes it incredibly hard to tackle big challenges. And we live in an environment of extremely large and complex challenges.

Our strategy of separation results in the proliferation of public and nonprofit entities, often doing similar work. To cite just one example, in Iowa there are over 1,000 general units of government (cities, towns, counties, school divisions, and so forth). Of that state's ninety-nine counties, eighty had fewer than 30,000 people as of 2006. But when Governor Tom Vilsack proposed merging some localities to increase efficiency and reduce the costs of redundancy (every jurisdiction has its own administrators, jails, police, and other functions), the state legislature quickly shot the idea down. When power is fragmented across so many units, we end up in situations where, to paraphrase the late cabinet secretary and Common Cause founder, John Gardner, there are 100 people who can veto a project, but no one person or office that can move it forward.

Multiple Funders and Categorical Funding

The way we fund social services, health care, and certain other programs contributes to fragmented services. When foundations and government provide separate funding for programs dealing with such problems as drug use, child abuse, gangs, and teen pregnancy, the result is a myriad of specialized services, each of which addresses one part of the problem. This (non)system of funding developed for understandable reasons: parents, advocates, providers, and public and nonprofit funders focus on specific needs of high-risk populations, and they don't want resources for their cause mixed into a larger pot where their interest could be lost. Thus individual programs develop intense and powerful constituencies, but those programs are often too narrow and fragmented to work.

One study of programs serving at-risk students in Los Angeles found 238 separate programs, each serving one aspect of the students' lives. As Lisbeth Schorr (1997) writes, "categorical funding that divides services into small, isolated pieces has made it almost impossible to prevent trouble before it starts" (p. 81). This kind of funding is a major challenge for service providers who want to take a holistic approach. The creative Patch program described at the start of this chapter, in which people from multiple disciplines and agencies form a team and work together closely to provide integrated services, is a delightful exception.

Specialization

As we gain more knowledge about certain technical issues, the professionals in that area inevitably specialize. That's appropriate, but it requires systems and processes that synthesize the specialized knowledge for the client. If you or a loved one has had a serious illness, you've experienced this issue. When an older cousin of mine became critically ill, his family dealt with different specialists who offered different diagnoses and different treatment options. The family needed a strong advocate to get the physicians to talk (and, even more challenging, to listen!) to each other, and they needed a wise internist to help them develop a holistic plan.

Lisbeth Schorr (1997) documents the same problem in human services. She describes a meeting with three professionals who were working with the same family. The social services counselor was concerned about the teenager's gang involvement, the school social worker focused on the seven-year-old's school absences, and the school nurse worried that both kids continually came to school with very dirty clothes. And the mother? She was upset that they'd gone six weeks without electricity in the house! Moreover, each professional knew of that problem but noted that it wasn't in his or her job description to call the power company. As Schorr comments, "Workers concentrating on specialized functions often lose sight of the family as a whole" (p. 82).

Elected Officials' Desire for Control

It's difficult to keep track of the number of committees and subcommittees in Congress, but it's not difficult to understand why there are so many. Control of committees and subcommittees conveys power: over money, over staff and priorities, and over policy development. When committees use their power to create separate programs for favored causes (each with its own staff and sometimes its own senior agency official), that only adds to the fragmentation of services.

Congress also contributes to fragmentation by making it difficult for agencies to share costs when working together on joint programs. As John Kamensky, former federal executive and Senior Fellow at the IBM Center for The Business of Government points out, a provision in federal appropriations law prohibits cost sharing on joint projects unless one agency is designated the executive agent or project owner (and when one agency is in charge, others are sometimes reluctant to share costs). Some agencies have received Congressional approval for cost sharing, but obtaining this approval is often a long, tedious process. Congress also adds to fragmentation through its committee process; when dozens of committees and subcommittees have control over parts of an agency, they sometimes send conflicting signals to the programs they oversee.

Information Silos

Our tendency to compartmentalize information is well known. Some strong leaders, like Thad Allen, are able to overcome or manage the problem, but every leader struggles with it. *The 9/11 Commission Report* emphasizes the problems caused by poor information sharing in the months prior to the 2001 attacks. It states that the "biggest impediment to all-source analysis—to a greater likelihood of connecting the dots—is the human or systemic resistance to sharing information" (National Commission on Terrorist Attacks Upon the United States, 2004, p. 416). A good deal was already known about the nineteen men who attacked our country on that horrific Tuesday morning, but the information held by one agency wasn't given to another or it was shared but got lost at some middle-management level or it was disclosed but in an overly compartmented fashion.

Each of these factors fragments information and service delivery, but none of them is insurmountable. Indeed, this book details cases of collaboration that overcome every one of them. The Virginia Retirement System developed ways to eliminate information silos in the 1990s (Chapter Ten). The analysts in a virtual team in the intelligence community work in different agencies but integrate their specialized knowledge seamlessly to help defend the country (Chapter Nine). Through the INEAP partnership, public and nonprofit managers in agencies that support small businesses are overcoming their different categorical programs to provide integrated solutions to shared clients (Chapter Six). Fusion centers are co-locating staff from all levels of government, nonprofits, and private-sector firms to share and analyze critical information and communicate it to first responders (Chapter Eleven). Washington State has even found a way to bypass the duplication of services created by thousands of units of government; the state has a powerful method for holding agency heads from different levels of government accountable for common goals (Chapter Twelve).

These and other examples can give us hope and teach us important lessons about surmounting the structural problems in our service systems. But there is another mega-challenge, not written into organizational charts but equally important: it's the individualism that's coded in our mental software.

Coping with the Expectations of a Highly Individualistic Society

Geert Hofstede, an anthropologist who has studied the cultures of over seventy countries, uses questionnaire data to identify their distinct natures. One of the factors he studies is the degree of individualism or collectivism in a culture, which is closely related to the ease of collaboration.

In individualistic societies, people are expected to look out for themselves and their immediate families. In collectivistic societies, people are integrated into strong extended families and in-groups from birth and are expected to give them strong loyalty. Here are some more specific core expectations:

In Individualistic Societies	In Collectivist Societies
Look out for yourself (and your family).	Take care of the group.
Speak your mind.	Maintain harmony.
Be independent.	Be interdependent.
Recognize that the individual is responsible and gets credit.	Recognize that the group is responsible and gets credit.

Table 1.2 shows the scores of selected nations on the individualism-collectivism dimension. The higher a country's score, the more individualistic it is. Of over seventy countries surveyed, the United States has the highest level of individualism—91 out of a potential 100. Although these numbers are striking, they shouldn't surprise us. American leaders from Jefferson forward

Table 1.2. Individualism Scale Scores of Selected Countries.

Country	Score	Rank
USA	91	1
Great Britain	89	3
Italy	76	9
Ireland	70	15
South Africa	65	19
Israel	54	28
India	48	31
Japan	46	Tied for 33rd
Mexico	30	Tied for 46th
China	20	Tied for 56th

Note: The higher a country's score, the more individualistic. For the complete listing of scores on this dimension and the other cultural dimensions, see Resource B.

have preached the importance of "rugged individualism." When French political philosopher Alexis de Tocqueville came to the United States in the 1830s to learn how democracy was working in the largest country yet to try it, he was struck by our strongly individualistic natures: "[Americans] acquire the habit of always considering themselves as standing alone, and they are apt to imagine that their whole destiny is in their hands" (Tocqueville, [1835] 1956, p. 194).

Tocqueville expressed great admiration for Americans, but he worried about the excessive individualism that democracy was creating in the new nation: "[democracy throws every person] back forever upon himself alone, and threatens in the end to confine him entirely within the solitude of his own heart" (p. 194). In their wonderful study of American individualism, Bellah and others (1985) concluded that "[i]ndividualism lies at the very core of American culture" (p. 142).

In many ways our individualistic streak has served us extremely well. The implications for collaboration in the United States and other highly individualistic countries, however, are challenging. Collaboration, after all, is about co-labor, not individual effort.

We're Also a Nation of Joiners

But there's another narrative to the American experience, one that Tocqueville also documented. This perceptive Frenchman described ours as a society filled with "voluntary associations" and concern for the public good. He noted that we're a nation of joiners, that when we get upset about something in our community we organize with others in order to take action. Tocqueville's great contribution was to note this ongoing tension or duality in American life—we embrace both a strong individualist ethic *and* a desire to join together for common purpose.

Psychologists David Waters and Edith Lawrence came to a similar conclusion from a different vantage point. Reflecting on their decades of experience with individuals and families in therapy, they identified two fundamental human needs: mastery and belonging. They argue that most people need to feel a sense of competence or mastery in some part of their lives and need to be recognized for that competence. People also need to be part of something larger than themselves, to belong to some group or organization or movement that reflects their core values.

Tocqueville discusses individualism and voluntary associations. Waters and Lawrence use the terms mastery and belonging. Different words, similar concepts. I believe there are two fundamental needs at play here: for *autonomy* and for *connection*. Collaboration helps meet the need for connection, but it seems to be at odds with the American urge for autonomy.

Me Versus We? Or Both?

"People must simultaneously be 'me,' an independent individual, and 'we,' an interdependent part of groups." That's the claim of Jessica Lipnack and Jeffrey Stamps (1997), two experts on networks and virtual teams. "Each of us grapples with an inevitable and continuous ten- *Autonomy and connection* sion between the need to *differentiate*—to *are complementary, not* enhance our individuality —and the need *contradictory, needs.* to *integrate*—to bond in groups" (p. 112). Their conclusion: cooperation requires individuality.

To reframe Lipnack and Stamps's words a bit, the two divergent themes in American life—individualism and collectivism or autonomy and connection—aren't necessarily contradictory. Rather, *me* and *we* are complementary parts of our psychological makeup. Many of us, including the most individualistic, have a strong desire to connect with something larger than ourselves. And, when that "something larger" is a collaborative team, team members can meet both the me and we needs as they contribute their special talents and unique knowledge and experience to a successful group project.

THE BOTTOM LINE

Collaborating across boundaries can be deeply exciting and maddeningly difficult, both uplifting and confusing. It calls on our best instincts and requires us to push back at some of our basest motives. The challenges to collaboration are wired into the very DNA of our organizations, and into our psyches. Yet the problems facing us in today's interconnected world can only be addressed through intelligent collaborative responses. And as

Thad Allen's example demonstrates, when we get it right we can lift spirits and save lives.

Fortunately, we have many examples of collaboration to study. The media are all too good at highlighting our collaboration failures, of course, and we do need to understand them. But it is more important to understand why some collaborative efforts succeed. Chapter Two describes one such example. It's about a collaborative leader, Roosevelt Johnson, and his extraordinary efforts to increase the numbers of minority students entering graduate school. Johnson, like Thad Allen, has a collaborative way of thinking. He also uses the principles that are present in most successful collaborative efforts.

2

AGEP

A Collaborative Project That's
Making a Big Difference

Changing an organization's culture isn't rocket science;
it's harder!

—John Hancock, Department of Veterans Affairs

A merica's universities are widely heralded as the finest anywhere, and many of them are truly gems, attracting wonderful young students from around the world. When it comes to fostering collaboration among faculty, however, most universities are case studies of how not to do it. University cultures are famous for rewarding individual performance and creating information silos, and most academics love their autonomy. Yet a federal manager named Roosevelt Johnson found ways to create collaboration among nine extremely competitive campuses in California and then successfully transferred the lessons learned to universities around the country. His is an inspiring story. It's also a first-rate example of using a collaborative mindset.

Alliances for Graduate Education
and the Professoriate

It was early in 2000, and Roosevelt Johnson faced a dilemma. Johnson, a National Science Foundation (NSF) veteran, was excited by the opportunity he'd just been given: leadership of the NSF's Minority Graduate Education program. The program was very much in synch with Johnson's values and life trajectory. An African American who grew up in the segregated South, he knew firsthand the challenges facing minorities who wanted to pursue advanced degrees, and he was passionate about the program's goal of increasing the number of minority students (Hispanics, Native Americans, Pacific Islanders, and Alaska Natives as well as African Americans) enrolled in U.S. doctoral programs in science, technology, engineering, and math (or STEM).

But he was also perplexed. His predecessor had changed the focus of the program from funding individual universities to using a collaborative model. How could he get the nation's universities to work together on this project? It was a challenge with no obvious answer. But Johnson loved it: "this is when the fun started," he recalled some years later.

Crafting a Strategy

Johnson's manager created a new name for the program; it was now called the Alliances for Graduate Education and the Professoriate (AGEP) program. The goal of the program was to increase the pool of well-trained minority graduate students earning PhDs in science, technology, engineering, and math. Johnson looked around for a *target*, a group of universities that might be open to the new alliance approach. He studied the map, and his eye fell on California. "This was pure intuition," Johnson reflected. "I had no formal background or training to tell me where or how to start. But the potential lured me into trying first with the University of California [UC] campuses. It's a gem of a system. If it worked there, I thought it would have a domino effect. And starting there would teach me a lot about how to create alliances elsewhere, how to get AGEP going."

Johnson wasn't naive about the challenges. The enormous UC system had nine campuses. Even though it was the largest producer of minority PhDs in the country, it would be the most difficult to deal with in terms of size and complexity. In 2000, three of the UC campuses—Irvine, Berkeley, and San Diego—had already received

NSF awards of $500,000 each for increasing minority graduate enrollment; although the three had said they would move toward an alliance model, they'd made little progress. And there didn't seem to be any benefit for them in moving toward a collaborative effort.

Johnson wasn't deterred. He remembers thinking, "Time is on our side; sooner or later each campus would have to be part of an alliance to get NSF funding" (that was a requirement under the alliance model). Johnson had something else on his side: the vote by California voters in favor of Proposition 209, which mandated that California institutions of higher education could no longer use race as a determinant for student admissions. UC leaders still embraced the goal of a diverse student body but had lost a key tool for achieving that goal. AGEP could be a method for achieving greater student diversity.

Engaging the President's Office

Johnson had a strategic decision to make: At what level to enter the UC system? He chose to start at the top. He called the UC Office of the President (UCOP) to see if the system's leaders were interested in the alliance approach. When he asked UCOP staff about minority enrollment issues, they turned the question around—What does the NSF want us to do? He offered to help them explore the feasibility of forming an alliance on their terms but refused to be directive. "I thought they knew their needs better than I did, so the best I could do was to help them figure out what they wanted to do given the fiscal and political constraints."

Johnson was working with a senior administrator in the UCOP who showed real interest in the program and the alliance concept. "She became a genuine champion for doing this program in a collaborative way," he noted. "UC didn't have a history of working as a system when it came to federally funded programs. She helped set up the key meetings that got us started."

Johnson controlled the grant funds, but he wouldn't tell the university leaders exactly what he wanted.

Engaging the Deans and Faculty: The Road Trip

It was easy to gain entry at the three UC campuses already in the program. But some of the other six hadn't yet begun to think about an alliance approach. Johnson had the campus leaders consider one question: If they formed an alliance, what would they expect to get out of it? "My thought process was simple: if I could find a common thread among the campus leaders, then I knew I could get them talking to each other."

Johnson arranged to spend a week visiting the nine campuses. The UCOP office charged each dean with identifying the key people who were interested in increasing minority enrollment in graduate education. Johnson made it clear that he didn't want to talk money in this first round. He emphasized that there would be a brainstorming session at each campus; he had no agenda, he was coming to listen. "I had fairly low expectations . . . no lofty idea of emerging with a mega-agreement. It seemed like a quick and easy way to learn about graduate education issues."

Johnson looked for a common thread to help the parties start communicating together.

Johnson went to California in May of 2000 and spent an exciting but grueling five days visiting all nine campuses (Figure 2.1). Typically, he met with deans, department heads, directors of minority programs on campus, and some interested faculty. At some of the meetings, money was among the very first questions raised by the deans and faculty. Johnson's typical response was, "Let's not talk money yet, let's see how much agreement we have on ideas first." If the ideas were solid, the money would follow.

At each meeting the dean introduced the topic, and Johnson listened as the group discussed what they might gain from forming an alliance. "I let them have a free-for-all at the meetings, to learn what was on their mind and what obstacles they faced: Too few applicants? Applicants who are accepted but don't want to come to your campus? Not enough support systems once minorities are on your

Figure 2.1. The Nine University of California Campuses.

campus?" Many of them hadn't thought about these questions, so the questions fostered important discussions.

Johnson recalled that "when I showed up at one campus, some-one told me that they had a running bet going that I wouldn't make it to all nine campuses!" As he made each one, the interest at the upcoming campus increased. In fact there were a few deans who'd planned to be on vacation on the meeting date but who attended when they learned that he was making each meeting. "The more seriously they realized I took it, the more seriously they took it. I later learned that I was the first NSF program officer to visit California" (this was largely due to NSF's poor travel budget).

After about the third day, Johnson started telling participants that he was finding certain

The deans and faculty had a number of common interests; the problem was that they didn't know it.

things in common among meeting participants across the campuses. Most important, they shared a strong interest in greatly increasing diversity in graduate programs. That changed the flavor of the meetings; the deans and the faculty hadn't realized they wanted the same things.

At the end of each meeting Johnson asked the participants if they thought there was any consensus, and what their next steps should be. He told them what he'd do next (determine what money was available), and he suggested some activities to consider that would be fundable under the program.

The Tipping Point: One Dean Steps Up

During Johnson's meetings at the three campuses already receiving NSF money for the program, he told participants candidly that the alliance might involve a temporary loss of resources for their campus's projects. He added that if they would sacrifice a little now, he'd get that money back to them. How do you get a group of deans to relinquish federal grant money they're currently getting, on the *promise* that the government agency will provide it again in the future? Johnson recalls a key event:

> There was a graduate dean at Berkeley who was extraordinarily respected. He stepped up and said, "We've got to do business differently. I'll take a cut." Because he was so respected, and because he offered to give up money, it persuaded deans at the other two schools to go along.
>
> When the word got out to the [other] six campuses that the "big three" were giving up some of their award money to help the others get into the alliance, that was a tipping point. It changed the whole complexion of everything, because this was unprecedented. You have to understand academia: these nine campuses are fierce competitors—for good graduate students, for faculty, for resources, for virtually everything. People hadn't seen one campus give up resources to help another.

Follow Up: Getting the Alliance off the Ground

Johnson returned to the NSF, put together a report summarizing what he learned from the nine meetings, and sent it to participants at each campus. The bottom line was, "Here are some goals you all want to accomplish. Some of these goals are only doable if you work as an alliance. And here are the items I can fund." He got the UCOP to provide some money for the alliance as well, which helped.

Although Johnson tried to avoid being overly directive, he did make a few recommendations to the nine campuses. One was to form a steering committee for the AGEP effort. He suggested that it be made up of the major players from each campus, that it be balanced in terms of numbers from each campus, that the chair should rotate, and that the meetings needed to rotate from campus to campus, so that everyone would share responsibility. The campus leaders took his advice and formed an AGEP steering committee. Everything done by the alliance is worked out by the steering committee. The California AGEP program was up and running in a year. It continues operating to this day, led by the steering committee.

The Results: Some California Accomplishments

AGEP's impact can be gauged in both quantitative and qualitative ways. Here are some qualitative indicators:

- *Recruitment of students*. Prior to AGEP, UC campus recruiters focused on their own school, went to conferences on their own, and didn't have a system-wide focus. Now they go to conferences as a team, sit next to each other at conferences, and share information and ideas about students and their needs.
- *Admissions*. When an alliance school doesn't accept a student, it sometimes forwards that student's application to the other alliance schools. The result: some students end up getting accepted to a school they didn't apply to! It's all done seamlessly.
- *Retention*. The alliance schools have a number of joint curriculum activities and workshops for their minority graduate students.

Table 2.1. AGEP Results, University of California.

Minorities	Before AGEP	After AGEP Started
In all graduate science, technology, engineering, and math (STEM) fields	Average of 149	296 (in 2007)
Receiving doctorates in STEM graduate fields	Average of 82	128 (in 2007)
As a percentage of total STEM graduate enrollment	7.4%	10% (in 2007)

Topics include interviewing skills, making public presentations, and how to select a postdoctoral position. Rather than being offered nine separate times (once at each campus), these activities are offered once or twice a year, and the students from the various campuses are brought together to participate in them. This approach also fosters networking among the students.

"California's experience solidified the concept of an alliance approach to increasing graduate minority enrollment. It really legitimized the concept," Johnson believes. "With California's success, there was no way other institutional leaders could say that this couldn't work." Table 2.1 shows some of the quantitative results for California.

AGEP's Impact Across the Country

When a group of Iowa universities showed an interest in AGEP, Johnson coached them on how to obtain NSF funding for an AGEP program and how to work together once they received their grant. In just a few years this Iowa alliance became a poster child for diversity. Table 2.2 has the results for one university in the Iowa alliance.

Beyond achieving these numbers, AGEP helped the University of Iowa develop a structure and culture to attract and retain minority graduate students. "Roosevelt stressed the need to take a holistic approach and aim for institutional change," remarks Phil Kutzko,

Table 2.2. AGEP Results, University of Iowa.

	Before AGEP	After AGEP Started
Minority enrollment in graduate math	9%	22% (7 years later)
Minority enrollment in graduate engineering	5	23 (2 years later)
Total minority enrollment in graduate science, technology, engineering, and math departments	35	70 (six years later)

Note: Rows 2 and 3 show actual numbers of individuals.

Table 2.3. AGEP National Results, 1997/1998 to 2005/2006.

	All Other Universities	AGEP Universities
Change in percentage of minority graduate students in natural sciences and engineering	15.6% increase	25.4% increase
Change in percentage of minority graduate students in all science, technology, engineering, and math fields	16.9% increase	26.3% increase

Source: George and others, 2007.

math professor at the University of Iowa. "He emphasized that in the first five years, the main thing was to build the structure to support AGEP students, even if numbers didn't go up. He focused on internal, cultural change in the institution to help minorities feel welcome and achieve at high levels, and that made a huge difference."

AGEP is also showing impressive results nationally. Data from sixty-one AGEP institutions, representing twenty alliances and covering the period from 1997/1998 to 2005/2006, are summarized in Table 2.3.

Note: To learn more about the twenty AGEP alliances, go to http://nsfagep.org.

Roosevelt Johnson: A Different Way of Thinking

One of this book's overriding themes relates to the thought processes of collaborative leaders. Phil Kutzko's comments on Roosevelt Johnson capture several aspects of this leader's collaborative mindset:

- Johnson took a holistic approach, aiming for institutional change.

- He took a long view of change.

- He suggested that the University of Iowa make its changes in phases (for example, advising Iowa to create an internal support structure in the first five years and then to build on that later).

- He understood that creating a genuine culture of collaboration in academia usually happens from the inside out.

Put another way, Johnson and other collaborative leaders take a comprehensive view of collaboration and change. They take the long view, the broad view (include all partners), the deep view (develop holistic approaches), and the strategic view (build the partnership from within and without). They also have excellent court vision.

THE BOTTOM LINE

AGEP is making a huge difference for hundreds of young people from minority groups who are eager to get PhDs in the sciences, technology, engineering, and math. And these students, in turn, are inspiring family members and friends to raise their hopes and goals. You would be excused for assuming that Roosevelt Johnson must be one of those exceptional people who operate at a different level from the rest of us. In fact, Roosevelt Johnson *is* a wonderful human being—warm, witty, bright, understated—but to move

AGEP forward he used strategies and skills that are available to anyone with a commitment to collaboration.

As I emphasized in the Introduction to this book, collaboration is most certainly learnable. It isn't magic. Nor is it the province of a few special people. There is, however, a discipline to this practice, and that discipline is the subject of the next three chapters.

3

A Framework for Collaboration

*Behind all the current buzz about collaboration is
a discipline. . . . If it contained a silicon chip,
we'd all be excited.*

—*John Gardner*

In 2004, Roosevelt Johnson spoke to one of my management classes about his experience in leading the Alliances for Graduate Education and the Professoriate (AGEP) program. His opening comment was telling. "You know, I didn't really have a clear game plan when we started working with the California universities. I knew there was a huge need, but I didn't understand that there's a structure or method to collaboration; we just kind of felt our way." I've met dozens of collaborative leaders who have voiced similar sentiments.

There's no one-size-fits-all approach to collaboration, no twelve-step method. But there *is* an underlying structure that's present in most successful collaborative efforts, a discipline that anyone can learn and use. In this chapter we'll look at the seven key factors that make up this discipline. Exhibit 3.1 lists these factors. Each was present in the AGEP case. (Figure 3.1 introduces the Collaboration Framework.)

Exhibit 3.1. The Seven Key Collaborative Factors.

1. The partners have a shared, specific interest or purpose that they are committed to and can't achieve (as well) on their own.

2. The partners want to pursue a collaborative solution now and are willing to contribute something to the effort.

3. The appropriate people are at the table.

4. The partners have an open, credible process.

5. The effort has a passionate champion (or champions), with credibility and clout.

6. The partners have trusting relationships.

7. The partners use the skills of collaborative leadership.

Figure 3.1. Collaboration Framework.

1. The Partners Have a Shared, Specific Interest or Purpose

Roosevelt Johnson didn't make the mistake of assuming that University of California (UC) leaders shared his enthusiasm about increasing diversity at the graduate student level. Rather, he began by asking questions and listening, which are among the collaborative leader's most important skills. In doing so he learned that the first factor required for successful collaboration already existed: leaders at the nine UC campuses had a strong shared interest in graduate student diversity. That was an important discovery. The fact that Johnson was passionate about this issue would have been irrelevant had there been little interest among the deans and key faculty. Fortunately, the first requirement for collaboration was in place.

Johnson learned how much these leaders had in common through his visits to each campus. To borrow from the language of foreign affairs, he used shuttle diplomacy, going from one stakeholder group to the next, listening, testing ideas, looking for commonalities.

> In the beginning the collaborative leader plays the roles of entrepreneur, detective, facilitator, and matchmaker.

This homework is invaluable at the beginning of most collaborative ventures. At this point the collaborative leader wears several hats and is part entrepreneur, part detective, part facilitator, and part matchmaker. Johnson did a superlative job of managing these roles; he had a goal and was up-front about it, but didn't push his agenda on others.

This isn't to suggest that the collaborative leader is evasive about his or her interests and purpose. Katherine Knowles, executive director of the nonprofit Zeiterion Theatre in New Bedford, Massachusetts, is clear about this point: "One mistake I've made is not laying my cards on the table at the start. You need to show who you are, what your mission is, up front, and invite other players to do the same. Then, ask if the proposed project is consistent with the missions of the other players. Asking this makes it easier for someone to say, 'We don't really fit in with this project.' Asking this allows the group to determine if they all understand the expectations."

Knowles and Johnson use different styles to get to the same end: determining if there is a shared interest.

2. The Partners Want to Pursue a Collaborative Solution Now

I once had a client who liked to talk about priorities. She preached priorities to her nonprofit agency's staff and board. When I asked her what the agency's priorities were, she smiled and proudly pulled out a piece of paper with fifteen neatly printed goals listed. Puzzled, I asked which were the agency's highest priorities. She replied, "*All* of them." But, clearly, when everything is a priority, you have no real priorities. A former CEO at Texas Instruments used to remark that "more than two goals is no goals." A bit harsh, but you get the point.

The second collaborative factor has to do with timing, priorities, and commitment. It's one thing to say that you and others have a common interest in a goal, and quite another for all of you to show your desire to contribute time and resources right now.

The key words in that last sentence are *contribute* and *now*. Having a shared interest means little if that interest isn't high on all the parties' agendas. Collaboration is hard work, and myriad forces can threaten to undermine the effort. There must be something that makes the goal a high priority in order to overcome those countervailing forces.

This isn't to say that each person at the table must be ready to sign on at the start. That's not realistic. Typically there will be people who come to the first meetings to check the idea out or who attend because their manager told them to go and represent their agency or because they were simply curious. And most people come to early meetings interested in learning whether the collaborative group's leaders have got what it takes to pull this off. For these and other reasons, members of the group may not be close to committing to the project at the start.

And that's an important challenge to the collaborative leader: How can you make the collaborative project a high priority for everyone at the table? How can you increase individuals' commitment to it?

Collaborative leaders use many strategies to establish a level of commitment and high priority. Exhibit 3.2 provides a starter list of ideas (see Chapter Six for more on this issue).

Roosevelt Johnson used several approaches to elicit commitment to AGEP from the University of California leaders. His soft-spoken passion for increasing diversity among graduate students was evident to all. Nobody in the UC system had seen a program officer from the National Science Foundation (NSF)

Exhibit 3.2. Strategies for Establishing High Commitment to a Project.

- Make the shared purpose real—bring in customers or other stakeholders who can talk about the problem being addressed and why it's so important to deal with it, now.

- Spell out, in clear terms, the cost of *not* acting—to the community or country, to the customers, to the agencies involved.

- Ask each of the parties, one at a time, what it would take for this project to become a high priority. Note: timing is critical here. Some people may not be ready to talk candidly about this during the early meetings—the necessary trust may not have formed yet. Consider doing shuttle diplomacy to get more honest responses.

- Find a senior leader who has a strong interest in the group's project and will devote time and perhaps resources to being a champion for it (see the end of this chapter for more on the roles of senior leaders).

- Identify those on the team who are clearly excited by the project; work with them between meetings to find an important role or task each can take on. Their enthusiasm and passion at the group meetings can become infectious.

- Build the project in *chunks*, and celebrate the small wins.

- Have the collaborative leader of the group demonstrate her passion for the project.

- Connect the project to a larger value.

come out to their campus previously to listen to them talk about their interests in an NSF program.

He also shared with them the reasons why he was so committed to this project, and he spoke about his experiences growing up in the segregated South and not having the option to go to a school like the schools in the UC system. He described being the first minority student in his graduate school's microbiology department, where he frequently felt isolated. It was personal for Johnson: "I didn't want students to lack what I lacked—the support services, mentoring, social opportunities, money, the sense of community."

When someone steps up and makes a personal commitment, it challenges others to do the same.

His sincerity and good listening skills also impressed the groups he met with. His work with the University of California Office of the President resulted in additional funding for the proposed alliance. He also took a risk by challenging the three large campuses that already had funding to give some of it up, for the larger good. And as we saw, a well-respected dean at the Berkeley campus responded positively and asked others to do likewise.

I'm often impressed with the impact on a group when one individual takes the first step and makes a commitment, offers something up and challenges others to make their own commitments. It gets people's attention. And it often generates similar commitments.

3. The Appropriate People Are at the Table

Allen Hard is a natural collaborator and a delightful guy to boot. He spent most of his career leading executive education programs for federal government managers. Since retiring, Hard has found a new passion: working with nongovernmental organizations (NGOs) in Southeast Asia to help local villages develop water sanitation facilities that are critical to improving their health.

One of his successful projects in Southeast Asia began in 1997 and involved four countries—China, Vietnam, Cambodia, and Laos—plus NGOs and academic institutions in those areas. The first task was to determine if professionals from these four countries could work together on water sanitation projects. As Hard noted, "NGOs can be very competitive. There are often big egos, power struggles, and conflicting ideas on how to do the work." He and his partners knew that the selection of professionals from the NGOs for the team was a critical step.

One of their first tasks was to decide which NGOs to invite to work on the project. More than that, *they identified the specific people they wanted* from each NGO. Hard explained that "you have to learn who works well on such projects, and (perhaps more importantly), who you really don't want on the project! Making these choices is only possible if you have lots of experience and know the individuals well."

In general the *appropriate people* include representatives of key stakeholder groups who will be affected by the collaborative project and individuals who have something to contribute to the project. Exhibit 3.3 details the qualities to seek when inviting people to collaborate.

Exhibit 3.3. Finding Appropriate People for a Collaborative Project.

For most collaborative projects, it's important to invite people who

- Represent an organization that has an interest in the issue, and can speak for that organization
- Have expertise and knowledge related to the issue
- Have a strong interest in the issue
- Can make time to work on the team
- Can bring resources to bear, if needed

In leading workshops on collaboration for over 3,000 people since 2001, I've learned that this factor is the one most managers identify as the toughest of the seven key collaboration ingredients. There are several reasons. For one, we usually lack any control over the people whom other agencies send to the table. For another, some of the appropriate people are probably involved in several other projects and don't have the time. In addition, we may not be in a position to know who the appropriate people are for a given project. (Allen Hard and his colleagues did extensive homework to identify the best and worst candidates for their project.)

Roosevelt Johnson knew that he couldn't identify the key people at each of the nine UC campuses on his own. So he asked his top contact in the UC Office of the President to talk with the graduate deans and ask them to identify others at their campuses who were interested in increasing minority enrollment. It worked. And the deans were given the latitude to decide whom else to invite. As Johnson knew, academics love their autonomy.

Getting the appropriate people to the table, and keeping them there after you've begun, is one of the most important collaborative tasks for any collaborative leader. We'll pursue this further in Chapter Six.

4. The Partners Have an Open, Credible Process

The word *process* generates a wide range of reactions from organizational types. For some it's a long four-letter word, an excuse for a lack of action and bottom-line results ("process for process's sake"), or a rigid focus on bureaucratic rules rather than results. Others see process as the key to producing results: good processes produce good products. In terms of effective collaboration, there's no question that a credible process is a key to success. For one thing, nobody knows whether a collaborative venture will work at

> *Process is a long four-letter word for some; others see it as the key to good results.*

the start, so the best predictors of success are often (1) the abilities of the person leading the effort, (2) the abilities of the people at the table (and their track records), and (3) the quality of the process being used. Because collaboration is difficult work, a strong process is critical for avoiding the many landmines along the way. Most important, the process used by collaborative leaders must build trust, reduce concerns, and gain the ownership necessary for the partners to commit to working together.

In the following paragraphs I'll describe some key elements of an effective process. (Chapter Six is devoted entirely to this topic; it details *how* to put these elements in place.) An open, credible process includes at least the following elements.

Joint Ownership

Some management consultants like to point out that people never wash their rental cars. It's true. We take care of things that we own, because we're invested in them. Members of a collaborative group are no different. They need a sense of ownership in order to feel invested in the project. And that means that the leader hasn't decided everything in advance.

Roosevelt Johnson gave the UC campuses a great deal of freedom to form their alliance and set their own goals, and urged them to form a steering committee that included the key people from each campus. He suggested that they rotate the meeting location and the committee chair to increase the sense of mutual ownership and that they allow this steering committee to make the major decisions. The UC leaders agreed, and that committee has made a huge difference in building trust, ownership, and commitment to the California AGEP program.

Agreed-Upon Norms or Ground Rules

When I consult with existing groups and ask them if they've formed any ground rules, the members' usual response is to study their shoes; their silence speaks volumes. It's not clear to me why many collaborative groups don't take the time to decide what norms they'll abide by, but what is clear is this: groups that do spend time establishing some norms or ground rules are usually far more effective.

There are many ground rules that collaborative groups find useful. Here are some of my favorites:

- Candor is essential, and there is no retribution.

- Everybody contributes and nobody dominates.

- Egos, and agency identities, are left at the door.

- Differences are kept professional, not personal.

- Decisions are made at the table (no behind-the-scenes deals, no surprises).

- The group uses the 70 percent rule.

I learned the last ground rule from a colleague whose collaborative group was struggling. Turns out the group had a number of strong-willed perfectionists. They couldn't come to agreement when key decisions had to be made because each held out for the "correct" or "perfect" solution. Of course there are no perfect solutions when people from different agencies and disciplines get together (just as there are no perfect bills in a legislature; that's why elected officials like to say that "the perfect is the enemy of the good"). The group started making progress when it adopted the 70 percent rule. When someone proposed a solution, group members judged it by whether they saw it as a good (not a perfect) solution, asking, "Can we each get roughly 70 percent of what we want from the proposal?" If so, it was good enough; they would adopt it and move on.

It should be the group's decision which ground rules to use. But I do find two absolutely essential: there must be candor, and there must be no retribution for candor. Once a group agrees on those rules, it's interesting how often someone will say, "Well, since we're being candid, I want to point out that . . ." (For an excellent discussion of collaborative ground rules and how to develop them, see Dukes and Firehock, 2001, Appendix H.)

Transparency

Recall Thad Allen's motto: "transparency of information breeds self-correcting behavior." There's much wisdom in those words. A transparent process builds trust and confidence, which are essential for collaboration to flourish. This is especially true when the partners don't know each other initially. Transparency also helps a team adapt to changing circumstances effectively, because the members don't worry about hidden agendas and can focus on what needs to be done. A process feels transparent when the partners don't surprise each other, when people follow up on their commitments, when the decisions are made at the table, and when everyone is asked for input on key issues.

One of the biggest challenges to transparency, and to an open process in general, is the perception of hidden agendas. This can be a difficult issue when there's a history of poor relationships among some partners and when a partner feels threatened by the initiative but doesn't surface that worry. Whatever the reason, it's in the leader's and group's interest to surface agendas.

In the last chapter I discussed how Roosevelt Johnson used shuttle diplomacy to learn the interests and agendas of those at the nine UC campuses. Tammy Rubel, a collaboration expert with the Israeli NGO Shatil, often brings up the issue of individual agendas when working with a project group. She tells the whole group that people usually have interests in a project that are separate from the stated goal (for example, they may want to expand their networks or learn of funding sources), and she asks group members to discuss their interests in the project openly. When they do, it builds transparency by getting concerns and issues on the table early.

Knowledge of Each Other

This last element of an effective process relates to the topic of the next chapter, building relationships. For now, suffice it to say that collaborative groups are much more effective when group members have some information about each other. When all we know about team members is their agency affiliation, we're flying almost blind. Or worse, we may be working with unfair stereotypes: "Bill works with the XYZ agency, and we all know what a bunch of egotists work over there . . ."

I observed the power of sharing information about team members at a meeting of two nonprofits. These agencies are partners to one of the U.S. national parks, and they provide excellent services to the parks. But these partners were in a serious conflict. They had overlapping missions and were fighting over turf. The meeting threatened to be very contentious, but it went well. One of the reasons: just as we began, one participant suggested we go around the table to learn about each other. Nobody objected. Several of the participants talked for two or three minutes about their work lives, where they went to college, their hobbies, and the like.

The group "lost" about twenty-five minutes because of this exercise, and as the meeting facilitator I was worried. I knew that some participants were very much "bottom-line guys" who would want to cut right to the chase. But the exercise proved to be a blessing. Participants gained valuable information about each other. It helped ease the tensions in the room. And participants frequently referred to items that they'd learned about each other during their later discussions.

The meeting participants "lost" 25 minutes from the long introductions, but they gained incredibly valuable knowledge about each other.

At the end of the meeting we did a recap, and many participants said that the initial exercise set an excellent tone that opened them up for in-depth discussions.

5. The Collaborative Effort Has a Passionate Champion (or Champions)

The fifth collaboration factor is a champion for the initiative, someone with credibility and clout who is totally committed to the project and makes it a very high priority.

Of the several dozen collaboration projects I've studied, I can't think of one that succeeded without a passionate champion. Champions often become obsessed with their project; they go to sleep worrying about it and get up each day totally focused on it. Of all the collaboration factors, this one may be the most important because a strong, committed champion is usually able to help the group put the other factors into place. Moreover, it often takes the persistence of a champion to overcome the inevitable hurdles and bureaucratic barriers that confront collaboration.

A champion can exist at either of two levels. He or she may be (1) a member of the core group doing the collaborative work, or (2) a senior leader who has responsibility for that group (or for the project the group is developing). Every core group needs a strong, committed champion at the table. Most large collaborative projects also need a champion at the senior level.

The Project-Level Champion

There is no set position description for champions; it depends on the project, the situation, and the kind of partners at the table. For instance, Roosevelt Johnson was working with academics, who quickly rebel when a peer (even one with money) becomes directive. Thad Allen could have been much more directive had he chosen to be, given the emergency authority granted by the president. That said, champions who are members of the core group, or project-level champions, *usually* have the roles and tasks listed in Exhibit 3.4.

The logical question at this point is how do you find a project-level champion? It's a reasonable question, but project-level champions aren't usually found. It's more likely that they will nominate themselves or be appointed by a senior leader. In my experience, the most effective champions are those who self-nominate. They have the passion, the drive, and the desire to do whatever it takes to make the project succeed.

There are times when you put the project on hold. Lack of a committed champion is usually one of those times.

Exhibit 3.4. Key Tasks of Project-Level Champions.

- Articulating the group's shared purpose, the benefits of succeeding, and the costs of failing

- Helping the parties see that they can meet the identified purpose only through joint action

- Keeping senior leaders informed of the group's progress and needs; asking for help selectively

- Helping to establish the key collaboration factors listed in this chapter

- Anticipating hurdles; helping the group address those hurdles

- Giving the group feedback on its progress

- Ensuring that every member is listened to; playing to the members' individual strengths (meeting the *me* needs)

- Helping the group celebrate successes (meeting the *we* needs)

- Taking occasional risks when moments of truth arrive

- Helping the partners remember what they share in common, especially when conflicts and differences threaten their progress

- Helping the group use collaborative problem-solving and decision-making methods

- Providing confidence, hope, persistence, and resilience

But what if no champion emerges from the core group? In such cases, it's usually wisest not to push it. Rather, the group can go forward in small steps, formulate its plans and line up its support, and see if a champion emerges. Sometimes, experienced members of the core group will go to one of the members who shows real talent and enthusiasm and ask that person to take on the champion role. Some potential champions are simply waiting to be asked. And if nobody emerges from the core group, it's reasonable to ask the group members if the project is a high enough priority to continue. There are times when the best strategy is to put the project on hold. Not having a champion at the table can be one of those times.

The Senior Champion

Exhibit 3.5 displays the usual tasks of senior champions. It's likely that the collaborative group will have to actively seek a senior champion to carry out these functions. Here are some questions to ask when trying to identify a potential senior champion for your group:

- Who has some leadership responsibilities for issues that our group will address?

- Who has the skills, clout, and control of resources to help us (or to block us)?

- Who has authority or influence over most of the members of our core group?

- Who has credibility with those who have a stake in our success?

- Who has a leadership goal or agenda that our group's success could significantly affect?

Exhibit 3.5. Key Tasks of Senior Champions.

- Demonstrating support for the initiative, through actions as well as words

- Showing the group members how their project connects to larger goals or priorities of the organizations involved

- Being a downfield blocker and helping the group to deal with hurdles that are beyond its ability to handle—political problems among partner agencies, policy hurdles, lack of senior support from certain partners

- Providing resources as needed

- Making needed changes in the systems that affect the group (for example, budget, human resources, and information technology systems), in order to provide more support for collaboration

- Providing recognition for the group's (and individuals') accomplishments, both within the agencies represented as well as among a larger, external audience

It may require some active intelligence gathering to answer this last question. Unfortunately, some senior leaders don't make their goals and priorities visible. But one of the best ways to find an eager senior champion is to locate a leader who not only has some responsibility for the group's mission but also has a vested interest in its success because the group's success will help move the leader's agenda forward. Savvy groups are always looking for allies whose agendas overlap with theirs. That's not manipulation; it's called effectiveness.

THE BOTTOM LINE

Collaboration is a discipline. Getting the key factors in place may seem like a lot of work. What's the payoff? In a word, results.

If you've learned to play an instrument, like to engage in sports, or take pride in any other endeavor that requires learning and practice, you're learning a discipline. You probably have a mental checklist of tasks that are central to success in that discipline.

When playing tennis I occasionally remind myself of the key factors for hitting a good backhand: arm back and elbow straight, knees bent, swing all the way through the ball, keep my head down. If I recall these keys on the days when my backhand is sloppy, the results speak for themselves. As the legendary pro football coach Vince Lombardi used to preach, "Practice doesn't make perfect. Only perfect practice makes perfect." And perfect practice requires knowing and practicing the key factors.

The goal for collaborative leaders isn't a perfect project, of course; that doesn't exist. But knowing and practicing the key collaboration factors will improve your results.

I've discussed five of the key collaborative factors in this chapter. There are two others—the formation of trusting relationships, and the use of collaborative leadership skills. Each is so important it merits its own chapter. We'll turn to relationships next.

4

The Power of Relationships
Built on Trust

When it comes to collaboration, it's all about trust.
—Tom Martin, Captain,
Virginia State Police (Ret.)

As Roosevelt Johnson, Thad Allen, and all successful collaborative leaders know, trusting relationships are at the core of most collaborative efforts. Collaboration, as I've defined it, involves people representing different units or organizations. Thus the parties must deal with the dual loyalty tension between the need to represent their home organization and the importance of becoming a participating partner of the collaborative group. Some of the parties at the table may represent agencies that compete for funds, mission, talented staff, and visible projects. How do you work with potential or real competitors in order to advance the partnership? It happens only through the power of trusting relationships.

This is true in the private sector as well. Noted Harvard Business School professor Rosabeth Moss Kanter studied alliances among thirty-seven companies in eleven countries. She found three major themes from her research. One of them is that successful alliances aren't managed through formal mechanisms; they're led through a "dense web of interpersonal connections" (Kanter, 1994, p. 97). Her key finding: "Successful partnerships manage the relationships, not just the deal" (p. 96).

Consultant Allen Hard's experience in working with international nongovernmental organizations (NGOs) leads to the same conclusion. "I've worked in many countries in Southeast Asia on water sanitation projects," he says. "When you do a lot of international work, you learn that in most countries *it's relationships first, business second.* . . . We always take time up front to learn about each other, share a meal, spend some social time together. We never jump right into the work. That goes directly against these cultures."

In many countries the unwritten rule is "relationships before work."

Why Are Relationships Critical to Partnerships?

Relationships are critical to partnerships for several reasons. First, they help the partners hang together when times get tough. Collaboration rarely works in a neat and tidy way. When there are setbacks, the group members need a strong sense of mutual trust to pull through. Nancy Carstedt, executive director of the Chicago Children's Choir, notes that "as we venture into unknown territory, it's critical to have that support [of a good relationship]" (Austin, 2000, p. 48).

In addition, collaboration inevitably requires negotiation, give and take, and compromise. Each is easier in the context of a trusting relationship. We're far more likely to consider another's point of view when there's trust, in part because we're not wondering what her "real" motive is. And third, trusting relationships increase the pace of collaboration and reduce some of the obstacles. Stephen M. R. Covey makes this point convincingly in his wonderful book *The Speed of Trust* (2006): "When trust goes up, speed will also go up and costs will go down. It's that simple, that real, that predictable" (p. 13).

And speed is often critical, especially in fields like law enforcement. Tim Longo, a police chief with experience in Maryland and Virginia, is strong on this point.

A few years ago we had a twelve-year-old girl missing in our community, and we had reason to believe she was probably with a guy two or three times her age. At about 4:30 on a Friday afternoon, the FBI's special agent in charge (SAC) for our region called me, offering to help. I was surprised; she was brand new in her position and we'd never met. I told her we could definitely use their help. At 10:30 the next morning an FBI agent called to tell me that they had already set up a field office in our town, and invited me to meet. I went right over and found that they had about twelve FBI agents and support people there, ready to do whatever they could to help. A short time later the girl was found alive.

That kind of rapid response often means the difference between life and death.

9/11 at the Pentagon: The Power of Relationships

I know of no more powerful example of the impact of relationships than the response to the 9/11 attack on the Pentagon. At 9:38 A.M. on that infamous Tuesday morning, American Airlines Flight 77 crashed into the west side of the Pentagon. It was loaded with 10,000 gallons of fuel, moving at 345 mph. Sixty-four people on board perished, as did 125 people in the Pentagon. We all know the results of the unforgettable day that the terrorists struck. What most people don't know is a very different story: the extraordinary collaboration of emergency responders at the Pentagon. Military, local, and state police agencies, firefighters, and other emergency management crews worked together seamlessly in the rescue and recovery efforts that went on for several weeks.

Emergency crews with special equipment arrived from as far away as Texas. The fire chief of the neighboring Alexandria, Virginia, fire department sent his deputy to Arlington County (home of the Pentagon) with this message for his colleagues:

"Whatever you need, you've got." Those representing the key agencies on the scene met at 6 P.M. on September 11. The FBI agent in charge told the group that the Arlington County Fire Department deputy chief was in charge; the fire was still burning, and that department would call the shots. The general representing the Pentagon quickly agreed. That might seem surprising, given that the Pentagon is a federal building, the nation was under attack, and a 1988 law permits federal control of emergencies in case of foreign attack. But each of the principals in the meeting quickly agreed.

Tom Martin, formerly commander of the Criminal Intelligence Division for the Virginia State Police, was the incident commander for the state police at the Pentagon after the attack. He has given many talks about the joint efforts on 9/11. In his view, "it's all about trust":

> One of the reasons that trust was high at the Pentagon was that most of the law enforcement responders knew each other. This was mainly due to the long-standing relationships that had been built among the agency supervisors. Most of us had attended numerous training sessions together. We had done some "table-top" exercises together and had a sense of how we'd respond to an emergency. Many of us had served on committees and task forces, too. So we knew each other, we had trained for emergencies together, and there was a strong sense of trust and mutual confidence among those people.

The after-action review of the events at the Pentagon confirms Martin's key point: "it is difficult to overstate the value of personal relationships formed and nurtured among key participants long before the Pentagon attack" (Arlington County, Virginia, 2002, A-31). By all accounts the level of true collaboration, the degree of information and resource sharing, and the lack of turf and ego problems among the principals at the Pentagon were extraordinary.

Trusting Relationships: Critical, Not Easy

Solid relationships are essential to collaboration, but that doesn't mean trust comes easily. There are institutional hurdles: the dual loyalty dilemma mentioned earlier, the reality that different partner organizations have distinct cultures and different priorities, and the possibility of past conflicts among these organizations. There are also personal hurdles: different personalities, oversized egos, personal agendas that people can't or won't share, and others. Finally, we need to always keep in mind the *me* versus *we* tension: the conflict between the fundamental human needs for autonomy and competence on the one hand and belonging on the other. If a collaborative group is perceived to be a barrier to meeting either need, that perception often leads to interpersonal problems among the partners. Exhibit 4.1 lists several significant challenges to forming trust among collaborative partners.

Exhibit 4.1. Challenges to Forming Trust Among Collaborative Partners.

- Prior conflict among the participating organizations
- Prior conflict among some of the individuals
- Hidden or different agendas
- Huge egos or difficult personalities
- Competition among individuals for leadership of the group
- Failure of some partners to follow through on commitments
- Lack of information sharing
- Bad chemistry among some individuals
- The dual loyalty dilemma
- A power differential among participating organizations

Forming and Sustaining Trusting Relationships

Exhibit 4.2 offers nine approaches for building trusting relationships. These approaches reflect an important insight described well in *The Speed of Trust*: credibility lies at the foundation of all trust. Covey (2006) suggests that our credibility is a function of two factors:

$$Credibility = character + competence.$$

First, when we judge another's trustworthiness, we try to determine if he is a person of character: Does he have integrity? Are his intentions positive or harmful? And second, we assess the person's competence: Will she follow through? Can we count on her? The approaches summarized in Exhibit 4.2 help build trust through demonstrations of character and competence. This is, of course, only a partial list. It comes from interviews with hundreds of managers in nonprofit and public agencies who have had considerable experience at relationship building during collaborative efforts. (Figure 4.1 emphasizes the importance

---

Exhibit 4.2. Character + Competence: Nine Ways to Build Trusting Relationship on Collaborative Teams.

- Share information, both requested and unrequested.
- Set aside time to work on relationship building.
- Model openness; use self-disclosure.
- Offer help during a crisis.
- Make good on commitments.
- Build the partnership in *chunks*.
- Take a personal interest.
- Engage in joint training.
- Earn trust by sharing credit, keeping confidences, being trustworthy.

of relationships in the collaboration framework introduced in Chapter Three.)

Share Accurate Information, Both Requested and Unrequested

When Tom Ridge was elected governor of Pennsylvania in 1994, he chose Tim Reeves to be his press secretary. Reeves was a newspaper reporter, and Ridge respected his work. When he hired Reeves, Ridge, a lifelong Republican, didn't know that Reeves was a Democrat. Nor did he care, but Ridge's senior aides weren't amused. They saw Reeves as an outsider.

Things got more dicey for Reeves when Ridge began including him in some meetings that didn't include certain other top aides. Reeves's close access to the governor on a range of issues not related to his press duties alienated his colleagues. Reeves, not a dull lad, quickly realized there was a reason he frequently had lunch alone,

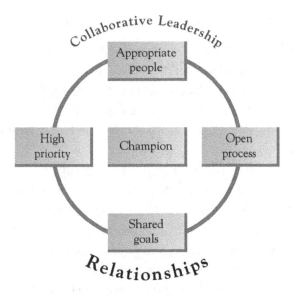

Figure 4.1. Collaboration Framework.

and decided it was time to build ties with others. So he started making a concerted effort to share information with his colleagues. When he attended a meeting that didn't include other senior people, Reeves briefed them about it afterward. When he obtained information that might affect them (for example, potential budget cuts affecting their areas), he shared that as well. Over time, Ridge's aides came to realize that Reeves was a team player and was looking out for their interests. Relationships warmed up considerably.

There are few more powerful ways to build trust than sharing information useful to others. And when that information isn't requested, it can be especially powerful. Some people may wonder what your "real" agenda is when you offer information that they didn't invite, but if you persist most people will accept the gesture for what it is, and some will reciprocate. Information sharing also becomes a symbol for something larger: your desire to build the collaborative team, to create something larger than the individuals.

Set Aside Time to Work on Relationship Building

Bob Stripling, a retired city manager, learned the importance of creating time for relationships at the end of his tenure as chief administrative officer of a town. He asked his town council members if he could interview them individually, asking what they really thought of him as a manager: his strengths, shortcomings, the whole nine yards. They agreed.

The most frequent and important comment Stripling received was this: "You only call me when you're trying to sell me on some issue; it's never just to talk." As he thought about this, he realized it was true. Stripling was fairly young, this was his first chief administrative officer role, he was passionate about a number of things, and when a council meeting was approaching he often called the members individually and told them why he thought it was so critical that they vote this way or that on certain items. These were the only interactions he had had with some members of the council. Some of them resented it.

Stripling took the message to heart and vowed not to repeat that mistake. In later city manager jobs, he started spending time with governing board members on nonwork issues and with no other agenda. Those exchanges served him well in his future jobs. Indeed, years later, Stripling started telling people in his profession that the city manager job is really "all about relationships." For a guy who's a strong introvert, who's always been very task oriented and focused on his strong technical skills, that's an impressive change.

Many busy managers can't imagine setting aside time explicitly for the purpose of nourishing relationships. Sometimes achieving this goal requires creativity. In 2005, ten professionals in Charlottesville, Virginia, created a child advocacy center, which involves the co-location of staff from several agencies. Gretchen Ellis, director of the area Commission on Children and Families, played a lead role in getting the new center started, and she knew it was critical for the key players to form solid relationships at the start. When someone suggested that the partners get training in child advocacy center matters, Ellis saw an opportunity. The training was offered in Huntsville, Alabama, 580 miles away. Rather than fly there, she got a van and the ten partners drove there together. "I wanted leaders from each agency to spend a lot of time together, and the long road trip forced that!" she recalled. It made a huge difference. The principals got very close and formed the trust that was a key factor in their center's success.

One of the most effective ways to set aside time for relationship building is also one of the easiest—break bread together. Sharing a meal (and drinks) is a near-universal way of forging bonds. Some collaborative leaders routinely bring food to meetings. Others schedule meetings over the lunch hour. In many parts of the country, law enforcement officials hold monthly luncheons for the top people in all the police agencies in the region. One agent from the Bureau of Alcohol, Tobacco, Firearms and Explosives (ATF) reports that these luncheons give him an immediate way to identify the key people in his network when he moves to a new community. "There's no agenda at these luncheons, no formal program or speaker. We just eat and talk. And the relationships formed there are incredibly important. After attending a few luncheons, it's no longer 'the ATF is on the phone,' now it's 'Al is calling.' It makes a huge difference."

Eating together is one of the easiest ways to build relationships.

Model Openness; Use Self-Disclosure

Anyone can model open communications; it's not only the job of the person nominally in charge (and in partnerships, everyone is in charge in various ways). Self-disclosure is a very effective way to demonstrate openness. It's almost always disarming, and it puts people on common human level.

Self-disclosure can be as simple as saying, "I'm confused about where we are right now in our project; can someone help me?" It also can surface issues that are easy for group members to avoid. Suppose a partner says, "I want to be positive about this idea, but I'm worried that we're all being too polite here. Frankly, I don't think this idea has any chance of flying! Am I the only one who feels this way?" Chances are that person isn't alone, and her candor may help the group avoid groupthink—agreeing in order to maintain group harmony, without any real debate or thought.

Another good way to model open communications is to acknowledge another's point of view, even when you disagree. Tim Reeves notes that he learned this lesson while serving as press secretary to Governor Tom Ridge. "You can't be an advocate for only one position. . . .You have to show respect for different perspectives— legal, legislative, policy, media. . . .Your colleagues will love you for it. This kind of candor builds relationships" (Linden, 2002, p. 97).

And that kind of respect also builds one's credibility and overcomes concerns about a hidden agenda.

Offer Help During a Crisis

It was October 20, 2002, and the D.C. Sniper was still at large, creating fear among the millions of people who live in Maryland, the District of Columbia, and northern and central Virginia. Ten people had been killed, and law enforcement agencies in dozens of jurisdictions were working overtime to find the killer or killers. Jay Gregorius, assistant special agent in charge of the Training Academy of the Drug Enforcement Administration (DEA), was looking for a way to help, even though tracking down snipers isn't part of the DEA's mission. So he called the sheriff of Stafford County, Virginia, a rural county not far from the scenes of some of the attacks, where Gregorius was also living at the time.

Gregorius explained that he supervised several law enforcement agents and that they'd do anything to help. The sheriff wasn't used to getting this kind of call, but he said that his deputies were spending a lot of time sitting at freeway exits and that when the next attack came he could use help in closing off every exit ramp and inspecting every vehicle. Gregorius said his agents would do whatever was needed, anytime, day or night. He added that the DEA agents would be taking orders from the sheriff. The sheriff accepted the offer, and the next day Gregorius and his agents were at the freeway exits, working with the sheriff's deputies. The sheriff, of course, was delighted. And since that time he would do anything to help Jay Gregorius (and vice versa).

One of the unusual aspects of Gregorius's story is that he found a way to form a relationship and start building trust in the middle of a crisis. People in the emergency management world know that the best time to establish relationships is *before* you have to work together. But Jay Gregorius also understands a different perspective. When someone's in trouble and you have a way to help, it's a great time to reach out.

Make Good on Commitments

In my management classes I often ask each participant to think of someone who is the epitome of credibility and then to identify what it is that contributes to that person's credibility. Inevitably, someone says, "she follows through" or words to that effect. It reminds me of Covey's formula for creating credibility: character + competence. Nothing demonstrates competence like making good on a commitment (and doing it well).

Making good on a commitment also helps people answer the question, What'll it cost me? Busy people often wonder if a collaborative team will waste their time. When they see that others on the team are competent and take their commitments seriously, it reduces the concern and builds trust.

There are two lessons here for collaborative leaders: (1) take time to identify each partner's strengths and interests, and (2) divide the overall project into a number of small tasks, giving the partners plenty of opportunities to make good on their commitments. Which brings us to the next way to build a trusting relationship.

Build the Partnerships in Chunks

Collaboration inevitably involves giving up something—some amount of control, autonomy, flexibility—in exchange for an outcome we can't produce alone. It's the first part of that sentence—the "giving up" part—that worries most of us. But our fear of loss at the start of a partnership decreases when we give ourselves a chance to take small steps together.

Katherine Knowles understands the power of taking small steps very well. Her experience leading a nonprofit theater group has taught her that "collaboration works best starting with baby steps, doing small tasks together, which gives us a chance to let trust grow." It's a smart strategy for several reasons. It not only builds trust, but also gives people a chance to learn what their partners can do. It can build credibility and accountability. And it gives the group some momentum and confidence for handling the harder tasks.

One of the best ways to take small steps is to create a product together. The initial product can be a Web site for the partnership, a shared intake form for agencies serving the same clients, a communications plan for informing key stakeholders of the group's progress. It needn't be large. But engaging in real work together can do wonders for a new partnership. As collaboration veteran Steve Schwartz likes to say, "Never underestimate the power of a product."

Take a Personal Interest

Chuck Short is special assistant to the county executive in Montgomery County, Maryland. Short's management style has been influenced in a powerful way by a man who wasn't known for his relationship skills. In 1981, Charlie Gilchrist was the Montgomery County executive. He was seen by everyone as an all-business type guy. He'd graduated first in his class at Harvard Law School and was incredibly bright, ambitious, powerful. He came across as a totally work-oriented, direct, very competent, in a hurry, and no-nonsense person. At the time, Chuck Short had a management position with the county. That year, his son was born blind, with a life-threatening condition, and for six months he struggled to live.

One day during that period, Charlie Gilchrist called Short and asked, "Chuck, how's your little boy doing?" Short answered briefly: "OK, his blood work looked good today, we're praying for him. . . . What can I do for you, Charlie?"

Gilchrist responded, "Nothing, Chuck. You can't do anything for me. I just wanted to know how your little boy was doing . . ."

That phone call had a powerful impact on Chuck Short, and that impact lasted for decades. When Charlie Gilchrist asked about Short's struggling infant, he was sincere. He wasn't in his typical fast-paced business mode. Since that day, Chuck Short has made a habit of calling or writing a note to a staff member *every single day*. The call or note is often about some personal aspect of their lives, sometimes about a professional accomplishment.

Decades after that phone call from his former boss, Short says, "It's amazing how many employees have thanked me for a note I sent on some important moment in their lives. Often I'd be 'managing by wandering around,' and inevitably someone would pull me over and show me a note that I had sent that meant something. Frequently it was pinned to a bulletin board and it was years old!"

It probably goes without saying that most of Chuck Short's employees had great loyalty and commitment to him because they knew he was committed to them.

Partners in a collaboration are typically peers, not part of a boss-subordinate relationship such as Chuck Short had with his employees. But the principle is the same. Remember the two fundamental human needs: for autonomy and competence (the *me* need) and for belonging (the *we* need). When we take a genuine interest in the other person, we're going a long way toward meeting the first need, which of course also helps create the sense of belonging.

Former employees still have Chuck Short's notes of appreciation and concern, decades later.

Engage in Joint Training

Charles Werner is a local government fire chief who has received multiple honors and high responsibilities in his career; among them have been chairing the executive committee of the Department of Homeland Security Office of Emergency Communications and Office of Interoperability Compatibility, and being named National Career Fire Chief of the Year in 2009 by *Fire Chief Magazine*. More than anything else, Werner is a team player who practices the art of relationship building every day.

Werner has used joint training to help his firefighters connect with different agencies. In one instance the neighboring police chief invited Werner's staff to attend a workshop on meth labs. Not long after, some of his firefighters were inspecting a building and smelled something odd. Because of the training, they realized that it was a meth lab and quickly reported it. That identification (and closure of the lab) wouldn't have happened if the police hadn't offered to share the training with the firefighters.

The secondary payoff of that training session, of course, went well beyond the content of the course: relationships were built and strengthened because the training offered a forum in which the parties could learn each other's perspectives and talk informally at breaks. When done well, joint training helps participants learn about other agencies and cultures and connect with some individuals they need to know.

Earn Trust by Sharing Credit, Keeping Confidences, Being Trustworthy

Perhaps the most powerful way to create trust is by being trustworthy. And one of the best ways to be trustworthy is to freely share credit with others. When we do that, any concerns about our "real" agenda tend to fade away. I'll discuss the importance of sharing credit widely and maintaining a modest ego in the next chapter, on collaborative leadership.

Len Faulk is a great example of earning trust by being trustworthy. When he retired from his administrative position at the State University of New York-Fredonia, a faculty colleague praised him at his retirement party. He noted that Faulk always maintained confidences when people discussed sensitive things with him. In an academic setting where rumors can spread quickly, Faulk was known for keeping confidential discussions to himself.

The ultimate way to build trust is to be trustworthy.

Len Faulk is often a behind-the-scenes leader, preferring to share credit and visibility with others. He never competes with his partners for visibility. People instantly sense that his only desire is to see the project succeed, and he downplays his own leadership role when it's time to hand out credit. Faulk knows how to keep his ego in check, which creates a lot of space for others' egos to get fed.

THE BOTTOM LINE

In his book *Trust*, Francis Fukuyama (1995) writes that "a nation's well-being, as well as its ability to compete, is conditioned by a single, pervasive cultural characteristic: the level of trust" (p. 7). Trust is as fundamental to collaborative projects as it is to a nation's well-being. If your team takes the time to develop trust, you'll be much better positioned to prevent or deal with such collaboration challenges as turf, information hoarders, different goals and interests, and competition for resources. Trust greases the skids; it helps collaborative team members overlook the small issues and address the larger issues directly. Without trust, little collaboration is possible. It's that simple. And that significant.

In a collaborative team or culture, everyone has the opportunity and responsibility for generating trust. But leaders (both formal and informal) are especially well positioned to create a climate of trusting relationships. In the next chapter we'll look at the characteristics and skills of collaborative leaders.

5

The Art of Collaborative Leadership

Collaborative leadership is about leading as a peer, not as a superior.

—David Chrislip

Thus far, we've looked at several examples that involve organization-to-organization collaboration. Getting two or more organizations (or units within one organization) to collaborate is tricky enough. Creating a collaborative mindset and initiative in a community is usually far tougher; dealing with various special interests, community leaders who are rivals for power, local politics, and shifting coalitions is no walk in the park. Here's an example of one such collaborative effort that has gone well and the collaborative leader who helped inspire it.

Revival in Jamestown, New York

Jamestown is a working-class city located on beautiful Chautauqua Lake in western New York State. In the nineteenth and first part of the twentieth century it thrived on a strong manufacturing base, but since the 1930s its population and economic fortunes have been declining:

- The city has a population of about 30,000, 30 percent fewer than in 1930.
- Only about 50 percent of the housing is owner-occupied (at least 15 percent lower than the national urban average).

- The total assessed value of Jamestown's housing went down by almost 7 percent from 1990 to 2002.
- Sales tax revenues declined over the same time period, reflecting in part the move of some retail businesses to the suburbs.
- Property taxes rose; businesses moved out.

In response to this deteriorating environment, the city's Strategic Planning and Partnership Commission (SPPC) decided to launch a strategic planning initiative in January 2002. The SPPC's membership included the city's key civic, business, elected, foundation, union, and community leaders. Jamestown's political leaders had been at odds in recent years, and many doubted that they could work together on the serious problems facing the city.

An Outside-In Strategy: Getting the Community Engaged

Given the city's political gridlock, the SPPC decided that a traditional, top-down approach would be fruitless. Instead, it decided to use an *outside-in* strategy: it would seek input from a large number of influential groups and individuals, write a strategic plan based on that input, and raise community expectations that the city's leaders would act on the plan.

The SPPC members interviewed the mayor, members of the city council, business groups, community activists, members of the clergy, foundation leaders, union representatives, and city department heads and other employees. People were uniformly pleased to be included; that wasn't the norm in Jamestown. The interviews produced a list of eleven key issues, including taxes, the need for jobs, community attitudes, infrastructure, and housing.

The commission took the unusual step of adding a newspaper reporter to its membership in order to make its work transparent to the community.

Then the commission took a most unusual step; it invited the local newspaper to put a reporter on the SPPC. The commission worked out a ground rule for the reporter's involvement: he would write about the SPPC's work but wouldn't quote members (allowing for candor at SPPC meetings). He followed through beautifully and made the SPPC's work visible to the community.

Engaging the Community Through the Media and Town Forums

Then the SPPC took another unusual and creative step. Some of its members wrote articles for the local newspaper about the eleven identified issues, including the recommended action items for each issue. The residents' responses were overwhelmingly positive. They liked reading about solutions, especially solutions offered by their neighbors and friends.

The SPPC then convened a town hall meeting to discuss the issues and action items with the public. About 150 people spent the evening learning about and discussing proposed actions. The SPPC revised the plan one last time, presented it to the city council and the mayor, and in the fall of 2002, the council adopted it unanimously.

From Plan to Implementation: Accountability by Keeping Score

The SPPC next created action teams for each issue, made up of council members, city staff, and community members. Finally, the SPPC developed a creative way to foster accountability. It posted a report card every quarter showing the status of each priority item, with a narrative section describing some of its efforts. The report card appeared in the newspaper and on the city's Web site and was also included in a mailing of the residents' utility bills. Figure 5.1 shows a few items from one of the commission's report cards.

Some Results

The SPPC members cite a number of accomplishments, including the following four points:

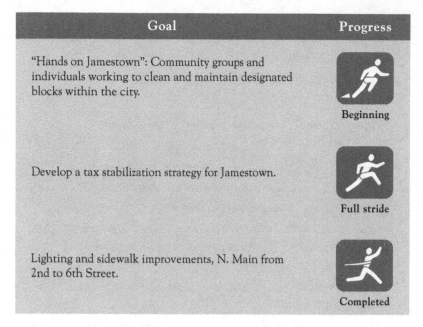

Goal	Progress
"Hands on Jamestown": Community groups and individuals working to clean and maintain designated blocks within the city.	Beginning
Develop a tax stabilization strategy for Jamestown.	Full stride
Lighting and sidewalk improvements, N. Main from 2nd to 6th Street.	Completed

Figure 5.1. Extract from a Jamestown SPPC Report Card.

- *Jobs and economic development.* The SPPC acquired funds to hire a marketing person, who helped bring many new firms to town (one of which has hired over 750 employees). Median family income has risen $4,200, and more new homes are being built now than before the SPPC began its work.

- *Education.* The SPPC spearheaded the adoption of the Chautauqua Educational Opportunity (CEO) program, which provides tuition and mentoring to promising high school students who weren't considering college. The program has funded an average of ten new students a year since starting in 2002.

- *Urban design plan.* The SPPC partnered with the city council and local foundations to develop the Jamestown Urban Design Plan, the guiding framework for the physical development of downtown Jamestown. It has won a national award and has contributed significantly to making Jamestown and the surrounding region attractive as a center of business and tourism and as a place to live.

- *Neighborhood revitalization plan.* This plan was developed to address residents' concerns about their declining neighborhoods. Several of its recommendations have been implemented, including development of a housing trust fund to support affordable housing.

Perhaps most important, many community leaders notice a clear improvement in community *attitudes*. Jennifer Harkness, who succeeded Lillian Ney as commission chair, sums it up this way:

"The commission strives for transparency in an environment that often fosters secrecy. Its objective is to bring strategic information and solutions directly to the citizens and local government, then foster partnerships and collaboration.

"What has made the commission effective, quite simply, is the leadership and example we have had in Lillian Ney."

Lillian Ney: Portrait of a Collaborative Leader

Many people played important roles with the SPPC during this critical time in Jamestown's history; none was more important than Lillian Ney. Ney was a member of the commission from 1996 to 2007 and cochaired it for most of those years. In the cochair role she worked closely with SPPC members and numerous community groups to overcome countless hurdles and short-term setbacks.

Ney comes by her service ethic naturally. Her father was an immigrant who continually preached the importance of giving back to the community, and she took her father's words to heart. Like her father, she became a physician. She eventually became the local hospital's medical director, then its vice president. In typical fashion she thought about how to be effective in her new management roles: "When I became medical director I took a course on how to be an effective administrator, and the skills I learned helped not only with doctors but with a wide variety of people in my other community roles." (The importance of collaborative leadership skills is emphasized in the collaboration framework, as Figure 5.2 shows.)

Figure 5.2. Collaboration Framework.

And the number of community roles Ney has filled is truly amazing. She's served on the boards of over a dozen nonprofits in the
community. She was on the Jamestown City Council for six years,
serving two of those years as council president. She cochaired the
Strategic Planning and Partnership Commission for six years. And in
2008 she was given the prestigious New York State Senate Woman
of Distinction Award.

When others are asked about Ney's exceptional leadership and
contributions to the community, they offer observations like these:

"She has great credibility and integrity."

"She reaches out and listens carefully to others."

"She plays for the long run—keeps her eyes on the prize."

"She understands the importance of the 'what's in it for me?'
question."

"She has a unique gift of bringing people of opposing views together for the common good."

"She displays an appreciation for others' views, but does not settle for mediocrity."

"In the end, focusing on the long term and achieving the goal is the only way to get it done," she says. "I try to help people think of the end product. Doing that helps us stop worrying about the petty things that come up in short term." And Ney has experienced more than her share of childish, often petty behavior. She's learned to "let it go," and her model has helped some of her colleagues do the same.

Leading in a collaborative fashion comes naturally for Lillian Ney. (Full disclosure: I've consulted with Ney and others on the Jamestown strategic planning effort, and have seen her exceptional leadership skills firsthand.) But this collaborative style is not natural for many leaders. What can we learn from her and others who excel at this art?

Five Qualities of Collaborative Leaders

Here's a thought experiment. Using David Chrislip's definition of a collaborative leader—someone who leads "as a peer, rather than as a superior" (Chrislip, 2000, p. 23), think of someone you've worked with whom you regard as an effective collaborative leader. We're talking about people who can excite a group to achieve a shared goal, who are adept at the art of influence, who can help other people find common ground. These are also people who are moved to fulfill larger societal needs, not for their career interests but because of their values and passion.

When I reflect on the collaborative leaders I've studied—people such as Roosevelt Johnson, Thad Allen, Charles Werner, Chuck Short, and Lillian Ney whom we've met earlier in this book—there are five qualities that appear over and over. They are listed in Exhibit 5.1, and I'll discuss each in turn.

> **Exhibit 5.1. Five Qualities of Collaborative Leaders.**
>
> Collaborative leaders
>
> 1. Feel driven to achieve the goal through collaboration, with a measured ego.
> 2. Listen carefully to understand others' perspectives.
> 3. Look for win-win solutions to meet shared interests.
> 4. Use *pull* more than *push*.
> 5. Think strategically; connect the project to a larger purpose.

1. Feel Driven to Achieve the Goal Through Collaboration, with a Measured Ego

One of the impressive things about Lillian Ney is her ability to work well with huge egos. As Len Faulk, one of her long-time associates, puts it, "She has a decent sized ego, but it *never* gets in the way. On the contrary, she never puts herself in a superior position to others at the table, even if she's the chair or president of the group."

Lillian Ney continually looks for people's strengths, which is one reason people love working with her.

It's not that Ney enjoys working with egotistical people; rather she finds ways to keep such behavior from sapping her energy and optimism. One of her approaches: she's always *looking for others' strengths and positive contributions*. As one of her associates puts it, "Lil's amazingly good at complimenting others. She does it routinely when people make useful contributions. The result is, people love working with her."

I've followed over fifteen successful collaborative leaders during the past ten years, and every one of them shares this first quality. These collaborative leaders are successful, in part, because of this uncommon but compelling combination: they're passionate about achieving the goal and also have no need to get the credit. This combination is also a winning one in the corporate world. Jim Collins found the same trait in his study of top business leaders. In his book Good to Great (2001), he describes what he calls "level 5 leaders," successful leaders who are a "study in duality: modest and willful, humble and fearless" (p. 22). Collins found in the most effective business leaders an "unwavering resolve" to achieve results, combined with a compelling modesty (p. 30).

2. Listen Carefully to Understand Others' Perspectives

When our daughter, Becca, was about eight, she returned home from school one day very upset. I was surprised, because she loved school and was typically upbeat when she returned each day and let go of her (too heavy) backpack.

"Becca, is something wrong?"

"Daddy, why don't teachers listen to kids?!" she demanded, tears starting to roll down her cheeks. I was so surprised I could only repeat her question.

"Why don't teachers listen to kids?"

"Yeah! I mean, I was ready for class today, and every time Mrs. Brown asked a question, I knew the answer and raised my hand. But she never called on me; not once! She called on all the kids around me, I know she saw my hand, but she just ignored me all day!!" More tears.

Becca, of course, wasn't asking a theoretical question about teachers and their listening skills. No, she had a very specific question: Why didn't *her* teacher listen to *her*, today?! Why, indeed?

It takes time and attention and a real desire to get past someone's immediate words and listen for the actual message. If I hadn't had my wits about me that afternoon, I might have launched into a minilecture on the questionable listening skills of some teachers I've known. But Becca didn't state what was actually on her mind at first. So my job was to decode the message, dig underneath the stated words, and look for the real meaning.

The skill of listening for the meaning under the words is powerful and often difficult to use. Powerful, because it allows us to get into another person's head, to see the world through her eyes. And in collaborative settings, that understanding is critical. It's virtually impossible to come up with solutions that will satisfy everyone at the table if we don't understand their underlying needs, interests, and perspectives.

But if this skill is powerful, it's also difficult for most people. Listening for others' perspectives takes real effort. It requires a genuine interest in learning why some people see things differently from us. And it can slow down a group process (at least at the beginning), so it runs the risk of frustrating some members who want to "get on with it."

Another reason this decoding skill is difficult has to do with people's history and the *stories* we carry around in our minds about our histories. A powerful example of this occurs each May in Israel, when that nation's citizens celebrate *Yom Ha'atzmaut*, the country's Independence Day. This day commemorates the end of the British Mandate of Palestine and the declaration of the State of Israel by David Ben-Gurion on May 14, 1948. It was an incredibly joyous (and perilous) moment for Jews. After 2,000 years of wandering, Jews again had a homeland. Coming just three years after the Holocaust ended, it was greeted by millions of Jews as a vital step toward justice and security.

For Arabs living in and near Israel, that date has a different name: al-Naqba, which means "the catastrophe." Many Palestinians who lived in Israel in May 1948 have a totally different memory of that time. Their story is one of being displaced, thrown out of their homes, threatened with death (and sometimes seeing loved ones killed) by Israeli soldiers. When the fighting ended, many Arabs learned that they had permanently lost their homes. When Israelis and Palestinians try to talk about the events of May 1948, they begin with radically different stories that have been passed down for over six decades.

Stephen Denning, a former executive with the World Bank, writes compellingly about the leader's need to understand others' stories. In *The Secret Language of Leadership*, Denning (2007) writes that leaders who want their followers to make a significant change "first need to understand the current story that their listeners are living. What's going on in that world? How does it hang together? Why does the world the people are currently living in make sense? . . . Leaders need to understand the world of their listeners, in all its peculiarity, its strangeness, its stubborn differences. The best—and perhaps the only—way to do that is to reconstruct the story the listeners perceive themselves to be living" (pp. 87–88).

Charles Werner, the fire chief mentioned in Chapter Four, excels at the art of learning others' stories. He always tries to remember a principle that Stephen Covey expresses in *The Seven Habits of Highly Effective People* (1989): "first seek to understand, then to be understood." Werner points out that firefighters face a challenge when trying to collaborate with law enforcement. That's because their cultures are so different. The firefighters' world is an open book; whatever they do is in the public eye. They're used to sharing information and working in teams; that's the culture. Police, however, often work individually. They must keep a lot of information to themselves. Theirs is a low-trust environment. So when seeking first to understand with police officers, firefighters need to begin with the knowledge that the nature of police work is very different from the nature of firefighters' work. That difference makes it even more important to foster relationships and trust and listen for others' perspective.

As Werner and other smart collaborative leaders know, listening "beneath the words" to uncover a person's real meaning isn't about trying to be nice; it's about being effective.

3. Look for Win-Win Solutions to Meet Shared Interests

In our polarized political life, it sometimes seems increasingly difficult to identify shared interests and look for solutions that satisfy all parties. But when we back away from the passions of the moment, it doesn't take an Einstein to identify shared interests, even in the most passionate of arguments.

Take abortion. People on the pro-life and the pro-choice sides will probably never agree on the morality of abortion. But many of the most ardent foes on this issue do definitely agree on the need to *reduce the number of unwanted pregnancies*.

Or consider gun control. The National Rifle Association (NRA) and gun control advocacy groups are bitter enemies, sometimes refusing to work together even when they actually agree on an issue. But when we step back, it's not hard to see that they both have a strong interest in *gun safety*.

There's nothing new about the concept of seeking shared interests and looking for win-win solutions. The question I find intriguing is this: Given that most of us understand the win-win concept and its potential power, why do we often forget to use it? Why do we get caught up in win-lose arguments, whether at work or home?

> *There's nothing new about the power of win-win solutions. So why do we often revert to a win-lose mindset?*

One answer to this question has to do with our socialization and mental "wiring." As we discussed in Chapter One, most Americans are raised in fairly individualistic environments. Kids learn early on to do their own work at school (although there is a growing movement toward group projects in some schools), the great majority of employees are still evaluated on their individual contributions, and many organizations maintain competitive cultures where it's simply not in one's interest to share ideas or information.

Another barrier to win-win thinking is the fact that some issues become politicized; individuals become reluctant to seek common ground because being associated with the "other" isn't in their political interest. In the Jamestown example, some of the city's elected officials who weren't of Ney's political party were reluctant to work closely with her at times, wondering if she would use her successes in a future run for mayor. Ney quickly understood this perceived threat. She met with the politicos and made very clear that she had absolutely no interest in the mayor's position. Because of her reputation for integrity, they believed her and got past the political rivalry.

Perhaps the most powerful factor influencing our ability to use win-win thinking is the fundamental stance we take to life: some people have an attitude of abundance; others assume scarcity. Think about the last time a colleague in your office was recognized for exceptional performance. What was your initial reaction? On the one hand, if you were pleased for the person, that could reflect an attitude of abundance—the other person's good fortune didn't threaten you; her reward didn't mean that there was less recognition available to you or to others. On the other hand, if you found yourself arguing with her recognition, that might reflect an attitude of scarcity (you might also simply think she wasn't up to the award, of course, but that's a different matter). Those who assume scarcity have a zero-sum view: there are limited goodies out there; that sum can't expand, so others' gains are our losses.

The assumption that another's good experience comes at your expense is sometimes based on reality, of course: a test that's graded on a curve means there are only so many A's to go around. At the same time, a strong scarcity mindset leaves us less likely to seek win-win solutions even when they're possible. It limits our ability to think creatively. It assumes that we can only cut up the pie. Effective collaborative leaders use a different assumption: that we can sometimes *grow the pie*. These leaders look for synergies, seek grants, and find partners with similar goals and complementary skills. Win-win is their default mode. That's a major reason for their success.

Next time you find yourself thinking that someone else's good fortune means there are fewer goodies to go around (in terms of the budget, new hires, plum projects, or opportunities to brief senior leaders, for example), check your assumptions. Are the resources truly fixed, or are there options to grow the pie?

To repeat, there's nothing new about the concept of win-win solutions. The question to ask yourself is, How can I remember to *look* for such solutions, especially when operating in competitive environments?

4. Use *Pull* More Than *Push*

When our son, Josh, left for college in 2004, my wife, Jackie, urged him to stay in touch by calling regularly. "Why don't you call us once a week?" she suggested. "Call on Friday evenings. We're usually home; it's the end of the week and a nice time to catch up." Josh said, "Sure," but it wasn't a very convincing "sure." Well, the first weekend came and went, and there was no call. Same thing happened the next weekend. Our daughter, Becca, happened to be home from college the following weekend, and asked us why we looked down. I explained that we'd asked Josh to call weekly, and hadn't heard from him yet.

Becca patiently explained the facts of college life to us. "First of all, Josh left home for a good reason; he wanted to get away! Second, you know he really doesn't like talking on the phone. And third, you want him to spend time calling you on *Friday nights?!*" By this time the error of our ways was more than clear.

"Honey, you're absolutely right," I responded. "What do you suggest?"

"It's really simple," she replied. "You just have to learn two letters: IM."

Well, I'm not the world's greatest techie, but I knew she was talking about instant messaging, a tool that Josh enjoyed using. Ten minutes later Becca had shown us how to get on IM. I saw Josh was online, and sent him a note telling him how we were doing and asked how his first weeks at school were going.

Josh's response: "Hey dad, what's up?" I considered it a great success!

The problem was, we'd been using *push* to get Josh to stay in touch. Push is direct, sometimes forceful, using the power of formal authority. It certainly has its place in management. But collaboration is usually the rule among peers, and collaborative leaders usually have no formal authority over their colleagues. (See Exhibit 5.2.)

Pull is different. Pull taps an inner need or motivation, it connects with something that the person already wants to do. In the martial arts, push is like karate—applying force to an object. Pull is like aikido—channeling the other's energy and drive to your advantage. With Josh, the pull was using a technology he thought was cool.

We've already seen several examples of pull. Thad Allen, who was in charge of search, rescue, and recovery efforts in New Orleans after Katrina, has generated extraordinary loyalty from his colleagues in the Coast Guard. One reason (among many): he treats people with enormous respect, irrespective of their position. When successful, talented managers communicate with front-line staff as peers, use their ideas, and take a team approach, they're using pull. And Allen uses pull in the most trying of circumstances—natural and man-made disasters (he also played a lead role in New York City on 9/11).

When Jamestown's SPPC leaders decided to use an outside-in strategy, they were using pull. They could have used push, by developing a strategic plan and presenting it directly to the mayor and city council. But they chose to pull hundreds of residents into the effort, and in doing so they also created a pull with the city's political leaders; they developed a *constituency* for their project, which made it safer and more appealing for political leaders to work together.

Exhibit 5.2. The Differences Between Pull and Push.

Push is more about . . .	*Pull is more about . . .*
Talking	Listening
Telling, explaining	Asking, inquiring
Meeting my needs	Trying to meet all of our needs
Getting you to do what I want	Creating conditions in which you and I want the same thing

As a collaborative leader, you can use pull to engage people in collaborative efforts in a variety of ways:

- Show your personal enthusiasm and commitment for the initiative.

- Give others control, autonomy, and lots of input.

- Describe the desired outcome, and ask the group to craft the best strategy for achieving it.

- Find and tap the strengths in each person on the team.

- Show how the project touches a core organizational or personal value.

One of the many benefits to using pull is that it gives others plenty of space to decide whether and how to get involved. When people feel free to act, the result is usually commitment, not passive compliance.

Pull also requires some strategic thinking and a secure ego. Effective collaborative leaders often ask themselves, Who is the

Push produces compliance; pull generates commitment.

best person to approach this individual whose help we need? They don't make the mistake of assuming that they need to be the one who makes the "ask." My favorite example comes from the world of marketing. South Street Seaport is an upbeat (and upscale) shopping area in lower Manhattan. In the 1980s, the developers bought several rundown buildings at a pier on the water and created a lively environment of shops, restaurants, and entertainment. It promised to be exciting.

But how do you get the word out about a new development in a city of eight million people? The developers thought strategically and used pull. They asked themselves, Which people in this huge city have the credibility to market our project? The answer was soon obvious. So a few weeks before the Seaport opened, its owners threw a huge beer and pretzel party for 6,000 New York taxi drivers, tour bus drivers, and their families! After that bash, several thousand people were singing the praises of the Seaport to their customers and friends, for free. That's the power of pull.

5. Think Strategically; Connect the Project to a Larger Purpose

Helmuth von Moltke was a nineteenth-century Prussian field marshal who was one of the leading strategic thinkers of his era. He believed that the main task of military leaders is to prepare extensively for all possible outcomes, so he drew up detailed plans before each battle. But von Moltke also knew that any plan must be revised because conditions inevitably change; that's why he used to say, "No plan survives contact with the enemy." More important than a strategic plan, he said, is the ability to *think* strategically.

Effective collaborative leaders think strategically, which requires good peripheral vision and the ability to think several moves in advance. They're not playing checkers; they're playing chess. And armed with von Moltke's insights, effective collaborative leaders realize that projects take on a life of their own, and the leader needs to both anticipate and respond quickly to change and challenges.

Thad Allen understands this intuitively. During his work on the Gulf Coast, Allen used different terminology for a similar approach. He told his partners that they would develop a "strategic intent," by which he meant a clear goal and general strategy, which the various partners would adapt and modify as conditions required.

Timing is another important aspect of strategic thinking. One of Lillian Ney's colleagues notes that Ney "has a great sense of group process. She knows what has to happen, who'll be needed to make it happen, and has a terrific feel for timing. She senses when a group needs to speed up or slow down, when to hold a retreat, when to talk with someone individually outside the group."

And effective collaborative leaders tend to excel at showing people what some call a line of sight, which means they demonstrate the *connections* between the team's project and a larger purpose. Roosevelt Johnson's work in increasing the enrollment of underrepresented students in certain graduate fields is a prime example. He's passionate about the mission of the Alliances for Graduate Education and the Professoriate, seeing it as a means to increase diversity not only among graduate students but also in higher education in general and in the broader society.

Collaborative Leadership Works in Hierarchical Settings as Well

The five characteristics of collaborative leaders aren't only about peer leadership; they can be equally effective in most hierarchical positions. Leadership scholars Zenger and Folkman (2009) studied 11,000 360-degree reviews of business leaders, in an effort to learn what led to poor performance in the corporate world. These reviews brought together survey responses from the leaders' peers, direct reports, and supervisors. For the 10 percent who were least effective, one of the top five mistakes was their lack of collaboration. Svara (2008) came up with similar conclusions in his study of mayors in small, medium-sized, and large cities. Mayors who provide a sense of direction and who use what Svara calls *facilitative leadership* are more effective than those who don't function in this way.

A study shows that one of the five top reasons for poor leadership performance is poor collaboration skills.

George C. Marshall, Army chief of staff during World War II and later U.S. secretary of state and of defense, excelled at using collaborative leadership in a hierarchical role. He was an extraordinarily talented man with a first-rate mind and character. And he had enormous formal power and popularity. The most admired American during the 1940s, he was named man of the year by *Time* magazine in 1944 and 1948, and he won the Nobel Peace Prize in

1953. Yet he often preferred to use his informal influence skills and frequently used pull. "Army officers are intelligent," he liked to say. "Give them the bare tree, let them supply the leaves" (Stoler, 1989, p. 112). Marshall had an enormous desire to serve in senior positions yet always kept his ego under control. When Congress wanted to award him a fifth star, he argued against it, believing that there were others who deserved it more.

James Madison, "father of the Constitution" and our fourth president, was another classic collaborative leader. A quiet, modest man, short and sickly, "he lacked the oratorical skills of an Edmund Randolph, Governor of Virginia. . . . He lacked the prestige and stature of George Washington. . . . And he lacked the eloquence and flair of Thomas Jefferson" (Newell, 2008, p. 3). Yet, he was the driving force behind the new Constitution. How did he do it?

Terry Newell, former dean of the Federal Executive Institute, notes that Madison was a behind-the-scenes leader who used his coalition-building skills to lead the Constitutional Convention and the subsequent effort to get the Constitution ratified. He asked Randolph to introduce the Virginia Plan to the convention, a plan that Madison wrote, because he knew Randolph had more credibility with the delegation. Madison also listened carefully to learn the positions and concerns of those from other states and used their input wherever possible.

Madison also relied on his broad network of relationships. "Years of legislative service had honed his skills of sensing the core of the debate and counting votes, and his contacts in all of the states were called into use" (Newell, 2008, p. 11). Madison was passionate about the need for a new, stronger national government, but he showed great flexibility at the convention, even incorporating some ideas he didn't support in the interest of forging the "great compromise" that brought most state leaders together.

We've seen other national leaders succeed through collaborative leadership skills, even though they wielded great power: Abraham Lincoln, Dwight Eisenhower, and Martin Luther King Jr. among them.

ON THE WEB

Exhibit 5.3. Collaborative Leadership Self-Assessment.

	Poor				Excellent
	1	2	3	4	5
1. Feel driven to achieve the goal, with a solid but measured ego	___	___	___	___	___
2. Listen carefully to understand others' perspectives	___	___	___	___	___
3. Look for win-win solutions to meet shared interests	___	___	___	___	___
4. Use pull more than push	___	___	___	___	___
5. Think strategically; connect the project to a larger purpose	___	___	___	___	___

Self-Assessment

How do you see yourself on these collaborative leadership characteristics? How do others see you? Exhibit 5.3 contains a set of questions that allow you to rate yourself on these characteristics (this self-assessment is also available online).

Given the environment you work in and the challenges you're dealing with, which of these characteristics do you most need to improve? And what steps can you take to get started?

THE BOTTOM LINE

There is no one personality type for effective collaborative leaders; some are outgoing and light up the room when they enter, others are so introverted and modest you'd never guess they are exceptional leaders. But most share the five characteristics I've just described. Unlike the heroic, individualistic leadership model of a General Patton or Lee Iacocca, a model that has long intrigued many Americans, collaborative leadership relies on skills that can be learned. And collaborative leadership skills are critical for address-ing the complex problems of an increasingly networked world.

In Part One we've looked at several collaborative leaders, includ-ing some who made a difference by increasing minority enrollment in graduate studies, rescuing Katrina survivors in New Orleans, and helping to turn around a Rust Belt city that had lost its manufac-turing base, some of its population, and much of its hope.

In Part Two I'll discuss more collaborative leaders who are mak-ing a big difference: reducing the health impact of tobacco, bring-ing Jews and Arabs together in Israel, serving small businesses, maintaining our nation's security, and more. And I'll describe the creative strategies they have used to deal with major obstacles. These leaders combine an ability to see the big picture—their court vision—with a fine eye for dealing with the details. We'll drill down into those details in the next section.

Part 2

Getting Started: Dealing with Process and People Issues

In Chapter One we identified two macro barriers to collaboration: our individualistic society and the fragmented structures that reduce the effectiveness of many agencies. This part of the book (Chapters Six through Ten) addresses the first barrier. More specifically, we'll look at the people and process issues that occur in collaborative projects, and offer strategies for addressing such questions as

- What, exactly, is the collaboration process?

- What do we do with people who don't play well with others?

- How do we work with people from different organizational (or national) cultures?

- How do we get strong-willed people to agree on a common direction?

- How can we handle problems of turf, huge egos, people who have different agendas, cultures that reward information hoarding, and the like?

- How do we help a set of individuals representing different organizations move from *me* to *we* (while still honoring their me needs and their home organizations' interests)?

I have already identified the key factors that support most successful collaborations, but how do leaders put those ingredients together in a coherent way? That's the broader question for Part Two. The focus will be on collaborative projects and initiatives. I'll continue to draw on examples from the public and nonprofit sectors, to ground the points in the reality of everyday management practice.

6

Getting the Collaborative Process Started

If you want to go quickly, go alone. If you want to go far,
go together.

—*African proverb*

This chapter deals with the challenge of getting a collaborative group started and developing a collaborative process. There are many fine books on leading teams. Here we'll focus especially on strategies for creating a collaborative team—one that includes people who represent different units or agencies.

There's no single strategy for getting started on collaborative projects. Smart leaders pay attention to the specifics of culture, politics, timing, the stakeholders, and the relationships among the leaders and stakeholders when designing a game plan. That said, many successful collaboratives follow this general advice:

Go slow to go fast.

That is, take time to do up-front homework, build senior leadership support, contact potential partners to learn their interests and concerns, and develop the norms that can foster trust once the team assembles. Figure 6.1 provides a graphic look at this approach.

The S curve was described by Richard Foster (1986) to depict the typical development and growth of many new products and

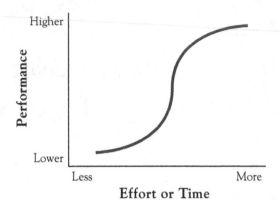

Figure 6.1. The S Curve.

processes. This curve is actually made up of two curves: the learning curve, where early efforts produce little improvement in performance until things start to take off, and the point of diminishing returns, where added inputs yield fewer outputs and improvement levels off. For instance, think of the miles per gallon we get on cars. When I bought a used Volvo in the early 1970s, it got about 22 mpg, considered good at the time. Engineers improved efficiency over the years (they moved up the S curve), and today it's common to get 30 mpg or more. But that's probably the limit for internal combustion engines; we've reached the top of the curve. We're now starting a new S curve, one that starts higher on the performance axis, to reduce fuel consumption based on new technologies—hybrids, electric plug-ins, and the like.

The S curve also reflects the *go slow to go fast* principle and the performance of many collaborative projects. The Jamestown strategic planning effort followed this curve: a lot of up-front time invested, then the takeoff point where visible results occurred, then a leveling off (and need for new projects—a new S curve). It takes time to build trust, to meet the *me* and *we* needs. Thus the go slow advice. As the group moves from a set of individuals with different agendas to a team with a common focus, performance takes off.

We'll start with a look at a very successful partnership, then use some of its lessons to describe the steps for starting a collaborative process.

INEAP: The Interagency Network of Enterprise Assistance Providers

Carroll Thomas is a warm, energetic, irrepressible person whose positive energy is truly contagious. Her official title at the Department of Commerce is *industrial specialist*, but when her boss asked her what she thought her job should actually be called, she replied, "partnership catalyst!" That probably says as much about Thomas and her personality as it does about her job description. Interestingly, her boss supported the different title, and it's now on her business card.

Thomas works for the Manufacturing Extension Partnership program (MEP), which is headquartered at the National Institute of Standards and Technology. MEP focuses on assisting small manufacturers in the United States. Early in her federal career Thomas realized that this program could succeed only if it actively partnered with a large network of other government and nonprofit organizations. But relationships with some of those programs were poor, and Thomas was determined to change that. How to do that wasn't so obvious.

Developing (and Redeveloping) the Concept

Thomas wrote a concept paper proposing a partnership of government and nonprofit agencies that serve small businesses, based on a core idea: establish relationships among the service providers *before* crises hit. She shared it with her boss, who liked it and encouraged her to develop the concept.

Thomas met with Antonio Doss of the Small Business Administration (SBA) to get his input. Their respective programs provided different services to small businesses, and they saw ways to complement each other. She rewrote the concept paper over a dozen times (!), shared a later version with her boss, and in October

2005 he gave the OK to work on the partnership. The basic concept was to create a network of public and nonprofit agencies serving small businesses that would share information and ideas and would create partnerships to better serve their common clients.

Getting the Appropriate People to the Table

Thomas and Doss then began a series of one-on-one luncheon meetings with people who worked in agencies that served small businesses. They used these meetings to discuss the network concept and get each person's reactions, suggestions, and concerns. They didn't ask for commitments, but the meetings helped them identify the people who had interests and skills to contribute to the partnership.

The lunch meetings made people feel special. They also gave Thomas and Doss the chance to ask who else should be involved, and the network expanded. The first group meeting was held in January 2006, and INEAP (Interagency Network of Enterprise Assistance Providers) was born.

Six people showed up for the first meeting. Some might have been disappointed by the small turnout, but Thomas was exuberant. "I thought it went great!" she said. "We spent three hours discussing ideas, asking, 'Why haven't we been doing this all along?' And, 'What kinds of information can we share?' And, 'What are the possibilities for partnerships?' People left on fire. Then in the following months it really started to take off."

Moving Up the S Curve—INEAP Starts Producing Results

Soon, fifteen to twenty people were attending INEAP meetings, and the enthusiasm kept building.

By 2009, INEAP's membership had grown to over 140 individuals representing forty-eight business and technical assistance programs. They include such government agencies as the SBA; Environmental Protection Agency; Export-Import Bank; and Departments of Commerce, Labor, and Energy; and nonprofits like the U.S. Women's

Chamber of Commerce, American Association of Community Colleges, and Association of Procurement Technical Assistance Centers.

As its membership grew, so did its impact. INEAP members have helped many small businesses gain access to services they didn't know existed. For example, INEAP has helped small businesses through the Green Suppliers Network, a collaboration between government and industry that helps small and midsized manufacturers learn to use "lean and clean" methods that reduce pollution, save energy, and cut costs (see Green Suppliers Network, 2009).

INEAP members have also partnered with the U.S. Women's Chamber of Commerce to produce Web-casts on lean manufacturing principles and their application to service organizations. And INEAP members are becoming a one-stop portal for their clients, helping them access valued information and services, easily and quickly. (For a more detailed write-up on INEAP, see Thomas, 2008.)

Getting Started: What to Do Before the First Meeting

Carroll Thomas is a wonderful collaborative leader, a passionate champion for INEAP. She and Antonio Doss were able to temper their passion with the need to bring their partners along slowly. Many of their early steps toward a collaborative effort are listed in Exhibit 6.1.

Let's look at these steps in depth.

Exhibit 6.1. Tasks Before the First Meeting.

- Do your homework. Be clear on the need and goal.
- Identify and talk with key stakeholders.
- Map the political terrain: Is the timing good to start? Does your boss (or bosses) support the project? What are the views of the key veto holders (those who can block the project)?
- Seek the support of a senior champion or executive sponsor.
- Plan the first meeting; invite participants.

Do Your Homework: Be Clear on the Need and Goal

I touched on this issue in Chapter Three, in my discussion of the first collaboration factor—having a shared, specific purpose that the partners can't achieve on their own. Every successful collaborative leader I know emphasizes the importance of gaining clarity on the need for change and the goal. Where collaborative leaders differ is on the best means of coming up with a clear goal.

Some collaborative leaders develop a clear goal in their own minds as they think through the initiative and start inviting people to join the team. In other instances a senior manager develops the goal and gives it to the team leader. And some collaborative leaders develop the goal through the process of holding initial discussions with the stakeholders. Each process has its place. In general, I favor developing the goal through early stakeholder conversations.

It's usually smart to develop (or refine) the goal through early conversations with the partners.

Carroll Thomas and Antonio Doss used this last approach. They started by documenting and discussing the need: small businesses didn't know the full range of government services available, and the service providers didn't know either. They also articulated a general goal but refined it through their early meetings with potential stakeholders. Such individual meetings take time, of course, but they can also start to build trust and give the leader very useful "intelligence" about the partners' hopes and (even more important) concerns.

Identify and Invite Key Stakeholders

Another key collaboration principle discussed in Chapter Three is getting the appropriate people to the table. But to do that, you have to first *identify* the appropriate people. Here's a general approach for identifying the appropriate people:

Look for partners who bring common goals and
complementary strengths and characteristics.

Obviously, you want the people at the table who represent organizations that share the project's goal. But if several of the parties bring the same strengths (in knowledge, skills, or technology), that invites competition. There are exceptions to this rule, of course. Some organizations may need to be represented simply because they have the power to block the initiative. But you may find other ways to include such organizations (for example, by consulting regularly with them or inviting them to participate on certain aspects of the project in order to use their skills without using too much of their time).

Collaboration scholar David Chrislip offers a different approach for identifying the key stakeholders. He looks at two factors: the *influence* each stakeholder has on the issue at hand, and the *stake* each has in the issue. I like Chrislip's method and have slightly modified it. In addition to influence, an organization might provide value to the collaborative group through its *expertise* on the issue being addressed. In Figure 6.2, these factors are shown graphically.

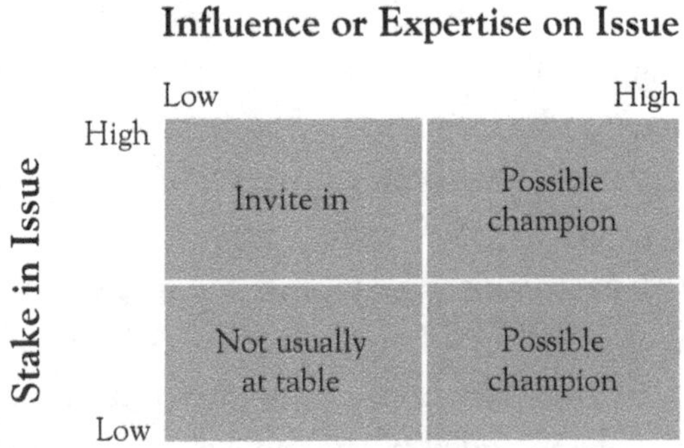

Influence or Expertise on Issue

	Low	High
High	Invite in	Possible champion
Low	Not usually at table	Possible champion

(*Stake in Issue* labels the vertical axis, High to Low)

Figure 6.2. Tool for Identifying Stakeholders.

Source: Adapted from Chrislip, 2002, p. 75. Reprinted with permission of John Wiley & Sons, Inc.

The horizontal dimension identifies those who have something to offer the collaborative group—influence, expertise on the issue, or both. The vertical dimension shows whether the stake in the issue is strong (high) or weak (low).

Individuals or organizations who are in the upper-right quadrant are obviously major players in the initiative; they have a lot to contribute and will be affected by the issue in important ways. They're often champions for the collaborative group because of this combination. Just as obvious are those in the lower-left quadrant. With little to contribute, and a small stake in the issue, there's usually no reason for them to be at the table.

Less obvious are those in the other two quadrants. The lower-right quadrant identifies people with a lot to contribute but little stake in the issue. They sometimes make very good champions. Because they have little at stake, they have high credibility and can be impartial in dealing with conflicts. People in this quadrant often include those in administrative roles, representing budget functions, information technology (IT) units, legal and human resource shops, and policy offices.

Finally, those with little to contribute but with a huge stake in the issue fall into the upper-left quadrant. Here we're talking about customers of the initiative, those in partner agencies and others who will be affected by the initiative but have few resources to offer. They need to be invited in because even though they don't have the clout to insist on being at the table, their voices can be a powerful and positive force for the team.

Another, less structured approach for identifying the appropriate people is to follow Thomas and Doss's lead and use shuttle diplomacy—meet the obvious stakeholders one at a time and ask who else should be included in the project.

Once you've identified the appropriate people, how do you get them to the table? Unfortunately, many would-be collaborative leaders don't think carefully about this question. All too often I've seen leaders simply contact the organizations that need to be represented on the team and invite them (often through impersonal e-mails) to the first meeting. That can work, *if* the leader specifies the individuals she wants on the team, *if* she has a good relationship with those being asked, *if* the initiative is compelling, and *if* those being asked have time to give to the issue. That's a lot of *ifs* to bank on.

Here are some approaches for getting the appropriate people to the table once you've identified them.

Sequence Matters: Think Carefully About Whom to Invite First

Collaborative leaders are wise to initially seek the involvement of individuals with great credibility in the issue being addressed. When such people sign on early, it attracts others, even if they have had reservations about joining. There's an excellent historical example of this approach. When James Madison started to plan the Constitutional Convention late in 1786, he knew how difficult it would be to attract state leaders to the meeting. Most had no interest in ditching the Articles of Confederation and starting over. So Madison made a key move: he began courting the most respected person in the land, George Washington. Washington agreed, and his involvement persuaded many others to attend.

Madison urged Washington to attend the Constitutional Convention, knowing his presence would lead others to come.

In addition to seeking highly credible people, it also helps to start with people who are talented and are known as team players. They can help the group get off to a fast start, generating some visible wins and attracting others to join the team.

Senior Leadership and Resources Matter

Senior leaders' support for the project can persuade busy people to join the partnership. Leadership support sends a symbolic message. The same is true of resources. When an initiative requires new funding, potential partners often wonder if they'll be "taxed" to pay for it. Some Pentagon planners like to say, "A vision without resources is a hallucination" (Friedman, 2008, p. 207). Conversely, potential partners are drawn to a project when the collaborative leader has access to resources. That was clear to Roosevelt Johnson as he worked with University of California deans on the AGEP program. They were eager to talk about his funding source from the start.

Passion Matters: Demonstrate Your Passion and Enthusiasm for the Project

Imagine that you're a very busy manager (which means, of course, most people reading this book). You've participated in some collaborative groups, with mixed results, and you have a very heavy workload. Thus you don't jump up and yell "of course!" each time someone asks you to join a collaborative group. But when someone like Carroll Thomas talks with you about a new venture, it gets your attention.

Why? She exudes excitement when discussing the INEAP partnership. Her enthusiasm is contagious, and passion strengthens partners' confidence in the project.

Shared Values Matter

A number of nonprofit programs serving the homeless around the country are led by faith communities. Dave Norris, a leader of the PACEM program, which provides shelter and meals for homeless people during cold weather, notes that "it's all about service, and service is a value expressed in the New Testament, the Hebrew Bible, and the Koran." Because of that shared value, PACEM has successfully brought clergy and lay leaders from dozens of faith organizations together to create and sustain the program. When identifying possible partners for your project, it helps to talk about the values involved and why they matter to you. If the potential partners share those values, that may be a powerful "hook" for bringing them to the table.

Map the Political Terrain

Most effective collaborative leaders understand the importance of doing their political homework. Lillian Ney was politically effective, in part, because she came across to colleagues as supremely *nonpolitical*. Her passion for collaboration, her eagerness to give others credit for any successes, and her appreciation of others' political sensitivities served her very well. Carroll Thomas has the same quality. They both excel at thinking politically, without appearing to be political.

Collaborative leaders need to address many political landmines in trying to work across boundaries. The best way to address them is to anticipate them and to understand the political rules of the road. Exhibit 6.2 is a starter list of these rules for would-be collaborative leaders.

The fifth political rule on this list is especially important when dealing with issues of turf and trust. Leaders can reduce concerns

---

Exhibit 6.2. Political Rules of the Road for Collaborative Leaders.

- Learn who the veto holders are; find out their interests and concerns early on.
- Keep the gatekeepers (those who provide access to key leaders) informed and involved.
- Find out whether some of the key stakeholders are rivals; use that knowledge when deciding whom to involve and how.
- Never surprise the key stakeholders.
- Avoid any appearance that the lead organization is in this to grab power or resources.
- Connect the collaborative initiative to the agendas of key senior leaders; make it clear how the initiative can help them.
- Keep timing in mind; is this the right moment to move forward?
- Remember one of the keys to political success: people usually gain influence when they share influence and credit.

over power and control by being very open about their interests in the project. Another way to lessen fears is to rotate meeting locations among the partners, as INEAP's leaders do.

In working with nonprofit and government managers for over three decades, I'm struck by the number of managers who don't like to focus on the politics of their jobs. Some people see politics as a long four-letter word, or simply aren't tuned into issues of power and influence in their agency. But effective collaborative leaders understand the importance of being politically savvy.

Lee Bolman and Terrence Deal documented this reality in their fine book *Reframing Organizations* (1997). Their research demonstrated that one can be an effective manager by focusing on the human and structural aspects of an organization. Being an effective *leader*, however, also requires good use of political skills.

Effective managers understand people and organizational structures; effective leaders also use political skills effectively.

If you're thinking that you simply don't have good political antennae, don't despair! Rather than make the effort to turn a deficit into a strength, consider getting close to someone who has a natural ability to think politically, and involve that person in your collaborative project.

Seek the Support of a Senior Champion or Executive Sponsor

Getting the support of a senior champion is usually a key step, yet there's no formula for doing it well. When and how to engage your senior managers is determined by your relationship, the senior managers' leadership styles, and how closely the project links to items on their agendas.

Carroll Thomas gave us one model for engaging senior people. She checked with her supervisor early in her planning and gained his support. She kept him in the loop as she started to meet potential

---

Exhibit 6.3. Making the Go/No-Go Decision.

- Mission test: Does this fit our mission?

- Financial test: Can we afford it (now and in the future)?

- Political test: Do we have the necessary political support?

- Feasibility test: Is this technically doable? Are the people with the required skills/knowledge and/or connections available to help?

- Relationships test: Is there likely to be a good fit between our agency and the others being invited to the table? *Fit* can include shared values, good work relationships, or a history of working together on previous projects.

- Timing test: Given the external environment, are we more likely to succeed by starting now? Would waiting or further preparation be wiser?

---

partners, then shared one of her final concept papers and got his approval to begin the INEAP meetings. Her supervisor was confident she'd keep him in the loop as the project went forward.

Another way to think about engaging your managers or leaders is to ask, What are their priorities, what's on their agenda, and can your initiative help them with their priorities and agenda? And the flip side of that question is, What is it that's driving your leaders crazy right now? If your project succeeds, will it take one of their concerns off their plate? As a nonprofit client of mine likes to say, "You need to know your leaders' 'edges' [boundaries] when taking on a collaborative effort."

Once the up-front homework is done, you have a decision to make: Should you move forward with the partnership? Exhibit 6.3 offers criteria to help you make that decision.

Plan the First Meeting; Invite Participants

If your decision is to move forward, think carefully about the first meeting. Here are a few tips to consider:

- Contact each person being invited personally. Yes, e-mails are very efficient, but they're *far less effective than a call or visit.*

- Decide if it's OK for invitees to send someone else in their place. If you don't want any substitutions, make that clear (some collaborative groups make this a ground rule).

- In your invitation, emphasize why this project matters to you and why it can make a significant difference for others.

- Send out the agenda for the first meeting in advance. If this seems obvious to you, I agree. I put it here simply because this "obvious" step is often neglected.

Developing a Collaborative Process During the First Few Meetings

Once you decide to move ahead with your project, the key question changes from Whether? to How? Here are several tasks that should be done during the early meetings to help the individuals at the table form a truly collaborative team. But first, a bit of theory.

A Model of Collaborative Team Development: Moving from Me to We

How do a set of individuals move from me to we? This is the classic question for all teams, but it's more complicated for collaborative teams than for teams from single units. Collaborative teams have to meet the needs of (1) the individuals at the table, (2) the collaborative team, and (3) the home organizations that the individuals represent.

Thus we need to reframe the question a bit: How do a set of individuals representing different units or agencies move from me to we *while meeting the interests of their home organizations?* The problem is shown graphically in Figure 6.3. When we consider this figure the question becomes, What happens in the cloud to help the individuals develop a team identity while maintaining their home agencies' interests? Let's demystify this process. In the Introduction to this book, I noted four key questions that most people ask

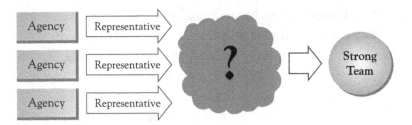

Figure 6.3. Partial Model of Collaborative Team Development.

(at least of themselves) when deciding whether to actively engage and identify with a collaborative team:

1. Do I have something to contribute that is needed, recognized, and used by the team?

2. Are we working on a project that is important to me and my own organization (important in terms of mission, priorities, values)?

3. Are we making progress; do we have a reasonable chance for success?

4. How will this project support or threaten any of my core needs or interests (and those of my home organization)?

As team members come to believe that their contributions are needed and appreciated, that will help to meet the fundamental human needs for competence and belonging. If they believe the project is important, that helps to justify the time and effort required. When the team starts making progress (moving up the S curve), many members start to identify more strongly with the team. Most people like associating with a winner. Finally, most team members need to see some tangible benefits to themselves or their home agency; if the project works against their interests, few people are likely to identify with the project or the team.

When team members become comfortable with the answers to these key questions, the attraction to the team outweighs the costs of belonging—loss of time, having to work out differences with other team members, and the like. Figure 6.4 shows the completed model of collaborative team development.

Every strategy that follows in this chapter, as well as those in Chapters Seven through Ten, can help people answer these four questions in meaningful ways, moving members from a me to a we mindset and identity. Exhibit 6.4 lists several tasks to get this process started.

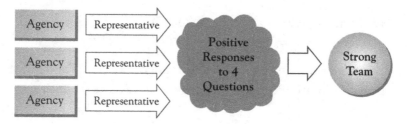

Figure 6.4. Model of Collaborative Team Development.

Exhibit 6.4. Tasks for the First Few Meetings.

- Shine a light on the problem or challenge.

- Create an open, credible tone to build trust—discuss everyone's interests and concerns.

- Discuss the process for working together; decide on team norms, the problem-solving approach to use, and the way decisions will be made.

- Develop a project plan together; establish steps or phases of the project, data needed, roles, criteria, and measures of success.

- Find out what the partners bring to the task, and play to their strengths.

- Invite members to take on initial tasks; decide how they will be accountable for their part.

- Shine a light on the successes; recognize contributions.

Shine a Light on the Problem or Challenge

When a collaborative leader invites people to work on an issue together, the leader usually views the issue as a high priority. But the issue may be a medium or low priority for the other group members. One way to get and keep the appropriate people at the table is to raise the priority by shining a light on the problem, demonstrating its importance and the cost of ignoring it.

Carroll Thomas did this in a personal way. At an early INEAP meeting, she told the group what it was like for her when, years earlier, she ran a business and tried to get government assistance. Thomas had been told that the federal government provided numerous programs to help small businesses, but none of the agency personnel she contacted seemed to know what services other agencies could offer. It drove her crazy and motivated her to seek change when she joined government service. Telling her personal story helped put a human face on the need that INEAP members had to meet.

Some leaders dramatize the problem or need by bringing in respected third parties to study and report on the issue. Others follow the Jamestown example and provide the media with facts and stories about the challenge and possibilities for change. And some bring in a senior leader who talks about the issue, why it matters, and how this team can make an important contribution. Exhibit 6.5 displays a sample agenda for a first meeting. Several of the agenda items relate to "shining a light" on the challenge being addressed.

Create an Open Tone to Build Trust: Discuss Everyone's Interests and Concerns

The INEAP leaders did an excellent job of talking about interests and smoking out possible concerns among partners when conducting initial one-on-one discussions. If you skip that step when choosing team members, it's important to do it once the partners are all at the table.

Exhibit 6.5. Sample Agenda for the First Meeting.

- Purpose of the meeting and of the initiative.

- Introductions—what are members' interests in the project?

- Senior leader's explanation of the importance of this initiative (if appropriate).

- Project champion's explanation of the problem or challenge (including data on the need or challenge, why it matters, cost or risk of not addressing it, benefits of dealing with it now).

- Group discussion—how do others see the problem or challenge?

- The goal or desired outcome of this project.

- Initial reactions—how do the parties view the project? Positives? Concerns? Questions?

- Ground rules for the group (if appropriate at this meeting).

- Next meeting date and the work to be done before then.

I was once advising a group of nonprofit leaders on a workforce initiative, and they weren't showing much energy for the project. It wasn't clear if it was a low priority, if they had major concerns, or both. So we agreed that members would come to the next meeting ready to respond to this question: What would it take for you to make this project a higher priority? Because the team's leader was open and candid himself, other partners were similarly candid. They talked about their concerns (for the first time), and the team made better progress once its members had cleared the air.

Jacki Bryant, executive director of a nonprofit child and family services agency, is a collaboration veteran. She stresses how important it is to help team members feel comfortable discussing their needs and interests from the start: "It really helps to invite candor and to be open yourself. What's in it for me to contribute to this? Most nonprofit folks don't want to be seen as uncooperative, so the leader has to engage people, invite them to talk honestly about the perceived benefits of the partnership

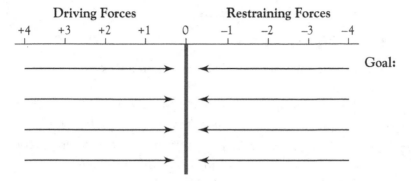

Figure 6.5. Force Field Analysis.

(to the members, their agencies, their clients), and she should model openness on this question. The more tangible the benefits, the better."

One tool that you can use for diagnosing strengths, challenges, and concerns is the force field analysis. Kurt Lewin, one of the early giants in the field of organization development and change, created a more formal way to flesh out a project's possibilities and challenges. He wrote that most organizational situations involve two types of forces: (1) driving forces and (2) restraining forces. *Driving forces* are those that can help move the organization in the desired direction. *Restraining forces* impede progress toward the goal (see Figure 6.5). If the situation is at equilibrium, not moving forward or backward, Lewin assumed that the sum of the driving forces equals the sum of the restraining forces.

When the leader is constructing a force field, the length of the lines indicates the strength of each force. For instance, if Carroll Thomas and Antonio Doss had done a force field prior to starting INEAP, it might have looked like Figure 6.6.

To change and move toward the goal, Lewin suggested, there needs to be an *imbalance* between the strength of the driving and the restraining forces. You can create an imbalance and move toward the goal by doing the following:

- Increasing some of the driving forces

- Reducing some of the restraining forces

- Using a combination of these two approaches

Kurt Lewin noted that most managers focus on the driving factors and neglect the restraining forces.

Lewin's key insight was this: most managers' default mode is to push forward by strengthening (or adding to) the driving forces. And there's nothing wrong with leveraging your driving forces . . . *as long as you work at least as hard to reduce some of the restraining forces.*

If you focus primarily on the drivers, you'll violate one of the lessons you probably learned in high school science, Isaac Newton's third law of motion: for every action, there is an equal and opposite reaction. If you emphasize the drivers, you'll increase the pushback, the resistance. Lewin emphasized the need to reduce restraining forces, which lessens the resistance to change (and doesn't produce any pushback). This isn't to say that you don't use the driving forces; both are needed, but restrainers are often neglected.

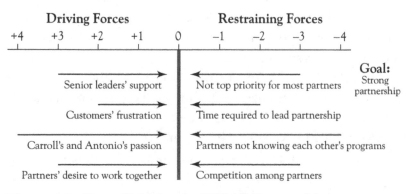

Figure 6.6. Force Field for the INEAP Partnership.

You can use this tool with your collaborative team to help flesh out any concerns members have. Once you (or a facilitator) explain the tool, ask the members to fill it out for your project. What are the key drivers and restrainers, and which restrainers can the team reduce or neutralize in the early phase of the project? The discussion will be more open if the team leader is candid about the likely restraining forces, including any concerns she has.

Determine Team Norms and Problem-Solving and Decision-Making Methods

We discussed the elements of an "open, credible process" in some detail in Chapter Three. But I want to offer a few thoughts here on the team's decision-making approach.

Many people emphasize the importance of reaching consensus when working on teams, and that's for good reason. When there's strong support for a particular decision or path, the team is more committed and more likely to succeed. Moreover, the obvious alternative to consensus—voting—is prone to leave a sense of winners and losers.

That said, I've also seen some teams struggle and lose energy because they define consensus as "everyone agrees." There's good reason to worry when all the people on the team say they agree. You're at risk of groupthink, which occurs when people are reluctant to surface opinions different from those of the (apparent) majority. You're also at risk of a plain vanilla, C+ solution. What to do?

An alternative to consensus is to discuss initial opinions on the issue at hand, then take a preliminary vote to learn who leans which way. A vote clarifies things; you may have more agreement than you thought. More often, I've observed, the team learns it has much less agreement than seemed present. Those who disagree with the direction being proposed are sometimes quiet when they sense that they're in the minority.

The first vote should be advisory, not the end of the discussion. If it's a close call, the team should discuss the pros and cons of the options on the table to see if any one option can be strengthened to gain more support.

Consensus works well for some teams. In other teams it sometimes masks disagreements that need to be aired. If you've fully aired views on an issue and there is widespread agreement, rejoice; you're closer to heaven! But if candid and energetic discussion reveals strong disagreement, a vote can clarify where people stand and lead to efforts to build greater agreement. And if a vote determines the final decision, it's important to ensure that those who "lost" feel that nevertheless they were fully heard. In addition, you may need to meet with those on the losing side, talk it through, and seek their advice on how to move forward and achieve the desired outcomes.

Develop a Project Plan Together

When a collaborative group agrees on a project plan and starts to implement it, it's a sign that the individuals are becoming a team with a common focus. Project plans for collaborative teams are similar to those of other teams. The plan should include goals, roles, timelines and deliverables, metrics, and individuals responsible for each task. There's one key difference about a collaborative team's project plan: it should include a clear communications plan that emphasizes external stakeholders.

Because collaboration involves people from different units and agencies, the partners have a special obligation to keep their agency or unit leaders and other stakeholders informed of the team's status. Thad Allen gave us a first-rate model of communications approaches during his time leading the cleanup of New Orleans.

Collaborative teams have a special responsibility to maintain close communications with external constituencies.

I urge collaborative teams to develop a communications plan for any large project. Every few months you should have a message to deliver: What have you learned and accomplished, what deliverables are

Exhibit 6.6. To MOU or Not to MOU?

There are several potential advantages to using MOU:

- They can reduce misunderstandings concerning who's responsible for what.
- They can be symbolically important (the parties typically sign the final agreement).
- In some cultures, they are a statement that this project is important.
- They can help increase accountability and follow-up.

The major potential disadvantages to MOUs are (1) that they may undermine trust ("if we have to put this in writing, we don't really have the trust and confidence we need in one another") and (2) that they may reduce flexibility.

scheduled next, when will your efforts become visible to others, how can others benefit from your work? Those are the practical questions that external stakeholders will ask about your project.

The communications should also let stakeholders know how the project is achieving its stated mission and how it is making a difference in the lives of real people. When you communicate to others at that level, you not only build external support, you also remind each other why you signed on in the first place.

Some collaborative teams find it important to spell out their mutual responsibilities in a memo of understanding, a MOU (or a memo of agreement, a MOA). As shown in Exhibit 6.6, such memos can enhance the communications process within the team as well as with the key partner organizations involved.

Find Out What the Partners Bring to the Task, and Play to Their Strengths

Playing to each other's strengths is always a good idea. When teams fail to do so, it's often because they haven't identified each member's strengths. Here's a story of a team that overcame that mistake.

"Barbara" was part of an intelligence agency liaison team that was sent to the U.S. Pacific Command. The members of the group received requests for information on a wide range of topics. Team members came from different parts of the agency and knew little about each other's skills and knowledge—as a team they didn't know what they already knew. The leader had Barbara interview the team members individually to gain a better understanding of what each brought to the table. Everyone was happy to talk. "One of the things I learned," Barbara reflected years later, "was how much people love to talk about their accomplishments!" Barbara compiled the results, and created two products:

1. A work summary for each member.

2. A matrix, listing member names on one axis and areas of subject matter expertise on the other (see the template in Table 6.1). She indicated on the matrix who had expertise in which areas.

Team members often don't know what they (collectively) already know.

The results were very positive. Barbara and the team members now had a better understanding of how they could help each other with specific requests. The team's performance began moving up the S curve.

As your team members develop their project plan, have them fill out the Skill and Experience Matrix. It will help in at least two ways: (1) the team members will be able to play to one another's strengths, and (2) the matrix will show the team if it is lacking skills or knowledge in any key areas.

Invite Members to Take on Initial Tasks; Decide How They Will Be Accountable

In Chapter One I suggested that our me and we needs are opposite sides of the same coin; in meeting the one we can help meet the other. This is the point in team development where meeting

Table 6.1. Skill and Experience Matrix for Collaborative Groups.

MEMBER	SKILL AND EXPERIENCE AREAS				
	Technical	IT	Facilitation	Project Management	Political & Marketing

both needs becomes both possible and imperative. Once the game plan is in place and you identify members' strengths, start inviting them to take parts of the plan and carry them out. This step offers members the chance to demonstrate what they can do and to show they'll be accountable for their promises. And it can initiate a virtuous cycle; members follow through on commitments, the team produces some products it didn't have before and experiences some success, and the identification with the team strengthens. This step helps answer one of the questions posed previously in the discussion of collaborative team development: Is the team making progress?

A note on accountability: this word often conjures up negative notions of warnings, consequences for low-quality work, or poor performance appraisals. That reflects thinking from a hierarchical perspective. In a horizontal, networked world, accountability takes on a whole new meaning. Here, it is an opportunity, not a dreaded event. Members are *invited* (not directed) to take on tasks; they're *encouraged* (not required) to opt for items that tap their expertise (or curiosity); they're *offered* (not forced to take) the opportunity to show what they can do that helps move the team forward.

Shine a Light on the Successes; Recognize Partners' Contributions

Robert Cialdini is an academic who writes about the art of influence. Once he did a study of college students, asking a sample of students each Sunday during the fall, "Who won the football game yesterday?" After most home team victories, students used the pronoun *we* in their responses—"we won big." And after most losses (you can see where this is going!), students reported that *they* lost the game, referring, of course, to their team (Cialdini, 1984). Cialdini's point: people love to be part of a winner, and they distance themselves from losing ventures. This is especially true of busy, successful people.

One of the best ways to address the me or we issue and help members identify with the team is to generate some early, visible successes and recognize members' contributions. The notion of generating early wins isn't new; many effective leaders understand it. But do they make those wins visible? When Carroll Thomas learned that the editor of the *Public Manager* was interested in an article on INEAP, she jumped at the opportunity. And the INEAP partners got a real boost when the article was published (see Thomas, 2008).

Some teams celebrate milestones over food, others keep a large project chart showing expected deliverables and progress made to date. And it isn't only the team members who need to see progress; as I noted earlier, the stakeholders and managers need this as well. However you chart your progress, be sure to keep senior people and other stakeholders well apprised.

THE BOTTOM LINE

There are many approaches for getting started on collaboration; the process spelled out in this chapter is hardly *the* approach (next time someone offers to sell you *the* approach, watch your wallet!). But the steps outlined here have worked for many teams. When you go slow to go fast by doing the important up-front work and when you address the four key questions discussed in the model for collaborative teams, you will reduce the many concerns that most people bring to collaborative efforts. Moreover, your team members will start identifying with the team, contributing their talents in ways that give the team the capability to make major change. The move from me to we has begun. And that is a major accomplishment.

Say you've formed a collaborative team, you're making some progress, but team members don't agree on how to move forward. They have different interests, and they disagree about the goal or strategies to achieve it. It's not that they don't know how to work together; they (seem) to want different things. How to achieve a common direction? That is our next topic.

7

Getting Commitment
on a Common Direction

*Don't push it if the parties have seemingly different interests.
It takes time to find common (or higher) ground. Hang in
there, move slowly, allow relationships and trust to form;
only that trust will help reveal what might be in common.*
                                                —*Frank Dukes*

In Chapter Six I introduced the concept of the S curve. In order
to move up the S and get to the point where performance takes
off, the team needs to agree on its goal and some strategies for
achieving it. This is the point in many projects when the members
move from polite discussions to direct and candid engagement.
What are the parties' underlying interests? What will success look
like? Can they talk honestly about their interests, about "what's in
it for me"?

When individuals forge common direction, they take a big step
toward developing a sense of *we*. But how do you do this important
work when the parties have a history of animosity, when their
interests seem to be fundamentally different? Here's an impressive
story about two groups that seemed to have nothing in common,
yet were able to forge a common direction.

Tobacco Growers and Health Advocates: Forging Common Ground Among Unlikely Partners

The decade of the 1990s was a difficult one for the tobacco industry. The amount of U.S. tobacco grown and sold was declining. And concern over tobacco's health impact was growing: in 2002, an estimated 400,000 Americans and 10 million people around the world died of tobacco-induced illness.

In 1994, two University of Virginia (UVA) health advocates met with Frank Dukes of the UVA Institute for Environmental Negotiations. They sought a way to reduce the harm caused by tobacco while maintaining the economic livelihood of Virginia's tobacco farmers. Dukes knew this was a long shot, given the animosity between the tobacco farmers and public health advocates, But he agreed to help with their project.

The Perceptions

As often happens when the sides harden in a dispute, members of both groups had developed black-and-white stereotypes about both themselves and the other side. Their stereotypes are summarized in Exhibit 7.1.

Exhibit 7.1. Perceptions Held by Tobacco Farmers and by Public Health Advocates.

Tobacco Farmers and Farm Leaders	Public Health Advocates
Tobacco is being singled out.	It's the big companies who are the enemy.
They want to ban our product.	We want to eliminate the harm done, and protect kids.
Our product is legal.	The big companies lie, the product is lethal.
They threaten our livelihood.	Farmers can grow something else.
They don't understand/respect us.	We're advocates for health.
They're the enemy.	They're the enemy.

Rebecca Reeve, one of the two initiators of the project, was able to get a grant from the Robert Wood Johnson Foundation. The purpose: study the tobacco farmers' economic needs, and share health advocates' perspectives on the health impact of tobacco. Thus started the Virginia Tobacco Communities Project (VTCP).

VTCP Phase 1: Getting Acquainted with Each Other and the Issues

As the VTCP was forming, the Virginia General Assembly created a committee to study alternatives for assisting tobacco farmers. VTCP leaders attended one of the committee's meetings, which included visits to a tobacco farm and warehouse and processing plant. The visits proved fortunate; the health advocates learned firsthand about the farmers and the pressures they faced, and the two groups had an informal way to start discussions while learning together.

The Roundtable Meetings: Shaky Beginnings, a Surprising Breakthrough

The VTCP leaders then held a series of roundtable meetings for the farmers and health advocates in 1994 and 1995. As Dukes recalled, "The farmers looked really uncomfortable throughout the meeting, and the advocates hardly spoke at all." Members of both groups faced strong criticism from colleagues for joining this effort.

At a second roundtable, participants heard from two economists who specialize in tobacco economics. The economists described the bleak prospects for U.S. tobacco. Again, there was no communication between the two groups. Then a breakthrough occurred. At a third roundtable, an advocate for the farmers got angry. Pointing a finger at the advocates, he said, "You 'antis' [the term that the farmers used for health advocates] are trying to eliminate our way of making a living!" Remarkably, nobody got defensive. Other farmers chimed

When the farmers complained about big tobacco companies, the health advocates learned they had a common enemy.

in, voicing their grievances against the tobacco manufacturers (who bought their products) and the manufacturers' lack of respect for the farmers.

This was a critical moment for two reasons. First, the outspoken farmer moved the group from tense separation to the start of authentic dialogue. Second, the health advocates learned that the two groups had a common enemy in the big tobacco companies. And that proved to be a golden opportunity.

VTCP Phase 2: Getting Focused on Key Issues

That meeting ended with an agreement to form four working groups. Months later, in December 1995, almost sixty people attended a VTCP town hall meeting in Roanoke, where the four working groups made several recommendations. Media from as far away as Atlanta covered the meeting.

One of their recommendations, for increased funding of cooperative extension agents, was later approved by the Virginia General Assembly. The other recommendations led to no action. However, the VTCP process helped its members open up communication lines. Moreover, they gained a much greater understanding of each other's concerns and interests.

The STCP: Going Regional

The VTCP stopped meeting when the grant ended in 1996. The Robert Wood Johnson Foundation provided a second grant, this one focusing on all tobacco-growing states. This broader effort, called the Southern Tobacco Communities Project, or STCP, began in 1997. The STCP's participants came from six Southern states and included many stakeholders (see Figure 7.1). The leaders invited representatives of the large tobacco companies, but they refused to come. That turned out to be a blessing; had representatives from the major companies attended, the farmers wouldn't have spoken so openly.

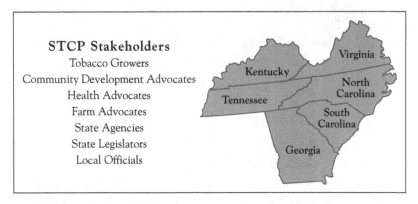

STCP Stakeholders
Tobacco Growers
Community Development Advocates
Health Advocates
Farm Advocates
State Agencies
State Legislators
Local Officials

Figure 7.1. Structure of the Southern Tobacco Communities Project.

Source: Adapted from "From Enemies, to Higher Ground, to Allies: The Unlikely Partnership Between the Tobacco Farm and Public Health Communities in the United States," by Frank Dukes. Published in *Participatory Governance*, Edited by W. Robert Lovan, Michael Murray, and Ron Shaffer. Burlington, VT: Ashgate Publishing Company, 2004.

The meetings were tense—formally joining the STCP could bring on the wrath of colleagues—and participants agreed to come only on a meeting-by-meeting basis. Hardly ideal conditions, but Dukes remained optimistic.

Fourteen Remarkable Roundtables

The STCP held fourteen roundtables between 1997 and 1999. This series of meetings included presentations on the economics of tobacco farming and the impact of eliminating the government's tobacco program (which set quotas and kept prices artificially high through price supports). The health advocates amazed the farmers by agreeing that the tobacco program should be maintained. The farmers began seeing the "antis" in a new light, and the two groups' understanding of each other's concerns and interests led to two major agreements.

The Results

1. *Core Principles Statement.* In 1998, the group produced its Core Principles Statement, which proposed a fund to diversify tobacco communities' economies, proposed laws to restrict youths' access to tobacco, and urged cooperation between the parties to improve safety and health, among other proposals. It also called for legislation giving the Food and Drug Administration (FDA) authority over tobacco products.

Then, on November 23, 1998, the attorneys general of forty-six states signed a landmark agreement with the five largest tobacco manufacturers. The states would receive over $206 billion from the manufacturers over the course of twenty-five years. Virginia was scheduled to receive $4.2 billion from the settlement. A group of Virginia legislators, farmers, and health advocates created a formula to divide up the funds. They agreed to seek 50 percent for tobacco farmers and their communities and 10 percent for youth prevention and cessation programs, leaving 40 percent for other programs, including public health initiatives. The state's general assembly unanimously passed a bill based on the proposed ratio.

2. *Presidential Commission.* In 2000, President Clinton appointed a commission to make recommendations on improving economic opportunity and protecting public health in tobacco-reliant communities. STCP leaders were instrumental in convincing the president to form the commission.

The commission's two major recommendations were adopted: (1) a buyout for value of the tobacco farmers' quota, and (2) permission to give the Food and Drug Administration regulatory power over tobacco (a change that had been strongly resisted for over a decade by the tobacco manufacturers). Congress voted to give the FDA such regulatory power in 2009, giving the agency enormous powers to control the contents and marketing of tobacco products.

Who would have believed that what began in 1994 at a tense meeting of farmers and health advocates would result in agreements contributing to legislation regulating tobacco and improving public health. Against significant odds, these two groups were able to find common ground.

Finding Common Direction

How do you get groups to forge common direction when the forces pulling them apart appear to be far stronger than the forces pulling them together? The tobacco initiatives offer important insights for dealing with this dilemma. Some of those insights are summarized in Exhibit 7.2.

Learn the Ground Truth Together

In the U.S. military, people often use the term *ground truth* to describe the reality of a tactical situation as opposed to what intelligence reports or senior leaders (far removed from the battle) assert the reality to be. When collaborative leaders try to help a group develop and commit to a common direction, they can start by designing experiences that give the group a taste of the ground truth.

Exhibit 7.2. Strategies to Gain Commitment on a Common Direction.

- Learn the ground truth together.
- Bring resources.
- Take the first step.
- Find a common challenge or enemy.
- Use a skillful facilitator.
- Widen the arena of engagement—bring in third parties.
- Be willing to try a different approach.
- Describe the criteria any solution must meet.
- Reframe the goal.

The health advocates and farmers built trust largely by looking at the same set of facts together. When the participants made visits to tobacco farms and processing centers, they (literally) learned ground truth. When they listened to well-respected economists describe the realities and prospects of tobacco farming, they deepened their understanding of the issues. These experiences helped them start to trust the facts being discussed, an important step toward trusting the process and ultimately each other.

In Chapter Six we discussed the importance of shining a light on the problem or challenge being addressed. If your team researches the facts and does an analysis of the challenge, that ground truth not only helps the team understand the problem but also gives the partners a common definition that can lead to a common direction.

Bring Resources

Public health champion Rebecca Reeve created the seeds of the tobacco initiative by bringing in two grants to support its work. As we discussed in the last chapter, collaborative leaders send a strong signal of support when they put money and other resources on the table. That, in turn, reduces one of the group's likely concerns and frees members up to search for common interests.

Take the First Step

At a key moment in the first tobacco initiative one tobacco advocate talked openly about his anger at the "antis" for being hostile to his way of life. In doing so he took a risk and an important first step. The health advocates appreciated the candor. That led some of the farmers to listen more carefully to the health advocates' concerns.

There are many ways to take the first step, and I discussed several in Chapter Four. Collaborative team members who model openness and candor are taking the first step. Offering others help when they're in trouble is also a powerful way to take the first step, as Jay Gregorius learned when he called a local sheriff to offer assistance during the 2002 D.C. Sniper crisis.

Find a Common Challenge or Enemy

Few things can bring a set of individuals together like a common challenge or enemy. We saw an example of this in the tobacco case, when the farmers started venting their anger at the big tobacco companies. Suddenly, the health advocates and farmers learned they had something in common. That helped reduce the level of animosity and raised the willingness to hear each other's concerns. Another way to create a common challenge is to work together to learn the ground truth of the issue. Yet another is to set a benchmark for performance: If another team worked on a similar project, can we do our work faster? Better? In a way that better meets customer needs? When team members make a powerful statement about the need being addressed—why it matters, who is being hurt, the cost of inaction—it helps to create a common challenge.

Use a Skillful Facilitator

Frank Dukes's participation was critical to the success in the STCP case. He was a model of the collaborative leader; unassuming but persistent, glad to give others credit, eager to understand others' perceptions. Dukes is also a caring and genuine individual, and many in the tobacco groups said that his obvious concern for them and their well-being meant a lot to them and helped them hang in when the meetings seemed to go nowhere.

When participants don't trust each other, they need to be able to trust the facilitator and the process used.

Years after the tobacco initiatives ended, Dukes reflected on some of the lessons he learned about facilitating contentious groups (see Exhibit 7.3).

Exhibit 7.3. Frank Dukes's Observations on Facilitating Difficult Groups.

- Persistence and resilience are critical. When you bounce back, others will be more likely to hang in with you over the long run. Dukes calls this "the power of showing up."

- Don't push for consensus immediately (this is related to having persistence). It takes time to find common (or higher) ground.

- "Appreciate the integrity of the others in the group." It's important to create an atmosphere in which people can see each other's basic honesty, to get past the positions and stereotypes of the other.

- The facilitator's basic belief that progress is possible is critical. People at the table will take some of their cues from the facilitator.

- "Show a basic, human caring for those in the group." Dukes's humanity helped group members feel respected.

Dukes also intuitively understands that in cases like these, the leaders and facilitator must use a great deal of pull. He says that "you don't push it if the parties have seemingly different interests. . . . Hang in there, move slowly, allow relationships and trust to form; only trust will help reveal what might be in common."

Dukes chuckles at the thought of leading the two tobacco initiatives "by the book." Consider: the membership changed from meeting to meeting; there was never a specific statement of purpose that all shared (they would craft one, then it would shift and shift again); ground rules were determined one meeting at a time; participants refused to formally sign on as members of the initiative. Only a highly flexible and patient facilitator could have succeeded in this context.

Dukes was also very careful at the start of each initiative: he made endless phone calls to explain the purpose and get input, he kept communications very open, he demonstrated great flexibility in revising the game plan according to participants' wishes, helping the participants see that they would own the process. When participants have no trust in each other, it's essential that they develop trust in the leader or facilitator, and in the process being used.

Widen the Arena of Engagement—Bring in Third Parties

When members of a collaborative group can't agree on a common direction, it sometimes helps to widen the arena of engagement (the term comes from Lucy, 1988, who discusses "widening the arena of conflict," p. 32), by bringing in customers, other stakeholders, and people with no vested interest to listen and offer their views. It was significant that the tobacco initiatives included meetings with key state legislators who were concerned about tobacco farming and health issues and with academics who briefed the parties on the economics of the industry.

Be Willing to Try a Different Approach

When members of a collaborative team don't agree on the goal or a strategy to meet it, they sometimes get stuck. People may have gone public with their views; they may see it as a loss of face to change their minds or seek common ground with others. One strategy to consider is for everyone to take a deep breath, put the current options on hold, and look for a new approach.

We saw an example of that in the tobacco initiatives. The first effort went about as far as it could; the group wasn't totally at odds nor did it have total agreement, but the grant ran out and the members did agree on a few items. Then a new initiative started, with representatives from a much larger region, and it built on the progress of the first group. To use the concept we introduced in Chapter Six, the second tobacco initiative created a new S curve. Because the first effort had produced some results and because many of the people from the first initiative joined the second initiative, the second (regional) initiative started at a higher level. Figure 7.2 captures this dynamic.

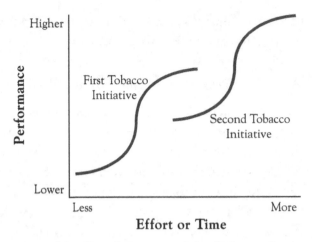

Figure 7.2. The Two S Curves of the Tobacco Initiatives.

Describe the Criteria Any Solution Must Meet

When a group is struggling to establish its goal or the strategies to achieve the goal, it's always useful to articulate the criteria that potential solutions must address. The tobacco participants were never extremely detailed in articulating their own goals, but they were very clear that any solutions they endorsed must honor the farmers' economic needs as well as reduce the health problems caused by smoking. For an excellent discussion of using objective criteria to help parties negotiate their differences, look at one of the classic books on negotiating: *Getting to Yes: Negotiating Agreement Without Giving In*, by Fisher and Ury (1981).

Reframe the Goal

If my wife, Jackie, and I get into an argument and the issue is very important to her, she sometimes pauses, looks me in the eye, smiles, and says, "Honey, would you do this for me?" I immediately relax, no longer in an argumentative mode, no longer feeling the need to defend my position. Especially if the issue isn't as important to me as it is to her, it's easy at that point to just say, "Sure." The goal is no longer arguing for my solution, the goal is now to support the relationship. As a friend of mine likes to say, "You can be right all the time, or you can have a good relationship. You can't have both." Jackie's using an approach that applies to professional and political conflicts as well as interpersonal relationships: she's reframing the issue.

In the political world, reframing the issue is one of the more effective strategies for overcoming conflicts based on deeply held values. Joe Szakos, the head of a nonprofit community organization, is a master at this art. Szakos's group helps low-income people push for policy changes that are important to them in such areas as employment, housing, and voting rights. In 2007, his group was working with a broad-based coalition that was lobbying its state legislature to raise the minimum wage. The state senate passed the raise, and it was now up to the state house, where the prospects weren't looking good. A representative of Szakos's group asked a conservative member of the key house committee what he needed to support the bill. The member said, "Stop framing this as a labor issue; you need to talk about it as a *moral* issue." The group took that advice, it proved easier for some legislators to support the raise in moral terms, and it helped to get the bill through the house committee.

THE BOTTOM LINE

I've outlined several strategies for helping collaborative teams find a common direction when the parties begin with different interests, goals, or priorities. Most collaborative teams don't start with the animosity and harsh stereotypes that were present among the tobacco initiative parties. But collaborative leaders make a mistake when they assume that those who agree to join a partnership are also in agreement on the stated goal. People join such teams for a variety of reasons; some even join because the team threatens their agency, and they have a strong interest in playing defense to stop the initiative.

When team members talk openly about their interests and goals for the project, they'll probably discover both agreement and differences. One of the collaborative leader's challenges is to create a climate of candor, surfacing all views and interests. Doing so helps a team seek common direction, and little is possible on collaborative teams without an agreement on the purpose.

The farmers and health advocates participating in the tobacco initiative came from radically different cultures. Their ignorance of each other's cultures was one of the biggest challenges they faced. The issue of working across different cultures is a huge one in many collaborative efforts and deserves its own chapter. That's our next topic.

8

Working Effectively Across
Different Cultures

*It's very powerful when people tell their stories to each
other. It's even more powerful when they work together on
real issues, on projects that affect them in their daily lives.*
　　　　　　　　　　　　　　　—Amiram Goldin, founder,
　　　　　　　　　　　　　　　　　　　Neighbors program

The American manager, an experienced and savvy negotiator,
was at his wits end. He was used to negotiating with other
Westerners, and understood the rules very well. You identify your
interests and bottom line, try to learn what the other negotiator's
bottom line is, get the best deal you can, and when you find a mutually beneficial agreement you shake hands. That shake is a signal
that negotiations have ended successfully.

This approach had always worked well, until he entered
negotiations in an Asian country. No longer could he "get right
down to business"; there had to be tea and time to talk about one's
family and other things. Once he and his Asian colleague finally
got into the negotiations, it took forever before they reached an
agreement and shook hands. To the American's amazement, that
handshake wasn't a sign that the deal was struck. As he later
learned, the shake meant only that his colleague was ready to begin
serious negotiations.

The Puzzle of Culture

Since the 1980s, organizational theorists have placed a great emphasis on culture as a key to understanding organizational performance. These theorists offer many definitions of organizational culture: the values espoused by an organization; the "unwritten rules of the social game" (Hofstede and Hofstede, 2005, p. 4); organizational ceremonies, language, and rituals; and others. One of the most significant aspects of culture relates to group members' fundamental *assumptions* about how their organization works and about the environment that affects it. Whatever the definition, there's no question that organizational culture is a major factor in determining performance.

Collaborative leaders frequently deal with partners from different agency or even country cultures. In doing so, they need to navigate a minefield of potential obstacles. That's what the Western negotiator learned when he assumed that a handshake in the Far East meant the same thing as in West. Dealing with different country or agency cultures requires patience and sleuth-like skills. It also requires a strong desire to learn the unwritten rules (and they are *always* unwritten!) about the other culture.

It's hard to find a place on earth where cultures are more at odds than in the Middle East. Yet some brave people there are making impressive efforts to bridge their enormous cultural, religious, and political divides. After describing this case, I'll discuss some of the strategies that helped the parties work together, and draw lessons for other collaborations.

Neighbors for Joint Development in the Galilee (Israel)

Amiram Goldin lives in the Galilee, the northern part of Israel. The son of Holocaust survivors, Goldin has had a lifelong passion to see Arabs and Jews in the Galilee learn to live and work peacefully together. Most of the villages in the Galilee are all Arab or all Jewish.

In many areas, Arab and Jewish villages exist within a few kilometers of each other, yet have almost no communication between them. Goldin created the nonprofit Neighbors for Joint Development in the Galilee program to change that.

Goldin says:

We were looking for a process that would lead to joint efforts and mutual respect among Jews and Arabs who live near each other. Many of the villages in the Galilee have the same needs—access to water and sanitation, better roads, recreational and social facilities, economic development and employment—but the Jewish and Arab villages rarely work together to meet their common needs. In 2002, we created Neighbors for Joint Development in the Galilee ["Neighbors" for short]. The goals were to raise their consciousness about their shared interests, to introduce them to the idea of joint development, to lend them the tools for joint planning, and then to plan the development of the land together with them, while building relationships based on trust.

The Neighbors Process

To understand Neighbors, we'll look at one of its projects: Planning for a Shared Landscape. In 2006, Neighbors began working with two pairs of communities: one pair was the Arab village of Sachnin and the Jewish village of Yuvalim and the other was the Arab village of Tamra and the Jewish village of Mitzpe Aviv. The Neighbors process included four stages:

1. The formation of groups of residents from each locality
2. A two-day intercultural dialogue workshop for each pair of communities
3. The identification of desired projects, joint planning for the projects, ongoing dialogue
4. An arts workshop involving the youths from the communities

Forming Groups of Residents. Neighbors staff sought groups of about fifteen in each locality. Once selected, the groups met separately for five sessions so the members could get to know one another and establish some internal chemistry. It was important for the members to have time to form strong bonds *within* their own groups before they began meeting with their counterparts from the neighboring village, because meeting with those from the other village was risky. They needed to feel supported within their own group first.

Holding a Two-Day Intercultural Dialogue. Next, Neighbors held a two-day dialogue workshop for each pair of localities. Assisted by Neighbors conveners, the participants first met separately in their municipal groups and talked openly about their hopes and fears, their frustrations and anger and desires. Then the Jewish and Arab groups came together to hear summaries of each group's feelings and to try to understand those feelings.

> *The Jewish and Arab participants first met separately and talked openly about their hopes, fears, and anger; then they met together to share those feelings.*

The discussions were very intense. Participants were candid and said things that were difficult for others to hear. But that kind of openness was critical for the process to succeed. These comments, made at the end of one of the workshops, reflect some of the emotions:

"I heard some very harsh things, and I said what I thought, true and honest things. Do I feel better understood? I think I do. It is very important to me to be in these kinds of discussions, as an Arab woman; it is a real mission."

"When comparing myself and the group then and today, yesterday it was all opinions and mutual recriminations that were hard to bridge. Today, I know that if we wish it, it is no dream: building bridges, thinking about things in common. Yesterday's fears have almost all disappeared."

The participants also spent time selecting issues for discussion and actions, such as building a meeting place between two of the municipalities to house recreational and cultural activities and developing more employment opportunities between municipal pairs.

Ongoing Planning and Dialogue Sessions. Next, the groups from each pair of villages met to begin concrete planning for their projects and continue their dialogue sessions. They met every two weeks for nine months. Each joint group meeting had a Jewish and an Arab facilitator.

Participants took tours of each other's communities, gathered data about the specific projects, set goals, and established criteria for evaluating their projects. For instance, the Yuvalim-Sachnin group decided to create a park to benefit both villages. Group members also worked out budgets for their projects.

Establishing a Youth Workshop. The Neighbors program also created an arts workshop for the localities. The goal was to bring young Arabs and Jews together for joint artistic activity and socializing. Youths were put into mixed Jewish and Arab groups led by facilitators. They created mosaics together; took field visits to each other's communities; learned about each other's culture, food, and religion; and got to know each other.

Implementation and Next Steps

The Neighbors program is ongoing. The Sachnin and Yuvalim villages found land to create a playground in Sachnin that will benefit both villages, and started raising money for the project in 2009. They're well on their way to a successful completion. The Tamra and Mitzpe Aviv joint discussions went well, but the groups identified a need that was highly controversial, making progress difficult. One of the lessons learned, the Neighbors staff concluded, is to be very careful in selecting initial projects.

It's remarkable that the Neighbors participants continue to meet several years after their initial meetings, developing greater trust and increasing commitment to their projects and to working together.

Amiram Goldin is optimistic about the program's future: "In the beginning of the project, it was very difficult to build trust. Our underlying aim was to build a basis for cooperation among people who don't have the same political agenda. We found that trust was only possible if we started at the grass roots and built it from the ground up . . .

"We also found that the *experiential activities*—field trips, seeing everyday life in the partner town, and especially creating joint projects—are critical."

The Neighbors process demonstrates the power of carefully building relationships through dialogue. Moreover, it demonstrates the importance of moving from dialogue to *concrete projects of mutual interest*. Neighbors is also testimony to the power of passionate, committed leadership—the impact of a champion. When Amiram Goldin says that it is critical to find a path to peaceful coexistence among Arabs and Jews in Israel, people listen to him. He has enormous credibility. You see, Goldin's son was killed in a terrorist attack in 2002. A short time later, Goldin created Neighbors. (For more details, see Neighbors for Joint Development in the Galilee, 2009. For information on a film about Goldin's personal story, see *Looking for the Lost Voice*, 2005.)

Adopting an Attitude of Curiosity

In two of the collaborative examples we've explored thus far—the Neighbors project and the tobacco initiatives—groups from radically different cultures were able to break down stereotypes, see each other as individuals with valid needs, and find and pursue common interests together. If they could get past their enormous cultural differences to collaborate on common goals, we can all learn something from their success. What were the keys to their efforts?

I believe that one of the keys had to do with an attitude. It's probably an attitude you've adopted when you visited another country (or a different part of this country) for the first time. Think about it: the food, rituals, dress, habits, and traditions are different, sometimes delightful and sometimes baffling. If you learned from the trip and enjoyed the differences, chances are you held an attitude of *curiosity*. That's precisely the attitude we need to adopt when collaborating with people from different organizational cultures.

But being curious about very different cultures can be a real challenge. Consider the Neighbors example. The Arabs and Jews in the neighboring villages have long memories of threats and violence perpetrated by "the other." How can you be curious about a group that you perceive as responsible for so much pain? It took enormous courage and discipline for the Neighbors participants to share their memories with the neighboring villagers and still be able to listen to each other's stories.

The mindset I find most powerful when working across different cultures is to think of the other culture(s) as a puzzle, a place that's different from my own experiences, one that I need to understand if we're going to be productive together. And developing such understanding requires genuine curiosity, even humility.

Some Strategies for Working Across Different Cultures

In addition to adopting the mindset just described, you'll need some strategies to help you navigate across different cultures.

Exhibit 8.1. Effective Strategies for Working Across Different Cultures.

- Respect differences; don't allow them to overshadow the commonalities.
- Work on relationships; take time to let trust grow.
- Become "bilingual"; take time to decode the other culture(s).
- Do real work together on a common goal.
- Co-locate staff from several agencies or units in the same space.
- Identify and use the strengths in each organization.
- Make needed systemic changes when trying to alter an organization's culture.

Exhibit 8.1 summarizes several of these strategies, some of which were used by the Neighbors leaders. I discuss each strategy in the rest of this section.

Respect Differences; Don't Allow Them to Overshadow Commonalities

Myra Howze Shiplett is a consultant who spent over thirty years working for the executive and judicial branches of the federal government, including holding senior positions in the Department of State and the Federal Trade Commission. She's worked with people in countries around the world and understands how cultural differences can blind people to their common needs and interests. She says:

> We sometimes forget the basic human things that most people want—take care of your children, have a family, see that those whom you love will have a better life than you have. Failures to bridge cultural differences often occur because people don't think they have the opportunity to be respected, to achieve these basic things for their families and others they care about, to have a secure and better life.
>
> Well, the differences among different countries and different ethnic groups are often enormous. But I've been struck by the many things that can and do bring us together. If we can focus more on what makes us similar we can do a great deal together.

Both the Neighbors project and the tobacco initiative succeeded, in part, because they respected people's differences and then built on that understanding to surface and address common needs. In the Neighbors instance, those common needs included recreation facilities, youth services, and work opportunities. One reason for Neighbors' progress is its focus on helping Arab and Jewish residents see that they have some of the same basic needs.

Work on Relationships; Take Time to Let Trust Grow

In 2007, Myra Shiplett began a two-year project for the chief of justice of Indonesia's Supreme Court. She worked as part of a team that included nongovernmental organizations, staff from Indonesian government agencies, and the chief of justice. The team's purpose was to help Indonesia come up with strategies to reduce corruption and then to implement those strategies. "This was meant to be a true partnership, not the old approach of offering aid to a country's leaders and telling them what they must do to get that aid," she reflected.

> Instead, the partners all sat down at the start and agreed to a plan of action for the first year, and they tried to make all decisions in the spirit of respect and partnership.
>
> It took a *full year* to establish a good level of trust, such that when the professional team offered advice the Indonesians would truly consider it. That year involved lots of meetings, demonstrations of respect, explanations of the data that the team developed, efforts to communicate and listen carefully to one another. At that point, the leaders of the court system were starting to implement certain HR recommendations.

Think about that: What was the team's deliverable after one year? A readiness to get started. A hard-driving leader might have fired this team. Fortunately, the team continued on and made considerable progress during its second year.

When working in other countries, it's usually "relationships first, business second."

Allen Hard, who consults with NGOs around the world, wouldn't be surprised by this team's experience. As noted in Chapter Four, Hard's work has taught him something that confounds many

Westerners: when doing work in certain other countries, he says, it's "relationships first, work second." Smart collaborative leaders understand that relationships and work aren't really separate activities in such cultures. The Neighbors leaders built this insight into their design. Their participants spent months in homogenous and mixed groups learning to listen to one another; those interactions developed into stronger relationships as they began doing work together on shared interests. Indeed, in many countries around the world, meetings begin with food and social banter, never with talk of work. Smart collaborative leaders find ways to ensure that meetings include food and drinks.

At this point some of you are probably thinking, "But we can't wait a year to get started; we have to demonstrate results fast!" Fair enough. And most interagency collaboration within the United States needn't go at such a gradual pace. But the principles are the same: If the partners come from different agency cultures and if they haven't worked together in the past, you need to take the time to build a certain level of trust and understanding for genuine collaboration to begin. Remember: to move up the S curve, you go slow to go fast.

Become "Bilingual"; Take Time to Decode the Other Culture(s)

Consider the following: a state police official was leading a joint task force made up of law enforcement officers from all levels of government. They were pursuing the leaders of a violent gang. When they located the gang leaders' hideout, the task force leader announced, "It's time to kick butt!" His intent was to arrest the gang leaders. But two members of the task force (who came from a local government police department) took his words literally and were about to storm the house with guns blazing, until the leader made his meaning clear.

Some might read this and wonder if this task force had spent any time training together, if they even had a game plan for the raid. Those are reasonable questions, but it's more likely that the communications breakdown occurred because the task force members

- Came from different agencies with different cultures
- Worked at different levels of government
- Were dealing with a high-stress situation (and probably operating on few hours of sleep)
- Didn't take the critical step of checking out the meaning of the person giving the order

Put all that together and it's a perfect storm for miscommunication.

Becoming "bilingual"—learning the other culture's values, policies and procedures, language, stories, politics, and structure—requires a real commitment and a genuine interest in others' cultures. It certainly takes time, but more than that it requires a willingness to suspend judgment and adopt that sense of curiosity. The collaborative leaders I've observed who demonstrate such qualities usually do so either because they're naturally interested in other people and cultures or because they failed to learn about another's culture at some previous point in their careers, to their detriment.

How do you decode another organization's or group's culture in order to avoid such mishaps and work effectively? We can learn from the Baltimore County Child Advocacy Center (CAC) in Maryland, where social workers team with police officers to deal with child sexual abuse. The center was formed in 1989, and police officers and social workers are co-located there. Teams of two—a cop and a social worker—work together to apprehend offenders and help the abused children. It's been a striking success, resulting in better treatment for the victims and more confessions and convictions. But the two professions have had to work very hard to understand each other's cultures. Table 8.1 summarizes the key cultural differences.

Table 8.1. Cultural Differences at the Child Advocacy Center.

Police		Social Workers
Separate self from others' feelings; stay objective.	*Training*	Connect with clients; tune into their feelings.
Don't trust; be wary, stay factual, and rely on hard evidence. The work is governed by laws; probable cause is needed to take action against suspects.	*Methods*	Form trust; be open; understand clients' point of view. The work is shaped by social science insights, experience, and intuition.
See police as higher on the food chain than social workers at the CAC.	*Pecking order*	Feel social workers must prove themselves (even though they usually have more formal education).
Most likely assigned to CAC during the first decade; didn't see it as career enhancing.	*Joining the CAC*	Chose to work at the CAC.
Think "lock 'em up; they can't be rehabilitated."	*Attitude toward sexual abuse perpetrators*	Think "work with them; change is possible."

Source: Adapted from Linden, 2002.

As Table 8.1 demonstrates, the cultural gaps between these two groups are enormous. Police live in a paramilitary, black-and-white world governed by laws. Social workers come from a far less rigid environment; they live in a world of grays.

The social workers and police at the CAC have used these strategies to decode each other's cultures:

- Shared rituals, like morning coffee together, lunches together

- End-of-day meetings to surface any issues or conflicts

- Open discussion of roles

- A lot of joint training

- Joint case reviews

- Joint development of protocols for interviewing

- Efforts to work on the relationship between the social work supervisor and her police counterpart

Do Real Work Together on a Common Goal

In 1954, a social psychologist named Muzafer Sherif conducted an experiment in intergroup relations. He took twenty-two boys to a Boy Scout camp in Oklahoma. The boys were similar in every important way. At the camp Sherif divided them into two groups, which lived in separate parts of the camp. Each group quickly developed its own identity, and soon the groups became highly competitive. Sports competition led to intergroup tensions and hostility. The staff had to work hard to prevent fights from breaking out as the groups started raiding each other's sites.

Before things got totally out of hand, Sherif changed the nature of the experiment. He gave the two groups several tasks that required them to work together on a common goal, tasks like unplugging a clogged water supply after they had gone several hours without water, and pulling the food truck out of a ditch as dinnertime approached. The boys soon let go of their animosities and started working together on these mutual "superordinate goals" (Sherif, Harvey, and White, 1961).

It's fascinating to see groups that are at odds, perhaps even hostile toward each other, join together when faced with an important common challenge. The Neighbors program helped Israeli Arabs and Jews identify common needs "on the ground," which led to joint work projects benefiting both. They didn't come together because they suddenly forgot decades of hostility; they joined out of a pragmatic desire to meet an important need, and their work together helped them break down stereotypes and identify other shared needs. As Amiram Goldin said, "Our approach goes way beyond dialogue. It is much more related to reality; they [the Jews and Arabs] work on real issues that affect them."

As I've noted earlier, working on shared tasks that lead to common goals is a powerful way to build trust, mutual respect, and a sense of team identity. It also helps partners learn about each other's cultures.

Co-Locate Staff from Several Agencies or Units

Sometimes more fundamental changes are needed than the strategies listed thus far. The police and social workers dealing with child sexual abuse, for instance, owe some of their success to the fact that they are co-located in one building, making it far easier for their two-person teams to meet frequently, form relationships, and share information on their shared cases.

Co-location can be a powerful strategy for groups with different cultures that need to work together on a daily or frequent basis. The U.S. Forest Service and the Bureau of Land Management, two land management agencies with similar missions and customers, have co-located field units in over thirty locations around the country. Through an initiative called Service First, they are improving customer service, saving resources, and improving land stewardship at these joint offices. The most effective co-located offices involve far more than shared space; they often integrate operations at the front desk and in such areas as human resources and fleet management, providing seamless service to customers who don't want to learn the bureaucratic ins and outs of which agency provides which service (for more on Service First, see Linden, 2002).

Some nonprofits around the country have also made considerable progress through co-location strategies. And since 2003, almost all fifty states have created fusion centers, which help emergency management, intelligence, and law enforcement officials to share information and work together. In Chapter Eleven, we'll look at fusion centers, nonprofits, and other groups that are co-locating.

Identify and Use the Strengths in Each Organization

When Joe Biden began his U.S. Senate career in 1973, Mike Mansfield from Montana was the Senate majority leader. By his own account, Biden was impatient and brash. He couldn't abide some of his colleagues' antics and clearly thought several of them weren't up to the job. Mansfield saw Biden's problem, but he also detected real potential in Biden. One day he pulled Biden aside and gave him wise advice along these lines: "These senators were elected by a large number of people who admire them. Your job, Joe, is to find out what it is that those constituents see in their senator." Biden took that advice to heart, changed his view of his colleagues, and became an effective senator and, later, vice president.

Cultural differences can put people on the defensive. Sometimes they also leave people feeling superior, as in Biden's case. Smart collaborative leaders help their colleagues move from *me* to *we* when they encourage the parties to look for the strengths in each culture, then tap and align those strengths with the project's mission.

Make Needed Systemic Changes When Trying to Alter an Organization's Culture

Myra Howze Shiplett, the consultant quoted earlier in this chapter, has thought long and deeply about the systemic issues involved in working across agency cultures. Her conclusions are on the mark:

> Until very recently there have been almost no incentives . . . that reinforce lateral communications and collaboration. Almost all of the incentives in the U.S. government are focused on the individual achieving a particular technical or policy outcome; those incentives must be changed to reward teams and collaboration. Take the promotion system. At the State Department, the criteria for promotion for foreign service officers do not include assignments out of your "cone" [a functional

division, political, economic, military, or the like].
Taking an assignment in another cone hasn't been career
enhancing at all. Secretary of State Rice tried to change
that, but too late in her tenure at State.

You don't need a PhD in organizational dynamics to realize
the folly of expecting employees to demonstrate teamwork and an
agency-wide perspective when their everyday reality and career
future relies on doing individual work in narrow areas. There are
several systems that can reward both individual and collaborative behavior—performance measures and performance appraisals,
training programs, promotions, and budgetary incentives, to name
a few. We'll look at two systemic methods that foster and reward
collaboration in Chapters Eleven and Twelve.

A Note on Doing International Work

This chapter has included examples of cross-culture work from
abroad as well as in the United States. What are the key insights to
keep in mind when working in foreign countries? I put that question to Michael Rawlings, a senior faculty member at the Federal
Executive Institute. Rawlings's thirty years of international experience include service in the judicial arm of the U.S. armed forces as
the U.S. Army Judge Advocate General Corps Officer at NATO
headquarters from 1986 to 1989. He also worked in the Office of
the Commission of the European Union, where he was able to
observe the emerging systems of the EU take shape—a fascinating,
once-in-a-lifetime experience. When I asked him to describe the
keys to working effectively with foreign governments and people
from other cultures, he offered a number of insights (Exhibit 8.2).

Rawlings's observations mirror those of Shiplett and many others who have extensive experience in different cultures. The same
themes emerge over and over: take time to learn the other culture,
understand that trust is critical, be humble, put "relationships before
work," learn others' assumptions and make your own assumptions

---

Exhibit 8.2. Michael Rawlings's Views on Working in International Settings.

- Relationships are critical: "Focus on the human before the work." One of the simplest ways to do so is to show an interest in the nonwork aspects of someone's life.

- Learn the culture and assumptions people bring to the task.

- When you think you're understanding some of the assumptions people hold, check with the people involved.

- Be sensitive to the paradigms of the people in the room; in international work there will be multiple paradigms, and it takes time to learn them.

- Be humble. You can't fully understand the culture(s) involved, you never will, but it's imperative to try to learn as much as possible.

- You can't just step in and start: it takes time, care, and lots of patience to learn the local culture, the country issues as well as the personal issues involved.

- Focus on the midterm and long term. Relationships and trust don't occur quickly.

- Always remain in a learning mode; you're never "there."

- Find someone who's native to the culture you're learning about—this person could be a friend or co-facilitator—and ask her to coach you.

- Be authentic.

- Ask, What is it that I don't see that you see that I might be missing and that's important to our success?

---

explicit, use the strengths of the local culture rather than trying to transplant what works in another culture, and play for the long run. And remember to maintain an attitude of curiosity.

These lessons reflect a wise comment from one of the most thoughtful organization development consultants in the United States, Marvin Weisbord, who writes, "The consultants' dilemma is that we always arrive in the middle of somebody else's movie and leave before the end" (Weisbord, 1990, p. 234).

Working across cultures requires the same perspective. It's someone else's movie (story), you're arriving in the middle (there's a past and a context that you don't know but need to learn), and it will go on long after you leave. You'll always have more to learn, and if you're curious enough you'll benefit from the inevitable mistakes and enjoy the journey.

THE BOTTOM LINE

Learning about different cultures can be painful work. Many people learn the unwritten rules of new cultures only by breaking them. You suggest a meeting with another agency to work out a conflict, or wonder aloud about bringing an innovative idea to the head of your agency, and people frown. "That's not how we do things around here" is how it's sometimes put.

When you adopt an attitude of curiosity and take the time to decode a new culture, what you learn gives you power—power to use the existing cultural rules to support your goals, power to understand what another's words means, power to grasp the assumptions underneath those words, power to understand why things are taking so much time, and power to develop strategies for finding common ground. Finally, decoding a different culture gives you power to address those four questions that usually determine whether members will move from me to we.

1. Do I have something to contribute that is needed, recognized, and used by the team?

2. Are we working on a project that is important to me and my own organization (important in terms of mission, priorities, values)?

3. Are we making progress? Do we have a reasonable chance for success?

4. How will this project support or threaten any of my core needs or interests (and those of my home organization)?

It is difficult if not impossible to answer such questions when you're working with people from cultures that you don't understand.

"Ah, but what about impossible-to-work-with Charlie?" I hear you asking. It's not an issue of being from different cultures—this person works in your agency, even in the same division. The problem is, he's a control artist, he won't share information, thinks he's always right, and can't play well with others (for starters).

There are plenty of difficult people in our organizations, no question. And some of them "honor you" with their presence on your collaborative team. What to do about difficult people and difficult situations is the topic of our next two chapters.

9

Dealing with People Problems in Collaboration

Don't fight forces, use them.

—Buckminster Fuller

There's an old joke: collaboration is a series of unnatural acts committed by nonconsenting adults.

It's far too cynical for my taste, but you get the idea. Collaboration goes against our personal and organizational DNA. In this chapter I'll discuss some of the "people problems" you'll encounter in your collaboration efforts. I'll begin with a major collaboration initiative that fell well short of its goals, largely because it didn't anticipate certain people issues. Then I'll describe a systematic approach to dealing with difficult people and behaviors, and finish with an example of collaboration that successfully addressed some major people problems.

The JIVA Program

In the mid 1990s, some key members of Congress grew frustrated with the intelligence community (IC). These members were concerned that the sixteen IC agencies didn't share information well, were overly competitive, and failed to take advantage of opportunities to collaborate. To address these concerns, the Defense Intelligence

Agency (DIA) developed an initiative to foster information sharing and collaboration across the community. To fund it, DIA reallocated approximately $40 million annually (taken from all Department of Defense intelligence organizations). It was called JIVA: Joint Intelligence Virtual Architecture.

Developing JIVA's Structure

As Chris Demme, JIVA deputy program manager for three years, describes it, the JIVA concept was to establish a virtual organizational environment and use advanced business processes to improve intelligence analysis, production, and dissemination. Demme thought the JIVA concept was promising, but he saw significant cultural hurdles in the intelligence community and wanted to improve the key business processes supporting information sharing. So JIVA added another element: the use of virtual teams (sometimes called *communities of interest*) made up of IC analysts and others who focused on a common mission area but worked in different agencies (Figure 9.1).

JIVA contracted with the Federal Executive Institute (FEI) to provide each of the sixteen virtual teams with a weeklong training session (disclosure: I was one of the FEI instructors for the JIVA program). FEI instructors helped each team clarify its mission, key objectives, and customers; do some team building; and establish team norms and practices for virtual communications. Each team had a leader, and the members were interested in working together on their shared technical interests.

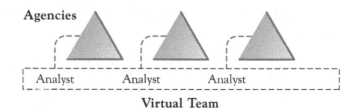

Figure 9.1. The JIVA Structure.

Team members came from most of the sixteen IC member agencies; they were mainly analysts from the middle ranks of the federal government. They formed teams on such topics as

- Regional issues in Colombia
- Theater ballistic missiles
- The Chinese military
- Regional issues in the Middle East

Each team had a mentor (usually a retired three- or four-star general or admiral) who met periodically with the team to help it deal with any political or resource problems it encountered. These mentors had access to the people leading the IC agencies and could intervene with them if a team needed assistance from on high.

Getting Mixed Results

Despite extensive efforts and major investments in the virtual teams, they didn't achieve their potential. An evaluation done three years into the program showed that about one-third of the sixteen teams were meeting regularly and were productive, one-third met periodically but produced little, and one-third no longer met.

It should be said that the overall JIVA program did produce some very positive results. But those of us who worked with the virtual team aspect of the program thought we should have gotten more out of the effort. Batting .333 in baseball is a very respectable average, but we weren't impressed with a one-third success rate, given the stakes involved. Clearly, something important was missing. Do you see it?

An Approach for Dealing with Difficult People and Situations in Collaboration

Think about the two fundamental human needs discussed in Chapter One: *mastery*—to be competent at something (and appreciated for it)—and *belonging*—to be part of something larger than oneself. In my experience, many of the people problems teams experience when working across boundaries are caused when one or both of these needs aren't being met. There were many factors that reduced JIVA's success, but the major one had to do with several middle managers' perceptions that the JIVA teams threatened these two needs. That shouldn't have surprised us.

After all, JIVA failed to offer middle managers any role in the initiative. They didn't have a seat at the table and had no control over the program. Yet they had analysts assigned to the virtual teams, sometimes doing work on another agency's mission area. That wasn't a formula for success, not given the fact that many of these managers had huge egos and control needs.

To the middle managers, JIVA offered few benefits and several potential costs. JIVA threatened the managers' need for mastery; they saw JIVA as reducing their units' competence. And JIVA certainly didn't help the managers meet the need to belong; in a very real sense they didn't belong to the program.

> When the middle managers looked at JIVA, they saw few benefits and a big loss of control.

As a result, some of these middle managers skillfully found ways to derail aspects of the project.

Collaborative initiatives can threaten the two fundamental human needs for a variety of reasons. The point isn't that you need to become an amateur psychologist but rather that you need to think in a systematic way about methods to ensure that these two needs are met. Doing so will go a long way toward reducing the impact of those with outsized egos, those who love to control resources and information, and those with the many other charming behaviors that bedevil even the most skillful collaborative leaders.

The following discussion takes you through a structured approach for addressing some of the major behavioral problems that arise in collaborative efforts. It involves five strategies (Exhibit 9.1).

Exhibit 9.1. Five Strategies for Preventing or Addressing Difficult Behaviors in Collaborative Projects.

---

1. Communicate your expectations and needs.
2. Use measurement, reward, and accountability systems that promote collaboration.
3. Raise the stakes of the initiative.
4. Check the roles (and role conflicts) involved.
5. Use pull to deal with difficult personalities.

My experience is that you'll have the greatest success if you start with the first three strategies, which are more preventive and proactive. If those don't address the problem, consider using the final two.

Communicate Your Expectations and Needs

Here's a fairly common conversation with some clients:

> *Manager:* We have a lot of talented staff, but many of them have a silo mentality and just focus on their work. I just can't seem to get my people to see the big picture.
>
> *Consultant:* Are you showing them the big picture?
>
> *Manager:* [*Long, embarrassed pause.*]

Sometimes leaders are convinced that they've made their expectations and priorities clear to others, yet conversations with their staff reveal confusion or ignorance of the priorities. In the JIVA program the goals and expectations weren't adequately communicated to everyone involved, which reduced overall impact.

In other instances the leaders' words about priorities are very clear, but those words aren't in synch with the agency's policies, informal rewards system, and the like.

When dealing with difficult behavior in a collaborative project, the place to begin is to examine both the collaborative leader's expectations and how they're being communicated. Here are two good examples. (An expanded version of the FMS example is available on the Jossey-Bass Web site for this book.)

Dealing with Difficult Behavior in a State Police Job and at the Federal Financial Management Service

Collaborating Laterally with Colleagues in a New Job

A state police sergeant was in a new job and new jurisdiction. She didn't know the local law enforcement leaders. She talked with neighboring police agencies about the importance of working together, but they were wary—what's her *real* agenda? So she started sharing information with personnel in other agencies without asking for anything in return. She kept at it until her colleagues realized she was sincere about working together.

A sergeant in a sister agency asked her to start attending that agency's weekly senior staff meetings, and the relationship took off. "It's amazing what a difference it makes to be at their meetings, learning how they deal with issues," she remarked. They began exchanging all kinds of information; some of that information helped solve crimes. As personnel in other agencies realized that she was eager to exchange information and had no hidden agenda, they started to reach out as well. By communicating her intentions and taking the first step, she helped a cold relationship become a positive one.

This sergeant had no formal authority over her peers. Moreover, she was the "newbie," and a female in a very male, top-down culture. But she was still able to forge a collaborative relationship with her colleagues, in part by signaling her interest and her expectations of sharing information.

Using Communications to Foster Collaboration at FMS

ON THE
WEB

When Dick Gregg was appointed commissioner of the federal government's Financial Management Service in December 1997, he took over a mess. The agency was as balkanized as any I've seen: units duplicated each other's work; the two senior leaders had different agendas; upper managers fought for turf; the agency didn't speak with one voice.

Gregg, a quiet, sincere (but not charismatic) man, wasn't overwhelmed, explaining that

> I brought over just one person from my previous agency, and made him my deputy. He and I had had some success together and I wanted to use basically the same approach here. So, on my first day at FMS, I made clear to the senior managers how I operate. I said that our first priority was to make the FMS culture one of teamwork. I gave examples of acting as a team. I said that we would speak with one voice, that information would be shared widely. I emphasized that we would have a few common objectives, and that we'd do business from an agency-wide perspective [Linden, 2002, p. 205].

Now, that all sounds very nice, straightforward, and terribly unrealistic, right? Perhaps. But Dick Gregg was determined to see change at FMS. He knew that collaboration was needed, and he was relentless in communicating and acting on that message.

Gregg recalled that the deputy he brought with him, Ken Papaj (pronounced "popeye"), "is a master at giving people feedback, both positive and negative. He can tell people what they need to hear much better than I can." So Gregg played to Papaj's strengths and had him sit down with each manager one-on-one, telling the manager

Dick Gregg understood that engaging people in meaningful dialogue requires small group, face-to-face meetings.

what he needed to continue doing and what he had to change in order to support the cultural change needed. Managers understood that Papaj and Gregg were speaking with one voice.

One manager later remarked that "Dick was very consistent with both words and actions. He told us what he wanted, why he wanted it, and that he expected us to do our part . . . he made his expectations very clear" (Linden, 2002, p. 206).

The words, of course, had to be supported by actions. Gregg and Papaj did a number of things to reinforce their expectations. They

- *Emphasized collaboration in the performance appraisals*. The first behavioral element in the appraisal became collaboration. The appraisal spells out in some detail what collaboration means and what's expected of the managers.

- *Made promotions based largely on people's demonstrated collaborative behavior*. This made it clear that collaboration was in people's career interest.

- *Made use of matrix teams*. The teams met weekly or more often to keep on top of operational issues. This helped staff learn how the agency's pieces fit together.

- *Communicated with staff in small groups*. They spent literally hundreds of hours meeting with employees in their own work units, talking about priorities and listening to the staff's questions. And because Gregg and Papaj are good listeners, staff learned they could talk candidly about their hopes and concerns.

Gregg understood one of the fundamental principles of organizational communications: if you want to make an impact on people's minds, you have to engage them in a two-way dialogue, which requires *small-group, face-to-face experiences*.

Leaders can't require collaboration, but they can expect it.

The results were impressive. In less than two years Gregg and Papaj helped transform a balkanized culture into one that is a model of openness, information sharing, and solid results. Although Gregg retired in 2006, the new culture retains these strengths. (For a detailed look at FMS and how Dick Gregg helped to change it, see Linden, 2002, chap. 12).

Chuck Short, a wonderful collaborative leader mentioned in Chapter Four of this book, has an apt saying: "You can't require collaboration, but you can *expect* it." Whatever your organizational role, it's important to ask yourself if you're clearly communicating your intentions to work cooperatively with others. It takes some thick skin (and a lot of persistence) to follow the approaches used by the police sergeant and by Dick Gregg. It's usually worth it.

Use Measurement, Reward, and Accountability Systems That Promote Collaboration

Some leaders and managers communicate their expectations and desires clearly, but their message gets undermined by the agency's measurement, reward, and accountability systems. This is an age-old problem. One way to ensure alignment between expectations and systems is to focus on the formal and informal systems that affect employees' careers.

For instance, the U.S. intelligence community (IC) was severely criticized after the 9/11 attacks for its failure to share information. As Ben-Har and Shiplett (2009) put it, despite many initiatives, "the current stove-piped system, which discourages . . . interagency cooperation, has hampered collaboration and policy implementation at historical junctures" of the intelligence community.

The IC has made several changes since 9/11, including a mandate that civilians cannot be considered for senior executive positions until they take part in a joint duty program, which involves rotational assignments in other agencies. The concept is that employees who rotate to other agencies gain a broader appreciation for how the parts fit into the whole system. NASA is one of several civilian agencies promoting a similar approach.

That's fine and good, you might be thinking, but I'm not the director of national intelligence; I'm not an agency director with the authority of a Dick Gregg. I don't have the power to require such systemic change. Fair enough. When you're leading a collaborative team you typically have no authority over the formal reward and measurement systems used by the team members' home organizations. But you *can* have a good deal of influence over the measurement and recognition of your team members' contribution to your project. Consider:

- Are team members briefing senior leaders about the project?

- Are their names appearing on the team's reports?

- Are you tapping their strongest skills and abilities?

- Are their superiors being informed of their contributions?

- Are you offering team members the opportunity to speak at conferences, write articles, or post blogs about the project?

I've seen members of collaborative teams significantly increase their commitment to the initiative once they talk about it at a conference or write about it in a respected journal or Web site. Formal measures, rewards, and recognition are important but never underestimate the power of informal recognition. That taps the power of peer esteem, and you can influence that irrespective of your formal position.

Raise the Stakes of the Initiative

Another strategy for dealing with difficult people and situations is to use a combination of pull and push by raising the stakes of the project. That is, find creative ways to make the team's work so important that it's in everyone's interest to play well together. You can raise the stakes in several ways. They're summarized in Exhibit 9.2.

Concerning the fourth point, Lillian Ney and the Strategic Planning and Partnership Commission in Jamestown (discussed in Chapter Five) found a savvy way to make their group's behavior

---

Exhibit 9.2. Methods for Raising Project Stakes.

- Invite a senior leader to meet with the team periodically.
- Bring in other powerful people to meet with (or join) the team, such as customers or stakeholders who will be affected by the team's work.
- Have your boss talk with the difficult person's boss.
- Make the team's project and the members' behaviors visible (shine a light on them).
- Connect the project to a higher moral purpose.

---

visible when they invited a reporter from the local paper to join the commission as a full-fledged member. Members of the commission were OK with his involvement because they knew he was fair-minded, and his coverage gave the commission increased visibility. A couple of commission members who were often very negative about new ideas modified their behaviors nicely when the reporter was present.

Len Faulk, one of the commission's key members, reflected that "it was a great idea to involve the reporter. There was real power to involving the media this way." Faulk added that the reporter's articles on the commission had a positive impact on the local newspaper's editorial coverage of the commission. The Jamestown experience brings to mind Thad Allen's wonderful insight: "transparency of information breeds self-correcting behavior." When you shine a light on a group, it often raises the level of maturity and performance.

And the last method, connecting the initiative to a higher purpose, is one of the most effective ways of giving collaborative teams a sense of urgency and improving the behavior of their members. We've seen many examples of focusing on a higher purpose in this book. For instance, at the Child Advocacy Center described in the last chapter, the police and social workers sometimes get on each other's cases. If the elbows get too sharp and the kidding gets personal, it sometimes ends when one of the staff reminds her colleagues that "we're all here for the kids, aren't we?"

Check the Roles (and Role Conflicts) Involved

One of sociology's more useful contributions to our understanding of human behavior is the concept of roles. A role can be defined as a position you hold and the expectations others have of you in that position. When someone acts unprofessionally, when someone you trust disappoints you, it's easy to personalize it. But it's almost always more useful to first ask: Given the role she's in, what are my expectations of her? And what are others' expectations? Are my expectations reasonable? Would others in this role act similarly?

During Ronald Reagan's first six years as president, Tip O'Neill was speaker of the House. Tip would often blast Reagan for his policies, for what he considered the president's eagerness to help only the rich. Some of Reagan's aides would get furious at Tip and insist he become *persona non grata* at the White House.

Reagan saw it differently. "That's just Tip being Tip," he'd say. He understood that in the role of Speaker (and leader of the opposition party), O'Neill would criticize, sometimes posture, and sometimes get genuinely upset over the president's actions. Reagan never personalized it. Indeed, he would have Tip over for a talk, they would tell some Irish stories, and often they were able to do important business together. They respected one another's roles.

In the 1960s, President Lyndon Johnson developed the same relationship with then minority leader Everett Dirksen, who was often very tough on LBJ in front of the cameras. But after dinner and drinks, they got important work done. They understood each other's roles, and knew what each needed to pursue his respective agenda.

The importance of roles in shaping behavior may seem obvious to you. Sadly, many leaders don't get this, and their effectiveness with their funders and other stakeholders suffers.

When you're working with a collaborative team and some members' behavior is causing problems, consider the questions in Exhibit 9.3.

Exhibit 9.3. Looking at Problem Behaviors Through the Lens of People's Roles.

- Does the person have a clear, important role in the team, a role that doesn't duplicate another's role? (You don't want two people competing to be "the expert" on a certain task.)
- If so, does that role play to the person's strengths?
- Is the person representing an agency or unit that has poor relationships with another organization represented on the team?
- Has the person been given a role or task by her boss that puts her in a negative or confrontational role?

Regarding the last question, it's critical to learn if your collaborative team has a mission that threatens one or more of the partners. That's exactly what happened with one of the JIVA teams. A manager, I'll call him "Al," had an analyst assigned to a JIVA team. Al learned that the team's leader was from a rival agency that coveted part of Al's mission. So Al told his analyst that if he participated positively on the team, Al would assume that he had a political agenda to help the rival agency. The analyst got the message and stopped supporting the team. As noted earlier, the middle managers who were threatened by JIVA found ways to seriously undermine it, often leaving no fingerprints.

When you see a reasonable person trying to play defense and slow down an initiative, talk with the person outside of team meetings to learn what pressures he may be feeling. Look for ways to reduce the perceived threat. In these cases it may be necessary to go to his boss(es) and candidly discuss the issue. Are there ways that the initiative can benefit his organization, and what can be done to reduce the costs or perceived risks?

Use Pull to Deal with Difficult Personalities

If the first four approaches don't produce results, it's time to consider the personalities involved. Many of my clients start at the other end of the continuum, assuming that people problems result from personality defects. That's understandable, but not helpful.

Trying to change someone's core personality isn't the work of a collaborative team, and it's a long process that usually fails.

There are, to be sure, some truly difficult people in this world. When I say *difficult people*, I mean those who are difficult with just about everyone, equal opportunity difficult people, if you will.

The most effective strategy is prevention: identify and actively seek individuals for your team who play well with others *before* other agencies or units decide for themselves who will represent them. If you have good relationships with the partner organizations, this can work. But you may have some very difficult people on your team despite your best efforts. What to do?

Here are two ideas to keep in mind:

> *"There are two types of problems in life: those you can solve, and those you have to manage."*
>
> *"Don't fight forces, use them."*

The first idea tells you that when dealing with difficult people, you need to realize that these are people whose behavior won't be solved; you'll be *managing* the behavior. As Robert Bramson notes in his interesting book *Coping with Difficult People* (1981), the goal with difficult people is to "contend on equal terms" (p. 5). It's very human to fantasize changing the truly difficult people in our lives (even more human is to imagine tossing them off a high bridge), but you're not going to do it, so let it go.

No, the goal is to deal with them and their behavior in a way that helps the team move forward, that meets your needs and those of the team.

If you're the difficult person's supervisor, you may try to insist that the person adopt different behaviors. But leaders of collaborative groups rarely have the formal authority to direct. Smarter is to adopt the approach attributed to Buckminster Fuller and "use" the person's force (rather than fight it). This is the same as using pull more than push.

Let's get specific.

Dealing with Contrarians

Say your difficult person is a contrarian, someone who takes pleasure in disagreeing with others. If you feel like taking the person by the shoulders and shaking him, you'll have a lot of company. But you won't be managing the problem behavior. Instead, ask your contrarian to look at some part of the team's game plan, and critique it (which legitimizes his role). Tell him, "We're pretty excited about our direction, and maybe we're overlooking something. . . . Ken, tell us where we may be heading

Ask the contrarian to critique the team's plan. That plays to his strengths, and may help the team.

for a landmine." Chances are, he'll be delighted. You're tapping one of his talents—seeing things differently from others in a negative way. If Ken is fairly sharp, he'll find a flaw in the plan and that helps you. Even if he doesn't find a major flaw, he's doing work that's potentially valuable for the team. That, for a contrarian, is progress.

Working with Egotists

One of the more frustrating types for me is the person who needs to impress others with her intelligence (it's especially frustrating, of course, when that person is usually right!). On the positive side, such folks' intelligence can help the team develop smart solutions. Unfortunately, they often alienate many people along the way. Such people are often challenging the leader for control or recognition. As Steve Schwartz, who's spent decades working with nonprofit and government partnerships, notes, "With these people you want to make an ally, not an adversary." Here are several approaches to consider when dealing with egotists.

Use pull by sitting down with the egotist, acknowledging her intellectual gifts, and then indicating your disappointment that she isn't being as effective with the team as she might be (and as you'd like her to be). Most egotists have a need to be competent and seen as such; that's how they meet their *mastery* need. Learning that they're not being effective gets their attention. Then try something like this: "Look, Barb, you know as well as I do that most people want to make an impact on a team's solutions. Your ideas are usually great, which is why it's frustrating that other team members frequently don't support you. When you have an idea for our team, how can you incorporate some of the other members' thoughts into your approach?"

If that doesn't help, here's another way to use pull. Give the egotist the power she desires. Tell her that she obviously knows how to have an impact on the group. If she wants, she can use her power to help the team make a huge contribution. And she also has the power to make the team truly ineffective. She can move it in either direction. Then ask, "What's your choice?" In Buckminster Fuller's terminology, this is an example of using forces (the need for control, in this instance), not opposing them.

I've used those very words with people whose egos and intelligence were destroying a team. And this approach helped turn the problem behavior around.

If you choose to talk directly with the difficult person on your team, you'll get wonderful guidance from a book titled *Difficult Conversations*, by Stone, Patton, and Heen (1999). The authors give very sound, practical tips on how to confront problem behaviors in a way that's both direct and nonthreatening.

An Example of Successful Collaboration with Difficult People

In the JIVA story, I noted the failure to actively involve middle managers in the initiative. Here's another example of virtual collaboration among intelligence analysts. In this case the needs of the middle managers were anticipated and handled well. There were very few people problems, and the initiative continues to be a major success.

IADS: Collaborating in a Culture of Huge Egos and Information Hoarding

In the aftermath of the 1991 Gulf War, members of the intelligence community who had worked on the analysis of another country's air defense systems learned that their customers needed them to produce more integrated analysis in many aspects of their work. At this time, if a senior official wanted to know how an enemy's air defense system worked, the intelligence agencies couldn't give a complete response. One agency could report on the country's early warning radar, another could analyze its surface-to-air missiles, but nobody integrated these reports for the customers. As one analyst put it, "The customer got parts of a jigsaw puzzle and had to put the parts together."

In 1994, some analysts at the National Air and Space Intelligence Center and other intelligence agencies began discussing this need, and within a year IADS was born.

IADS, or Integrated Air Defense System, involves analysts from intelligence, defense, and related agencies who work as virtual teams to analyze enemies' air defense systems. IADS has a two-part structure made up of (1) a coordinating group of managers from the involved agencies and (2) a group of working-level analysts from the same agencies who use collaborative software to work together on common problems.

IADS' Two-Part Structure

The Coordinating Group is made up of division chiefs from the IADS agencies. Twice a year this group's members identify the highest priority countries for analysis. The Analyst Group then schedules

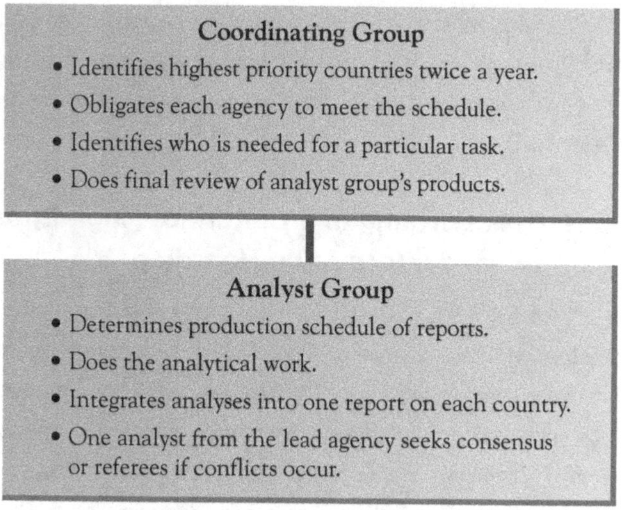

Coordinating Group

- Identifies highest priority countries twice a year.
- Obligates each agency to meet the schedule.
- Identifies who is needed for a particular task.
- Does final review of analyst group's products.

Analyst Group

- Determines production schedule of reports.
- Does the analytical work.
- Integrates analyses into one report on each country.
- One analyst from the lead agency seeks consensus or referees if conflicts occur.

Figure 9.2. The IADS Structure.

the reports on each country and sees that the studies are completed (Figure 9.2). Ninety percent of the analysts' communications are done via collaborative software or phone.

Ty Johnson was the first chief of the Coordinating Group after IADS was formed. The participating agencies had a host of concerns, but Ty handled them well. Like other collaborative leaders I've described, he anticipated and reduced the worries early on. He did this by patiently listening to the middle managers, by addressing their concerns as they raised them, and by negotiating with each of the partner agencies to get them committed to IADS. The creation of the Coordinating Group helped meet most of the managers' control and belonging needs. And IADS has been a wonderful success, providing its customers with integrated, high-quality, and timely reports on very important intelligence issues.

If you look back at the five approaches described in this chapter, you'll see that the IADS model uses four of them:

1. *Communications and expectations are open and clear.* Because most of the analysts' managers are in the Coordinating Group, each of the two groups understands what the other expects.

2. *Collaborative behavior is measured and rewarded.* The Coordinating Group evaluates the Analyst Group's work. Analysts are assessed and rewarded both for their team's products and for their individual work. The IADS structure also holds the managers accountable. The Coordinating Group is accountable to IADS's customers, which include members of congressional committees, the Office of the Secretary of Defense, and the Air Force chief of staff.

3. *The stakes are very high, and the products are visible to all.* Reporting to members of Congress and at the secretary of defense level tends to get people's attention. More important, the IADS products are used by troops fighting in the field, whose needs raise the stakes for all IADS members.

4. *Roles are clear, and the role needs of each group are met.* The managers have a seat at the table. They have control over which analysts will work on each study. The analysts know that the managers are obligating their agency to contribute, greatly reducing their concern that some agencies aren't pulling their fair share.

As a result, those familiar with IADS report few problem behaviors. The managers are committed, and the analysts are producing quality products on national security issues.

THE BOTTOM LINE

Author Michael Shrage (1990) tells a story about an experienced manager who applies for a senior executive position. He interviews for the job, and by the end of the interview he has clearly impressed the interviewer, who asks him one final question. "As you know, we use the team concept here. Are you a team player?"

"You bet," he replies confidently. "Team leader!"

Such people often cause far more problems than they solve. They may make up only 5 to 10 percent of those on collaborative teams, but they can consume 50 percent or more of your time and emotional energy. If you adopt the attitude of curiosity and if you follow the strategies listed in this chapter, you can spend considerably less time on these delightful folks. More important, members of the team will be more likely to believe that the team has real potential for success, one of the four criteria that determine whether people will make the shift from me to we. Collaborative leaders who prevent or address problem behaviors build confidence in the team.

At this point you may be thinking, "Yes, but what about the times when . . ." My experience is that the methodology described in this chapter will help you with the great majority of difficult people and difficult behaviors. But there are some people and situations so difficult that these approaches won't suffice. We'll turn to the most difficult situations next.

10

Dealing with the Most Difficult Situations

Huge Egos, Empire Builders, Information Hoarders, and Cultures That Reinforce Them

The past is never dead. It's not even past.
—William Faulkner, Requiem for a Nun

At the start of Chapter Four I described the near seamless collaboration that occurred at the Pentagon on September 11, 2001, and for the next two weeks. Egos and turf were put aside; nobody cared what agency others represented; the operative attitude was, "Whatever you need, you've got." Because of previously established relationships among the principal agency leaders, 9/11 at the Pentagon was a case study in collaboration . . . except for the relationship between the Federal Bureau of Investigation (FBI) and the Bureau of Alcohol, Tobacco, Firearms and Explosives (ATF).

These two agencies have fought over turf, resources, and egos for years, and they continued to fight on 9/11. Astonishingly, when thirty ATF agents arrived at the Pentagon that morning, an FBI agent at the scene told them to leave. This was only the most amazing of several run-ins between these two law enforcement organizations. Over the years they have created competing programs that have the same objectives, failed to merge similar databases (despite orders from their superiors to do so), and actually threatened to arrest one another at crime scenes in battles over jurisdiction. For members of these two strong organizations, the epigraph at the head of this chapter rings all too true: "The past is never dead. It's not even past."

When I ask participants in my workshops to identify the most challenging hurdles to collaboration, they mention these three more than any other:

- Turf

- People with huge egos who amass power or resources

- Fear of losing control

Each of these hurdles is involved in the FBI-ATF relationship. Their feud is about stubborn personalities, but it's also about overlapping missions (which creates fear of losing control and turf). "It's just a constant battle" for control, as one ATF agent puts it (Markon, 2008, p. A1). How can collaborative leaders work with such egos and cultures?

Here I'll explore two examples of cultures in which turf, control, and outsized egos thrived, and we'll see how some very creative collaborative leaders dealt with these situations. I'll analyze each and then discuss the common themes later in the chapter. (An expanded version of the first example, which concerns the Internal Revenue Service, is available on the Jossey-Bass Web site for this book.)

Powerful Managers Used to Getting Their Way

John Springett is a fascinating study in contrasts. He's tall, extremely bright, has a savvy understanding of organizational dynamics and politics, and has functioned at very senior government levels. He also has a tendency to land squarely on his feet after events that derailed others' careers. If this was all you knew about Springett, you would be forgiven for assuming that he is a domineering figure who has a strong need to control people and resources. That's hardly the case. If you met him at a party, you'd probably be struck by his wonderful listening skills, his modesty, and his genuine interest in others; you wouldn't come away thinking that he had been the leader of very large organizations. John is an excellent example of the collaborative leader persona I described in Chapter Five. He needed all of those collaborative qualities and more in the 1970s when he took over a failing technology initiative at the IRS.

Changing People's Behavior When They Don't Want to Change

In the 1970s, senior leaders at the Internal Revenue Service (IRS) were painfully aware that the technology supporting the agency's handling of returns and taxpayer service functions was falling apart. The IRS established a multimillion-dollar program to replace this technology with a modern, integrated system. Senior IRS officials made the proposal to Congress for a new tax administration system.

But the Government Accountability Office (GAO) reported to Congress that the IRS's cost-benefit studies on the system didn't support the enormous expenditures required. Two congressional committees were harshly critical of the new system's potential privacy issues and technological risks. Try as they might, IRS leaders couldn't revive congressional support for the program. Over three years and thousands of hours of staff work went for naught. Not long after, the director of the new system had a heart attack and died.

Bringing in a New Leader

John Springett was brought in to help revive this critical project. He was only thirty-five but he brought excellent technology experience to the job. However, he knew little about the IRS culture and operations. One of the most powerful managers—I'll call him "Carl"—ran the Audit Division. Audit was responsible for most of the cost-benefit studies that the GAO had bashed. It was also considered the most powerful IRS division. Carl was a large, imposing powerhouse of a man who knew how to control resources and was used to getting what he wanted. He looked and acted like a man who ran the agency's most powerful organization.

Springett reported to the assistant commissioner for Data Services, and was one level below Carl (see Figure 10.1). Springett's staff assured him that being very direct with Audit about its flawed studies would be "organizational suicide." They told him that they would have to make any changes that needed to be made in Audit's studies.

Springett was charged with developing and implementing a strategy to upgrade the IRS's automated tax system that would be supported by that system's key stakeholders. His challenges included

- Improving the hardware and software supporting the tax systems.
- Gaining the confidence of key congressional committees, the GAO, and industry.
- Forming positive relationships with the IRS commissioner and his own staff.

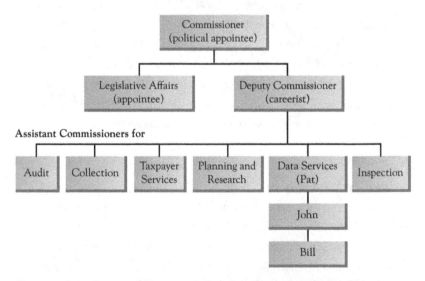

Figure 10.1. Internal Revenue Service Organizational Chart, Late 1970s.

- Developing solid relationships with the key IRS divisions.
- Gaining credibility within the IRS culture (as an outsider who didn't understand many of the terms and forms used, he started with two strikes against him).

Moving Forward on the New System

Springett started by doing his homework and a lot of base touching. He met with his new reports and his manager, then did a ninety-day rotation as acting deputy director of the Atlanta IRS service center, where he learned a good deal about the IRS operations and culture. This stint gave him some credibility with agency veterans. He also spent time meeting with staff of the key congressional committees that would review the IRS's technology requests, and met with the IRS commissioner and assistant commissioners.

Next, Springett decided he had to be direct with Carl. His secretary called and requested a few minutes on Carl's calendar. It was clear from the response that Carl had little interest in a personal meeting, and would have his top staff present when Springett came over. Now the question was how to communicate the message, appear as an equal, and maintain the creditability of his new office.

> In an inbred culture like the IRS, Springett realized that he needed to start by learning the agency's operations and culture.

Springett chose to do something dramatic. He decided to attend the meeting with none of his staff. He got a shopping cart, put all the faulty Audit analyses into it, and walked into the meeting pushing the loaded cart! "The old system had failed," he recalled later, "and Audit's reports were part of the problem. My message was, 'these are your reports, we want to work with you, but to get our new system funded we need you to make changes.'"

Carl's senior staff chuckled at the shopping cart, but they were not amused with the message. The discussions were brief but to the point. Audit needed to fix its own studies, Springett said. He would work with Audit once the studies were changed. Carl appeared somewhat taken aback, but he said that he appreciated Springett's directness and that his staff would review the studies to see if any changes were really necessary.

Springett's staff knew the results of the meeting by the time he returned to his office! Audit staff were already calling to identify ways that Audit could work with Springett's office to strengthen the studies. From that point, Springett and his staff had an increasingly collaborative relationship with Audit as well as other IRS executives. In addition, Springett enjoyed a strong relationship with his own staff.

Over the coming months Springett and his staff developed a plan for upgrading the IRS systems. The plan included Audit's revised cost-benefit studies. Their plan was bolstered by a National Academy of Sciences panel report on the IRS's taxpayer system (Springett had set up the panel). The report noted a significant risk if the current system wasn't upgraded. Congress accepted the new IRS plan and funded it for several years as it was successfully implemented.

Analysis

How did John Springett succeed with someone who overpowered others, in a culture that rewarded domineering managers? First, he learned the agency culture and met with the people who had control over his mission to learn their interests and concerns. Then he thought about Carl's situation: "Nobody wanted to go back to Congress and be denied again, so Carl had an incentive to go along," Springett remarked. Moreover, Springett understood a key fact about people like Carl: they respect others who are strong. "I think I surprised him by walking in that way. I was willing to say that his vaunted unit wasn't doing proper analyses."

Third, Springett didn't threaten Carl. "I said that we would work with them. I wasn't confrontational; since I came by myself he didn't feel attacked." In addition, Springett was creative. "The shopping cart? They probably thought I was insane! I thought it would have a symbolic impact. Carl probably raised holy hell with his staff, but they knew they needed our help." Finally, Springett had the facts on his side, and a prestigious third party (the National Academy of Sciences) agreed.

John Springett handled a powerful manager very well. His goal wasn't to change the IRS culture or change Carl. Rather, he followed the advice noted in the last chapter: when dealing with a difficult person, your goal is to meet your needs and move on. Springett did that and more. By being straight with Carl and keeping him informed of his unit's efforts on the new system, Springett was able to work well with Carl and his staff on other projects.

Transforming the Culture of a Top-Down Agency Where Information and Resources Were Hoarded

Bill Leighty is a most unusual guy. A former Marine with a BA degree in economics and an MBA degree as well, he has held several leadership positions in state government—he was deputy commissioner of the Virginia Department of Motor Vehicles and director of the state's retirement system. In 2002, Governor Mark Warner tapped him to be his chief of staff, and four years later Warner's successor, Tim Kaine, kept Leighty on as his chief. Few civil servants make such high-level leaps into politics; probably none has been asked to stay on as chief of staff by a second governor. It was as director of the Virginia Retirement System that he had first shown his tremendous ability to handle the most difficult situations.

The Virginia Retirement System: A Stovepiped Agency in Deep Trouble

One of Leighty's key leadership challenges was running the Virginia Retirement System (VRS). The agency offers pension benefits, life insurance, and related services to over 270,000 public-sector employees working in state and local government, school systems, universities, and other bodies.

VRS was an agency in turmoil when Leighty came in 1995. It had been investigated for three years because of a scandal, and Virginia's leaders thought it was politicized. Legislative support was plummeting; media reports were negative; employee morale was terrible. And the stakes for Leighty and the agency were huge: VRS was the twenty-ninth largest public or private fund in the United States, managing over $30 billion at the time.

What Leighty found when he arrived were locked doors and information silos. "You literally couldn't get into certain units," Leighty recalled. "I mean, they had *locks* on a number of doors, and unless you knew the code, you couldn't get into that section of the building!" The locked doors were symbolic as well as real. Information wasn't shared laterally in the agency. "The perception was, 'you stay in your unit, we stay in ours,'" recalled Donna Shumate, human resource director at VRS during Leighty's tenure.

"People had very narrowly defined jobs," Leighty recalled. "The culture had been old school for decades: you learn a job, do it better than anyone else, get promoted, then you learn that job, and so on. Employees told me that they were specialists in this area of risk management or that, and that 'this is how we do the work, we can't change it in any way.' I knew we had to make major changes, fast."

The Key Changes

Eliminate Locked Doors. One of the first things Leighty did was to get rid of those locks. It was an important early move: "we had to radically change the ways communications worked in the agency," as he put it.

Use MBWA. Leighty is a high-energy guy, almost always on the move. He began "managing by wandering around" (MBWA) in order to learn the culture, the operations, and the people. Most employees had never seen the agency director come to their office or cubicle (those locked doors were pretty effective). Some of the employees were taken aback at first ("What's he doing here?" "Are we in trouble?"), but when Leighty showed a genuine interest in their jobs, that struck a chord. As Shumate says, "People take pride in their work."

Conduct Road Shows. Leighty took groups of VRS staff to meet with a large number of employers in the state. The purpose was to help staff learn what employers expected of VRS, what problems they encountered with the agency, and how VRS could help the employers make life better for their employees. Getting this external information was a totally new experience for the staff, who were accustomed to sitting at their desks and churning out paper. Leighty also met with key members of the legislature who had power over his agency.

Start a "Dumb Rules" Contest. This contest invited employees to identify rules, regulations, even laws that were getting in their way. Leighty noted that "we found about a third of these were outside our control, a third were rules we had written ourselves, and a third weren't rules at all! We got rid of those fast!" Leighty worked with the legislature to change some laws, and employees appreciated his advocacy.

> *Of the many dumb rules hindering performance, one-third came from the agency itself.*

Conduct Strategic Planning. Leighty created a strategic planning process to give the staff a broader understanding of their environment and to provide clear priorities. Staff from all functions and levels were involved, meeting with stakeholders to learn their expectations and creating a new mission. The process helped employees understand whom they were serving, and it got them out of their narrowly focused worlds.

Moreover, the process led to one of the early uses of a pay-for-performance system in a government agency (this was in 1996). The system focused on agency core values developed by the employees. One of those values was "adapting to change." As Shumate noted, committing to that value was an enormous change at VRS.

Use PIT Crews to Implement Change. The strategic plan identified six concrete issues that needed improvement. Leighty and his executive team developed process improvement teams (PITs) for each issue. People on the teams came from all levels and units—from mail-room clerks up. Each team had an executive sponsor who obtained resources and helped teams do what they couldn't do for themselves.

Many of the teams' solutions were implemented, which gave employees a sense of empowerment. More than that, they learned about the agency's processes and the people who managed those processes. The blinders started coming off staff members' eyes because of the cross-pollination.

Emphasize Communications. Leighty instituted two kinds of formal communication methods: (1) a monthly director's meeting for the entire staff, where he informed employees of important factors affecting the agency, and (2) a quarterly director's meeting with each work unit, where Leighty and unit staff discussed work performance. Both kinds of meetings gave Leighty a chance to communicate the values and priorities. These were two-way sessions, and staff could ask questions directly or in writing.

Some Results

"The executive team revolted a few times that first year," Leighty says. "They told me that I was just too radical for them, that these ideas wouldn't work. I was patient but let them know that their roles were going to change because we had to change. And the teams were a great tool for the execs to see what their own staff could do."

The changes at VRS are now legendary in Virginia government. The impact was visible by the start of the second year. There were many positive results, according to VRS staff and observers. They're listed in Exhibit 10.1.

Three surveys documented the impact of the VRS changes on its employees. In every category but one, VRS employees were more positive than other state employees and employees nationwide. Some results from the surveys are displayed in Table 10.1.

In one of the most telling signs of the extraordinary change at VRS, some private-sector firms began asking Leighty to share the VRS "formula" for success. And years after Leighty left VRS, the culture of collaboration continues to grow.

Exhibit 10.1. Some Results at VRS.

- A big increase in information sharing and collaboration, both internal and external
- Much broader thinking, more creative ideas
- The identification of future leaders
- A major focus on customer needs and perceptions
- Improved performance

Table 10.1. VRS Employees' Satisfaction Compared to Satisfaction of Virginia and U.S. Employees.

	National Average	Virginia State Employees	VRS Employees
High level of trust in leadership	35%	36%	43%
Confidence in leadership	37%	51%	76%
Have access to information needed	61%	88%	89%
See direct link between pay and performance	28%	25%	35%
Have resources to adequately perform job	70%	73%	68%
Satisfied with level of communication	28%	40%	46%

Sources: Data from Leighty, 2001; and from Watson Wyatt Workforce USA, 1998, and Watson Wyatt, 2000.

Analysis

Bill Leighty may seem to be unique. His move from civil service to high-level politico, his energy and creativity, may leave you thinking, "someone like Leighty could do those things, but I couldn't." That's a natural reaction. And I think it's wrong.

Consider: Leighty did things that any manager or leader could do: he carried out strategic planning, developed process improvement teams, emphasized communications, and engaged in MBWA. Nothing new there. Yes, doing away with locked doors and sponsoring a dumb rules contest seem unusual, but they're not that far fetched. If you're determined to make major change, you could implement these initiatives.

No, it's not the novelty of any single change that explains the transformation at VRS. Rather, it's the fact that Leighty made *all* of these changes and that they all were part of an *integrated package* that focused on clear and needed agency goals.

One last point: Leighty proudly points out that he rarely had to confront employees who didn't get the changes. Their peers took care of that in most cases because there was so much employee ownership after the first year that most employees didn't like it if others got in the way.

And what about those who weren't affected by peer pressure and who continued to stand in the way of change? There were a few such cases, and Leighty gave each of them a clear message. He said it was clear that the person wasn't in synch with the agency's direction, that he had done everything he could to communicate the reasons for the changes and had listened to everyone's feedback, and that they both knew there was no way he could fire the person. Then he made it clear that his one option was to make things uncomfortable each day for that person. As you would guess, these individuals found other places to work.

Reflecting on these encounters, Leighty says that "as difficult as that conversation was, failing to address the renegades is letting down the employees who are performing. It is the leader's job to address this aspect of the agency culture." Leighty took no pleasure in taking such actions. And the renegades as well as the agency were better off as a result.

Dick Gregg encountered the same issue during his tenure at the Financial Management Service (described in Chapter Nine). Gregg also found a few managers who wouldn't, or couldn't, adapt to a collaborative culture. He moved them to different positions and replaced them with people who wanted to be team players. Nobody was fired, most people got the message, some chose to leave, and other staff respected Gregg for acting on his stated values.

Rewarding those who "get it" won't matter if those who hoard information and accumulate power continue to be rewarded.

Rewarding those who "get" collaboration isn't sufficient if people who amass resources and hoard information continue to do well in their careers. I've worked with many leaders who prefer to do work-arounds rather than directly confront the kind of difficult people and culture described here. Sadly, a focus on rewarding the positive isn't enough to change this kind of culture. You also have to demonstrate that hoarding information and resources will side-track one's career, not enhance it.

Some Common Themes

What do we make of the leaders in this chapter who confronted some very difficult people and situations? Exhibit 10.2 identifies a few commonalities; I invite you to generate your own.

Exhibit 10.2. Dealing with Powerful or Control-Oriented Personalities and the Cultures That Reward Them.

- Use collaborative leadership skills.
- Find ways to be creative, take prudent risks, and use political skills.
- Respond to basic self-interests.
- Start at the individual level, *then* move to systemic change.

Use Collaborative Leadership Skills

Recall the discussion of collaborative leaders in Chapter Five. Effective collaborative leaders usually have these qualities in common. They

- Feel driven to achieve the goal, with a solid but measured ego.

- Listen carefully to understand others' perspectives.

- Look for win-win solutions to meet shared interests.

- Use *pull* more than *push*.

- Think strategically; connect the project to a larger purpose.

Both John Springett and Bill Leighty demonstrated these characteristics. You can't deal with oversized egos and entrenched, information-hoarding cultures without a solid ego, but you need to keep it in check. You have to seek win-win solutions, which requires an excellent ability to learn others' perspectives and underlying interests. In terms of the fourth characteristic, Leighty and Springett used *both* push and pull. To deal with these kinds of challenges requires a good dose of confidence and a willingness at times to move forward with your agenda despite the initial pushback.

In addition, these leaders were very good at thinking strategically and helping others see the higher purpose to their efforts. They thought about the impact of their early actions, and planned those actions to make the maximum statement about their goals.

Find Ways to Be Creative, Take Prudent Risks, and Use Political Skills

These two leaders were also quite innovative. Springett had to find a way to get the attention of a powerful, domineering manager (who was one organizational level higher up than Springett), without threatening his ego or power. And Leighty had to shake up a culture that was allergic to change and new thinking: thus his road shows, dumb rules contest, and early use of pay for performance.

VRS was also the first public pension fund in the country to develop a Web site.

The situation in each of these examples also involved a degree of risk. Bill Leighty could have lost the respect of his senior managers at the start when he took steps like doing MBWA (which many of his senior managers opposed). Springett took a risk the day he walked into Carl's office pushing a cart full of the Audit staff's discredited analyses. Like most successful risk takers, they also understood the importance of *assessing and managing* those risks up front, which involves doing your homework. Springett and Leighty did their homework by getting to know key staff at the start, learning the culture, and identifying a few activities that would send early, positive messages to employees. They also managed risk by ensuring strong support from key external stakeholders. And that brings us to their use of political skills.

Those who take on the challenges that Springett and Leighty addressed need considerable political savvy, which includes having a good sense of timing and lining up support from stakeholders. Springett knew he had support for change from the IRS commissioner, who was upset that Congress had rejected the agency's funding request for the new computer system. And he created another kind of support when he requested the involvement of the prestigious National Academy of Sciences. That group's report gave Springett ammunition to use in dealing with people like Carl. Leighty met with the state legislature's leaders, the retirement and compensation subcommittee chairs, and the chairs of the appropriations committees to get their early input and support.

Leighty understood that "a crisis is a terrible thing to waste."

They also were sensitive to timing. Bill Leighty understood the wisdom in the saying that "a crisis is a terrible thing to waste." He used the crisis atmosphere at VRS as a mandate for change. And he adapted when senior managers told him he was pushing too hard, too fast. John Springett also wanted to move quickly, but he knew he needed time to learn the agency procedures and culture in order to have some credibility, so he spent ninety days in the Atlanta IRS office to learn the ropes.

Respond to Basic Self-Interests

When creating change in top-down, information-hoarding cultures that reward managers with huge egos and power bases, it's essential to anticipate the pushback from those who have a lot to lose (as they see it). Collaborative leaders need to be very candid about the benefits for people in these situations. One of the best ways to do that is to address their most basic self-interests. For the powerful, domineering types, that means their power and resources. Their basic interests also include their reputations. At the IRS it was in Carl's interest to help the agency obtain the necessary congressional funding; it was not in his interest to be seen as the reason funding was lost in the first place. Springett gave Carl a path to retain his influence—fix the faulty reports.

In cultures like the old VRS, the self-interest can be the reestablishment of employees' lost pride and respect. Former HR director Shumate noted that Leighty quickly became an advocate for the agency with external stakeholders, which sent a very positive signal to the employees. Some employees thought Leighty was wasting his time when he created the road shows. But they often got good feedback from their visits, and when Leighty brought back positive comments about individual staff and the impact they had on customers, some employees started to believe in the change.

Begin at the Individual Level, *Then* Move to Systemic Change

The two initiatives in this chapter resulted in major, ongoing change. The IRS implemented a major new hardware and software system that was critical to its core business processes; the Virginia Retirement System continues to be a model of collaboration, known for great customer service and strong performance.

For those of us who are interested in how to institutionalize major change, these stories are impressive.

---

*Change begins with relationships;
it is sustained through institutions.*

Interestingly, each of these change stories began at the individual and interpersonal level, not with the institution of new structures and methods. Bill Leighty started doing MBWA and taking staff to meet key stakeholders. Springett spent time getting to know his staff and other key individuals at the IRS. The same pattern held true in several of the other examples of major organizational change noted in this book.

Jean Monnet, who spent decades working toward the creation of the European Union, once said that nothing begins without relationships, nothing lasts without institutions. That's a final lesson from this discussion of dealing with truly difficult people and situations. *Start at the individual level*—get to know the staff, get the right people in the key positions, learn who your stakeholders are, and build relationships—*then* move to the broader level of systemic change. This is the approach used by John Springett and Bill Leighty; it is the approach used by several other collaborative leaders I've followed.

Management guru Tom Peters once remarked that organizational excellence requires great people and great systems. You need both, he said, but if he could have only one, he'd go with great people. To make collaboration work, to make meaningful change in the lives of others, I believe we need both people (strong relationships at the individual level) and systems (that reward collaboration). It's very difficult to do both simultaneously. Getting the sequence right is important.

THE BOTTOM LINE

In Chapter Five I discussed five characteristics of collaborative leaders. One of those characteristics is their pursuit of win-win solutions. They tend to assume abundance; they believe that by working together with others they can grow the pie (through improved performance, greater funding, more recognition, and interpersonal effectiveness) for all partners. Life isn't a zero-sum game for these leaders, and they continually look for ways to share what they have in order to increase the pie for all.

The difficult people and behaviors we've looked at in this chapter reflect a very different mindset. Difficult people tend to see the pie as fixed, not expandable; they see life as a zero-sum game. Thus it makes sense from their perspective to hoard information and resources, to keep new ideas to themselves, to work independently rather than interdependently. Most of us have a mixture of the zero-sum and win-win perspectives. But some people, perhaps because of painful life experiences, lean strongly to the win-lose, zero-sum mentality.

In my experience, working with people to change their win-lose perspectives is a long shot. Less difficult, however, is to help people change their win-lose *behaviors*. That's what John Springett and Bill Leighty did. It didn't work with everyone; Leighty had to make life difficult for those who refused to change behaviors. But it worked for many. The payoff? Surprisingly positive change in individual behaviors and in an agency culture.

Dealing with control artists and other truly difficult people and their behaviors isn't for the meek. But it can be done. And doing this hard and important work will win the hearts and minds of your colleagues.

Part 3

Developing Sustainable
Collaborative Cultures

Part Three focuses on some of the largest collaboration questions, those related to the organizational cultures that hinder or support collaborative work. This final part of the book addresses the first mega-challenge to collaboration introduced in Chapter One, the fragmented nature of our agencies and the systems that do more to separate than to integrate people. How can we create systems, methods, rewards, and structures that foster truly collaborative cultures, that attract and support people whose default mode is to share? In the following chapters we'll explore several exciting systemic changes that are demonstrating success.

Note that although managers can use these approaches to good effect, their greatest leverage occurs when organizational leaders get behind them. Cultural change, ultimately, is the work of leaders. In these chapters I'll also discuss the leadership implications for large-scale cultural change, and look at one leader who has done an exceptional job of instituting such change in a way that supports the two fundamental human needs for autonomy and belonging.

Finally, I'll discuss one of the most interesting and optimistic trends in organizational life—the entrance of the Millennial

Generation into the workforce, which has been going on since the early 2000s. This cohort is characterized by behaviors and attitudes that are beautifully in synch with our organizations', and nation's, most pressing needs. It is a generation that will give you great hope for the future.

11

Co-Locating Operations

Using Shared Space to Foster Information Sharing and a Culture of Collaboration

When you step into an intersection of fields, disciplines,
or cultures, you can combine existing concepts into a large
number of extraordinary new ideas.
—Frans Johansson, The Medici Effect

The quotation that starts this chapter is from a fascinating book about the origins of the Renaissance. As Johansson tells it, the Medici family and a few others like it helped fund a large number of creative souls—architects, sculptors, scientists, poets, painters—and brought them from the far reaches of Europe to fifteenth-century Florence. Once they started finding each other, they broke down barriers, learned from one another, generated exciting ideas, and contributed to one of the most innovative periods in human history. This is what Johansson calls the *Medici effect*—the creativity unleashed when people from different disciplines and cultures come together.

There's something about proximity that helps reduce barriers and spur creativity.

E-Mail-Free Fridays and the Wonders of Talking to Each Other

The power of proximity. That's an insight that U.S. Cellular employees gained when they adopted e-mail-free Fridays. U.S. Cellular is a telecom company, selling wireless communications including e-mail. A few years ago employees told their chief operating officer that they were overwhelmed with e-mails. The COO said, OK, we'll ban e-mails on Fridays. He got lots of pushback (watch what you wish for, employees!), but he persisted. He was also flexible: if there's an urgent need to e-mail, fine. And nobody's fired if she e-mails on Friday for other reasons. But most have followed the rule.

The result? Soon employees were telling the COO how much they loved coming to work on Fridays. It was their most productive day. And some discovered that the person they'd been e-mailing for years . . . worked down the hall (Schaper, 2008)!

It turns out many people like to be released from their e-mail jails once a week. U.S. Cellular employees truly value their face time now; many say that these conversations are more creative and useful than exchanging e-mails. Yes, there's something about proximity that creates bonds and reduces barriers. Of course the opposite also happens sometimes. But without proximity the *probability* of genuine communications is lower. According to one study, researchers in the same department working on the same floor are more than twice as likely to collaborate as those who work on different floors; and researchers from different departments working on the same floor are *six times* more likely to collaborate than those working on different floors (see Kraut, Egido, and Galegher, 1988, for more on this). As two scholars of networked government write, "for all the advantages that modern technology provides for sharing information, nothing surpasses old-fashioned, face-to-face interaction" (Goldsmith and Eggers, 2004, p. 96).

Co-Location: A Structural Approach to Increase Collaboration

This chapter is about the potential for people to connect at a more authentic level by co-locating employees from different organizations, that is, putting them in the same space. Many agencies are using the co-location model to increase information sharing and trust, to generate creative ideas, and to improve service to customers and clients. What can we learn from organizations that co-locate and share resources and information, even staff? What are the different kinds of co-location approaches, and what are some of the challenges involved in making it work? We'll look at three co-location examples—involving arts organizations in Buffalo, New York, a Child Advocacy Center, and fusion centers. I'll explore the benefits and issues involved, and discuss some critical success factors for getting started.

Co-Location Among Nonprofit Arts Organizations

Just Buffalo Literary Center, CEPA Gallery, and Big Orbit are three nonprofit arts organizations in Buffalo, New York, that have shared space and certain administrative functions since 2005. Just Buffalo offers an array of literary arts and arts-in-education programs. CEPA Gallery presents contemporary photo-related art and supports working artists. And Big Orbit has an art gallery and programs in the fields of experimental theater, literary performance, new music, and sound art.

Once they co-located their administrative offices, they quickly started to realize a number of advantages. Financial savings was an obvious one (they share equipment, a software contract, phone and Internet services, and more). Physical proximity also helped the three executives develop a strong sense of trust and respect, and they soon looked for other ways to collaborate.

Early Wins: A Shared Grantwriter, Big Gifts

Their first shared staff was a full-time grantwriter, whose time is allocated among the three organizations based on the size of their budgets. Sharing a grantwriter is potentially risky: What if she finds a grant that all three might seek but only one can get? After all, competition over resources is one of the biggest collaboration challenges among nonprofits. Laurie Dean Torrell, Just Buffalo Literary Center's executive director, says, "We worked out guidelines to deal with the possibility that two or all three of us would go for the same grant. Being in constant dialogue helped us a lot; we developed a lot of goodwill among the three execs, which made a big difference whenever a potential issue came up."

The grantwriter helped the three organizations increase grant funding. Building on that success, the agencies brought on more shared staff: an administrative assistant, a development associate, and a part-time receptionist.

A Variety of Benefits

Could they also share information on their respective donors? That's a risky area, but they've been able to make impressive progress. A consultant who worked with them on their collaboration advised that "each organization ends up with its own flock" (its own donors). They don't solicit each others' donors. Rather, they focus on sharing knowledge and on developing stronger gift programs *within* each agency. "We share information and ideas on how to best approach development. We've made joint pitches to donors to fund a joint program done by two of our organizations, resulting in larger grants than we would have received had we gone in individually," Torrell says.

Beyond the tangible benefits, there are important intangibles. "Being together works against the sense of isolation you can get with a small staff," Torrell comments. "Having a shared staff helps us coordinate things that we might not see if we were separate, like doing mailings." This is all possible because of the executives' strong relationships.

When it comes to donors, the three organizations share knowledge, not names.

One of the biggest benefits from close proximity is central to their missions: increased creativity. Torrell describes the relationship as a think tank. "We work so closely . . . it's helped us come up with new thinking to expand our capacity and create a built-in brain trust and support system for problem solving and practical help." Exhibit 11.1 lists the major benefits.

Exhibit 11.1. Co-Location Benefits for Buffalo Arts Organizations.

- Financial savings: Just Buffalo saved at least $63,000 in 2008 (out of a total budget of $650,000).
- Increase in individual contributions: individual contributions are up 500 percent and corporate funding up 300 percent over a three-year period (compared with a baseline period prior to co-location).
- Improved artistic programming.
- Creation of a support network for the executives and staff.
- Synergies, which have contributed to each of the previous benefits.
- Full-time access at part-time expense, through the sharing of skilled staff.

Several Years of Careful Planning

Initially, the three leaders moved toward co-location slowly. Their key funders began talking about collaboration at the start of the 2000s. The organizations secured a planning grant in 2003 that helped them work with their boards on the co-location concept. Boards are by nature conservative, and some board members worried about losing identity, about trying to meet the very different needs of each organization, and about funding. Then Erie County, one of their major funders, went through a major financial crisis in 2004 and 2005, reducing arts groups' funding drastically. That got the boards' attention, and pushed them to move faster toward accepting co-location.

The three organizations formed a collaboration committee of the executive directors and a few individuals from each board. It meets quarterly, providing expertise and progress reviews and communicating to the individual boards. With the help of a facilitator, this group was a key to the process. Another key was how the organizations framed their goal: *to strengthen each individual organization*. That helped their boards let go of some worries about competition.

The arts agencies' goal isn't collaboration; it is to strengthen each individual organization (through collaboration).

Laurie Dean Torrell concludes that co-location can work beautifully, but it has to be genuine and can't be funder-forced. That said,
funders played an important role in this story. One foundation funded
a facilitator who skillfully helped the agencies' boards get comfortable
with the concept. Gail Johnstone, former director of a Buffalo-area
foundation that supported the arts co-location, points out that part
of the reason collaboration in the nonprofit world is often done poorly
is that many staff and boards simply don't know how to pull it off. So
funders need to provide support to create a collaboration capability.
That support helped this arts organization co-location to succeed.

Is the Goal of Co-Location Several Stronger Agencies? . . .

If you're thinking about co-locating, you need to address a fundamental question early on: What's the goal? Is this about combining
to create a new organization, or about making each individual partner more effective? The Buffalo arts organizations are very clear
about their goal. When there's a proposal, they ask, "Is this in line
with strengthening our individual arts organizations?" Torrell calls
that "the centerpiece of our approach."

. . . Or a Joint Venture?

At the other end of the co-location spectrum is what we might call
a joint venture. Private-sector firms sometimes agree to jointly form
a new company to create a product or service. These joint ventures
are often formed for a specific project (for example, high-tech competitors might start a joint venture to create a new hardware or
software product). And some become ongoing entities.

For instance, IBM and Toshiba created an ongoing joint
venture in the 1980s to design and manufacture liquid crystal displays (LCDs). They used their respective (and different) compe-
tencies. Toshiba had a world-class manufacturing process and had

demonstrated success making small displays for cell phones but lacked experience using this technology with larger screens. IBM had adapted the displays to larger screens (like computer monitors) but lacked Toshiba's manufacturing experience. Their joint venture, Display Technology Inc., began manufacturing displays in 1989, and three years later it was one of the world's leading LCD manufacturers, building the flat panel displays now found in many of our homes and offices.

Figure 11.1 offers a continuum of co-location options, with some features of each.

We've looked at just one co-location so far: the Buffalo arts organizations. This model, with its emphasis on strengthening the individual organizations, is the least daunting change (the left-hand side of the continuum). Because most staff are not shared and the partners retain their separate programs and customers, there's little threat to agency identity. Staff continue to work for

Continuum of Co-Location Options		
Independent Units ------------------- Joint Venture		
Goal:	Strengthen individual units.	Create a new entity.
Staff:	Some are shared, most work for their separate agenies.	All are shared and work as part of the new entity.
What else is shared:	Space, equipment; programs are coordinated.	Most resources, training, decision making, and joint programs and accountability for their results.
Governance:	Each agency governed separately.	The organization has its own governing or advisory board.
Customers:	Each agency serves its own.	All serve same set of customers.
Buffalo arts organizations ----- Fusion centers ----- Child Advocacy Center		

Figure 11.1. Continuum of Co-Location Options.

Note: This continuum doesn't imply a "most desirable" place to be. Success is possible at any point along the continuum.

their home agency, under its policies and procedures. Tracking and accounting for funds is also less complex than it is in other parts of the continuum.

At the other end of the continuum is the joint venture model, which creates a new organization with the potential to create its own programs and services. In a joint venture, where staff are all shared by the new organization and work full time in the same space, the possibilities for trust and synergy are enhanced.

However, joint ventures also can present major challenges: How to deal with different funding streams (and the different limitations of each)? How to maintain accountability? How to help employees deal with their different professional cultures? What to do when the agencies' policies differ?

We'll look at a joint venture that has addressed these challenges. Baltimore County's Child Advocacy Center has demonstrated the potential of a joint venture since its creation in 1989. And it is demonstrating impressive outcomes.

The Child Advocacy Center: A Public-Sector Joint Venture

The Baltimore County Child Advocacy Center (CAC) (mentioned in Chapter Eight) was formed by the Baltimore County Police Department, Health Department, Office of the State's Attorney, and Department of Social Services (DSS) in 1989. As in other child advocacy centers around the country, each two-person CAC team consists of a police detective and a DSS social worker, who work together in the CAC offices to investigate child sexual abuse cases, ensure that abused children are protected, work toward successful prosecution of child sexual abusers, and refer victims to treatment. These teams leverage the two partner agencies' respective strengths. For instance, the social workers usually take the lead when interviewing the child; the police lead when interviewing suspected offenders.

Governance and supervision of the CAC can be a challenge. A police lieutenant and a DSS social work administrator serve as co-directors of the CAC, overseeing daily operations. A committee made up of managers from the key stakeholder agencies serves as a governing board. It meets quarterly and focuses on longer-term planning and policy matters. Some people have suggested the need for a single center director, but that doesn't seem to be in the cards. Codirector Kris Debye, representing the DSS, notes that "each department wants to maintain its own leader and its own accountability here." In line with that approach, the center's staff are paid and evaluated by their home agencies, although they tend to develop an identity with the CAC.

> *The Child Advocacy Center police officers and social workers work in two-person teams, combining their complementary skills.*

Beyond that, each agency contributes in its own way, based on comparative strengths and advantages. For instance, the Department of Social Services is 80 percent state funded, whereas the Police Department is locally funded. It turns out that there's far more flexibility in the county's budget than in the state's. So the county funds a number of positions and items that would be difficult to get through the state bureaucracy, like the office lease.

It can get complicated: many staff use state-funded computers that rest on county-funded furniture. As Debye says, "There's no set formula stating who pays for some items. We work it out." Special items, like state-of-the-art digital recording devices and monitors, have been acquired through specially secured grant funding. Working these issues out requires considerable communication and trust, which Kris and her police counterpart work hard to maintain.

CAC Results

It's hard to argue with success, and the CAC has demonstrated excellent results. Using the unique combination of social work and law enforcement skills as well as the chemistry and trust that the teams have developed, the CAC has been able to generate major

Table 11.1. Baltimore County CAC Results, for Indicated Cases.

	Baseline	1992	1999
Arrest rate	27% (1988)	73%	95%+
Confession rate	20% (1990)	40%	50%

Note: "Indicated cases" are those in which the social workers found abuse likely to have occurred.

increases in confession and arrest rates, as the numbers in Table 11.1 indicate. And these results have continued to this day.

What Made the Difference?

These results stem partly from the CAC model and partly from a number of smart steps taken by the CAC's police and social work leaders over the years. The key steps have included

- Ongoing discussion of roles
- Joint training
- Joint case reviews (which also provide a needed venue in which team members can ventilate, given what they learn about the horrific experiences many victims go through)
- End-of-day meetings to surface any issues or conflicts
- Use of jointly developed interviewing protocols
- Continual work on the relationship between the codirectors

It's very important for social workers and police officers to see the middle managers working well together. The emphasis on building and maintaining relationships has been critical to dealing with the huge differences (discussed in Chapter Eight) between the police and the social work cultures. (The CAC is described in more detail in Linden, 2002, chap. 2).

Another example of a joint venture involves fusion centers, which have been one of the federal government's encouraging responses to the September 11 attacks. More information about fusion center issues and critical success factors is available on the Jossey-Bass Web site.

Fusion Centers

The 9/11 Commission pointed to the failure to "fuse" domestic and foreign intelligence as one of many information-sharing lapses prior to the attacks. To help fill that void and provide a coordinated way to share and analyze intelligence and law enforcement information, over forty-five states have created fusion centers.

These centers typically bring together employees from a variety of state, federal, and local government agencies dealing with law enforcement, emergency management, intelligence, homeland security, health, and other areas of concern. These staff members are co-located and share information on an ongoing basis. Sharing information within and across the law enforcement and intelligence communities has long been an enormous challenge. One of the major hurdles has been trust. A key fusion center strategy is to foster trust among these and other personnel in order to help them share information and thus prevent crimes and attacks.

How Fusion Centers Work

Employees from the various agencies work in the same center. The goal: detect, prevent, and respond to criminal and terrorist activities. Some centers also deal with gangs, drugs, and natural disasters. The centers try to achieve their goals by accessing and fusing information from twenty or more databases, analyzing that information, and sending the analysis to first responders and other stakeholders.

Their customers include law enforcement, public health, public safety, and homeland security agencies (at all three government levels). They also serve certain private-sector firms, which own as much as 85 percent of the nation's critical infrastructure. In many states citizens can call a fusion center to report concerns; the Maryland fusion center, for example, receives 60 percent of its calls from citizens reporting a suspicious activity. Other service calls come from law enforcement officials.

Most centers are run by and financed by the states. They also receive funds from the Department of Homeland Security and the Federal Bureau of Investigation. The centers use a variety of governance structures, but most have established some kind of governance board representing the major agencies providing staff to the center.

I consider the fusion center approach a hybrid model of co-location, for two reasons. First, at many fusion centers employees rotate in and out every few years. Second, in some fusion centers employees are situated with others from the same agency (rather than working next to individuals from other units). This can limit information sharing and can heighten the dual loyalty tension: Is the employee there primarily to support the center (and its customers) or to serve his home agency?

The open floor plan at MCAC; analysts can view each other's monitors.

Source: Maryland Coordination and Analysis Center; used with permission.

The watch section in many fusion centers is staffed on a 24/7 basis. The photo shown on page 208 was taken at Maryland's fusion center—the Maryland Coordination and Analysis Center (MCAC)—which integrates employees from several agencies. The data screen on the wall can project the images or data from any analyst's monitor.

Fusing and Disseminating Information: An Example

Fusion centers offer the unique combination of access to large numbers of existing databases, the ability to analyze this data from multiple perspectives, and also the ability to then act quickly to provide first responders and other government officials one source of information. This saves agencies' time and cost (most police agencies can't afford to maintain twenty-plus databases).

Here is one example of the many available. In 2004, Baltimore County police officers riding in a marked police car observed a passenger in another vehicle videotaping the structure of the Chesapeake Bay Bridge. When the police were pulling ahead of the vehicle, the passenger dropped the camera, then began videotaping the structure again after the police car had passed. The officers contacted the watch section of MCAC, which quickly found that the driver was an unindicted coconspirator named in a federal indictment issued in Chicago and involving the terrorist group Hamas.

MCAC personnel contacted the Maryland Transportation Authority police (the law enforcement agency responsible for the bridge and the closest first responder), who stopped the vehicle. Simultaneously, they contacted the Maryland Joint Terrorism Task Force and also an assistant U.S. attorney responsible for national security matters in Maryland. The assistant U.S. attorney called the U.S. Attorney's Office in Chicago and that office obtained a material witness arrest warrant for the driver in relation to the outstanding indictment. The driver was taken into federal custody and thereafter ordered to appear before a federal magistrate in Chicago.

"None of this would have happened without the fusion center," noted Harvey Eisenberg, the assistant U.S. attorney for the District of Maryland. "Many entities were involved, all of them followed the established protocols. And because of Maryland's fusion center, it happened quickly and effectively. That demonstrates the power of fusion centers."

Fusion Centers: Great Potential, Significant Issues

Those who champion fusion centers point to a number of benefits, listed in Exhibit 11.2.

However, fusion centers also pose some challenges. Because of the vast amount of information they collect, some civil liberties advocates worry that these centers may misuse the information (Peters, 2009). MCAC employees all receive civil liberties training and undergo annual recertification training, but actions of some other centers have raised concerns about overzealous monitoring of minority, academic, and other groups.

In addition, the federal government's role in supporting fusion centers needs to be clarified. In addition to providing funds and some staff and training, should it set national standards and promote a model that all centers must meet? Should it hold centers accountable? And who reports to whom—the centers to the feds, or vice

---

Exhibit 11.2. Fusion Center Benefits.

- Build trust; reduce turf problems among people from different agencies.
- Foster information sharing between agencies at all three levels of government.
- Capture information from multiple databases that state and local agencies cannot afford to maintain themselves.
- Fuse information from multiple databases, which can provide quick analyses to first responders.
- Give first responders one-stop service on potential threats and suspects.
- Provide analysts with a greater ability to spot trends and prevent crimes and attacks.
- Promote mutual learning for employees from different professions.

versa? Another major issue has to do with the fusion center hybrid model. Can co-located units achieve their goals when many staff rotate in and out every few years?

Perhaps the most significant issue is this: Can a law enforcement culture, which focuses on solving yesterday's crime, coexist with an intelligence culture, which aims to prevent tomorrow's attack? On the one hand, Chicago judge Richard Posner argues strongly that these two cultures are fundamentally different, that they can't and shouldn't be merged (see Posner, 2007). On the other hand, Chuck Rapp, former director of the Maryland fusion center, reflects the view of many fusion center supporters: "I agree that law enforcement and intelligence are different cultures. However, the two must be merged. Intelligence information becomes more valuable when law enforcement information is joined with it, because it puts it in context, and clarifies some of the assumptions being made."

A major fusion center issue: Can the law enforcement and intelligence cultures mesh?

These issues are important, but I think they will be worked out in the years to come, primarily because of the high stakes involved. The fusion center model holds great promise for dealing with a critical national need: the sharing and analysis of information from various sources to benefit first responders and others in times of crisis.

Why Co-Locate? And What Are the Critical Success Factors for Co-Locating?

Many leaders and elected officials consider co-location a great way to save money. Having looked at more than a dozen co-located examples, I'm not persuaded by this reasoning. Some co-located efforts save very little money. And agencies can remain co-located and save a few bucks a year, yet realize none of the other important benefits of co-location.

The real promise of co-location has to do with its potential for collaboration, and its impact on your mission—improved customer service, increased tempo of operations, higher quality products. If it helps you improve such outcomes, then co-location can be a powerful strategy to pursue. Exhibit 11.3 lists some critical success factors for co-locating.

In thinking about these factors, I've been struck by the impact that apparently small decisions can make. One example is the use of space. If you and two partners are going to co-locate, will there be one reception area or three? If there is one reception area, the people working there need to be cross-trained so they can answer all questions. Will there be one administrative area (supplies, mail, copy machines, and the like) or three? If you and your partners

---

Exhibit 11.3. Critical Success Factors During the Co-Location Planning Phase.

- Look for partners with similar goals and complementary strengths.

- Generate senior leadership support.

- Be very clear on the goals at the outset: (1) What can you and your partner(s) accomplish together that can't be done separately, and (2) what's the model? To strengthen individual entities? To create a joint venture? Some of each?

- Learn from others who have co-located, but remember there's no one-size-fits-all structure or strategy.

- Create a governance structure that represents the partners.

- Determine how the partners will fund the move and then share the costs of the space.

- Maintain continual communications (up, down, and sideways) during the planning and move.

- Consider memorializing the agreement in a memo of understanding (MOU) that contains the work plan and clear descriptions of how the space will be divided up, goals and roles, benchmarks, the timeline, and the criteria of success. One person or a small group should plan and execute the move.

- Plan and execute the move in chunks, a strategy that offers opportunities for learning.

collaborate on one administrative area, does that mean purchasing supplies together? Sharing equipment? Can one person handle certain administrative duties for all three partners? None of these questions is impossible to answer, but all must be addressed.

When two natural resource agencies co-located their field units in a Western state, they decided each agency needed its own training room and its separate kitchenette area. It seemed reasonable at the time. The unanticipated consequence? There's far less informal mingling of staff in this center than in another co-located building where the natural resources agencies have shared such spaces.

It's impossible to anticipate all consequences from decisions about use of space, of course. Once you've learned from a few other agencies that have co-located, the best strategy is to make your decisions, move in, and plan three-month and six-month check-ins to discuss how it's going and whether some decisions need to be revisited. Exhibit 11.4 lists several practices to consider when co-locating.

Exhibit 11.4. Critical Success Factors Once Co-Location Is Operational.

- Manage the symbols to support a sense of equality among the partners: consider how agency logos are used, who chairs the meetings, who represents the co-located entity to the media and public, and the like.

- Hold early and ongoing discussions of roles and business processes: Are there some operations that can be integrated?

- Take time to learn each partner agency's culture, including its core values.

- Ensure that the default concerning information is "when in doubt, share."

- Share credit on jointly produced products.

- Communicate successes widely to external stakeholders and employees.

- Engage the employees in developing a few (emphasize *few*) metrics that are meaningful to customers and other stakeholders as well as to employees.

(Continued)

Exhibit 11.4. Critical Success Factors Once Co-Location Is Operational (Continued).

- Follow the money carefully, so each funder knows how its money is spent.
- When major differences arise, the key criteria for resolving differences should be (1) what best serves the mission? and (2) what generates the most stakeholder support?
- Ensure that the various managers show their mutual support in front of employees.
- Nonprofits need to get their boards on board early in the effort.
- If some of your staff belong to a union, involve the union early so there can be useful input and no surprises.
- It's all about relationships, so provide ongoing, formal and informal trust-building activities. The most critical relationship in co-located units is the relationship among the partners' on-site leaders. They set the tone.

Moving into a new space with people from other units can have an emotional impact on staff. The leaders of two agencies that co-located in the mid-1990s were surprised that their employees were so anxious about the change. For the staff it wasn't about a new space. No, the issue had to do with *identity*; they liked being part of their home agency. The agencies' leaders wanted to integrate as many operations as possible—the front desk, training, IT support, and more. But most of the staff weren't ready for that. So the leaders decided to keep those operations separate at the start, and didn't integrate some functions until the second or third year. Rather than create one new logo for the operation, they kept the two agency logos on their letterhead and fax cover sheets, alternating which one was in the "power" position on the left. As they explained, "the 'small' was huge at the start. So we managed the symbols."

> *Co-locating employees raises anxieties,*
> *and the "small" can become huge.*

Clarifying and managing expectations also becomes important once the move is made. If you're operating as the Buffalo arts organizations were, it's important to remind staff that the goal isn't to form one organization; the goal is to share space and information to help each of the separate organizations boost its performance. Indeed, that should be the ultimate criterion for any co-location, regardless of the model: Does this change make a positive impact on our clients; does it help us better meet our mission?

Reality Check: Co-Location Poses Potential Risks

We've looked at examples of three different kinds of co-location. Each has shown considerable success. None was easy to create. Co-locating with other units poses some risks, and they need to be discussed at the outset.

- *Is there a good fit with the respective cultures?* Police and firefighters are both in the public safety business, but they operate in markedly different cultures. Some municipal leaders have merged the two into one agency, often to their later regret. If the partners' core values aren't in synch, co-locating isn't likely to succeed.

- *What information can or should partners share about customers?* The Buffalo arts organizations chose to share information on how to approach donors, but they don't exchange their actual donor lists. That's a reasonable decision for organizations that sometimes compete for the same people's support. In contrast, if human services agencies co-locate, one of the benefits should be improved information sharing about shared clients (with appropriate safeguards for privacy).

- *Do key stakeholders support the change?* The executive directors of the Buffalo arts agencies were excited about co-locating; the agencies' boards were slower to accept the idea. Many funders are eager to see their recipients move in together, but some special-interest groups oppose co-locations, worrying that the agency they monitor will be less accountable for its actions. It's important to listen to your stakeholders' concerns and help them see co-location's benefits.

- *Do the agencies' leaders work well together?* When the U.S. Bureau of Land Management and the U.S. Forest Service began co-locating field offices in the 1990s, they learned that the field office managers' relationships were critical to success. In general, when those managers worked well together and had the same vision for co-location, it worked well. That said, nobody stays forever. In some instances the managers who created the co-located unit later left and were replaced by people who didn't form strong relationships with each other and who didn't value a co-located model, and performance suffered. The key lesson? Senior leaders at the top of each agency need to be committed to co-location and to selection of managers who will support it.

- *Is loss of autonomy a concern?* If two units occupy the same building, one on the first floor and one on the second, autonomy won't be a problem. But why co-locate if you're immediately going to separate? The most effective co-locations include some sharing of space, of staff, of information, and of other resources. And that's where the worry about lost autonomy kicks in. The easy response to this risk is to be very clear at the outset concerning who does what, and form a strong governance committee that deals with such issues. But the more important answer is this: there *will* be some loss of autonomy. Less when partners maintain separate and distinct agency identities, more when partners move toward a joint venture model. The question is, Are the co-location benefits significant enough to warrant this loss? If relationships among the leaders are solid and if the partners have similar values, this issue can be handled.

THE BOTTOM LINE

Co-location is a growing trend, not a fad. It has demonstrated real value in such disparate fields as firefighting, human services, policing, the arts, education, natural resources, and homeland security. The major payoffs aren't financial savings, although that sometimes occurs. The biggest benefits for employees are the trust, shared information, creative ideas, and energy that are produced. For clients, other stakeholders, and our communities, the payoffs include faster service, easier access to information, and one-stop operations (no need to shop around for the right service provider).

Moreover, co-location can be a powerful response to the problem of fragmented organizational structures. When co-located units do much more than share space—when they share information, produce programs and products together, even share some staff—they substitute integration for fragmentation. This is one of the most powerful ways to move people from me to we, because they see the evidence of their joint identity every day.

In his 1982 book *Megatrends*, futurist John Naisbitt coined the term *high tech/high touch*. Before we even knew how to spell *Internet*, he saw that in a world of ever increasing technology, people have greater needs for human contact: "We must learn to balance the material wonders of technology with the spiritual demands of our human nature" (p. 40). Co-locating and integrating people from different units provides the opportunity for both high tech and high touch. And as our government and nonprofit organizations confront ever more complex and interconnected challenges, we'll require hefty doses of both.

Co-location is an example of a structural change that helps leaders create a collaborative culture. Another way to generate a culture of collaboration is to adopt certain management methods. In my view, the most powerful method for improving performance through collaboration is sometimes called CompStat. It doesn't change an agency's structure, but it has proven to be a powerful lever for changing people's behavior. We'll look at one excellent example next.

12

Using CompStat

A Structured Method for Generating Collaboration and Accountability

The most important thing you can do to drive interagency collaboration is to make all agencies accountable for improving outcomes.

—David Osborne

Many people would agree with David Osborne's comment that mutual accountability is central to achieving collaboration. But how to achieve accountability among different agencies? For a growing number of organizations, the answer is to use CompStat (also called PerformanceStat or CitiStat), a method that combines structured meetings focused on goal achievement, fact-based analysis and decisions, senior leadership involvement, and rigorous follow-up. It's making a difference in a number of communities. One of the most impressive is in Washington State.

Washington State's GMAP: Fostering Collaboration Around the Governor's Priorities

When Christine Gregoire took office as governor of Washington State in January 2005, she wanted to bring a structured method for improving overall performance to state government. Gregoire, a three-term state attorney general with a passion for results, had just won the closest governor's race in U.S. history. She had used a management method called CompStat in the attorney general's office with good results, and wanted to adapt it to the whole state because of the way it creates accountability for outcomes.

CompStat (short for Computer Statistics) was initiated by the New York City Police Department in 1994, and it helped the department to reduce the city's crime rate dramatically (violent crime declined more than 70 percent in a decade). Although some law enforcement professionals argue that CompStat wasn't entirely responsible for this turnaround, many police agencies in this country have had success using key elements of the CompStat method. Martin O'Malley adapted the method to an entire city when he became mayor of Baltimore in 2000, calling it CitiStat (Behn, 2007; Henderson, 2003). Soon the Stat method took off around the country. Exhibit 12.1 lists its key characteristics.

Gregoire was the nation's first governor to expand the Stat method across state government. In June 2005, she launched her version of the method, calling it Government Management Accountability and Performance, or GMAP.

Exhibit 12.1. Key Stat Characteristics.

- Focuses middle and senior managers on achievement of certain agreed-upon goals.

- Makes heavy use of data to assess performance and inform decisions.

- Includes regular, structured meetings where senior leaders question agency managers about recent performance and outcomes, and managers discuss what they're learning and how they're working together to achieve the outcomes.

- Emphasizes persistent follow-up and produces action plans for improvement after each meeting.

- Is managed by a small unit that tracks and analyzes agency performance between meetings.

- Provides a disciplined approach to senior-level decision making.

How Washington State's GMAP Method Works

Under the GMAP process, each agency director reports quarterly to the governor or her chief of staff on agency performance. The meetings focus on the governor's six high-priority areas. For instance, agency directors responsible for health care priorities must report on the percentage of Washingtonians who are insured and the rate of deaths from heart attacks or strokes (among other concerns).

Unlike many management meetings, these sessions focus primarily on data. An internal GMAP team provides a report for each meeting that details the stated goals and measures for the priority area the meeting is focused on, performance toward those measures over the past quarter, the action plan agreed to by agency directors to improve performance, and the current results. When it comes to GMAP and performance, you can run but you can't hide, as the old saying goes. And that's what the governor wanted.

The GMAP method focuses state managers on the governor's priorities, and holds them accountable for results.

Perhaps most important, GMAP focuses on the governor's major priorities, which gives her a powerful tool to continually remind state employees what she expects of them. Governor Gregoire frequently tells agency managers that "the public is holding me accountable for this outcome, and I'm holding you accountable for it as well." The governor's six priorities as of 2009 were

- Economic vitality
- Government efficiency
- Health care
- Safety
- Transportation
- Vulnerable children and adults

GMAP Builds on Other Stat Applications and Adds Impressive Features

Washington State is probably the most innovative government entity using the Stat method today, taking what others have done and adding key features. Most governments using this approach focus on individual agency objectives, such as number of pot holes filled in a given period of time, number of overtime hours worked, response times, and the like. Gregoire and her staff designed GMAP to focus entirely on broad-based *outcomes* that no single agency can achieve on its own, thus requiring ongoing collaboration. In another innovation, GMAP uses logic models (explained later in this chapter) to help agency managers and staff understand how their specific activities and outputs—say, the number of inmates trained in certain work skills—lead to larger outcomes such as community safety. A third innovation is the way GMAP actively engages citizens in identifying priorities for state government. Exhibit 12.2 lists GMAP's distinguishing characteristics.

Unlike some public figures who love to use the A-word (*accountability*) but who duck for cover at the first hint of trouble, Gregoire is serious about accountability. Citizens and the media are invited to GMAP meetings, and anyone can view the meetings

---

Exhibit 12.2. Characteristics That Distinguish GMAP from Other Stat Methods.

- It focuses entirely on broad outcomes.
- It requires active interagency collaboration to achieve those outcomes.
- Its outcomes reflect the governor's priorities.
- It allows citizens to be actively involved in establishing GMAP priorities and performance measures.
- It uses logic models that show the connections between agency programs and the governor's priority outcomes.
- Its meetings are open to the public and accessible through the Web.

---

through the Web (go to http://www.accountability.wa.gov and click on "Watch a performance report"). When *Governing* magazine named Gregoire one of its Public Officials of the Year in 2007, it noted that "she runs one of the most open state governments in the country" (Walters, 2007a).

A GMAP Meeting

The governor or her chief of staff presides over each GMAP meeting. Two large screens project the performance data for the outcomes being discussed. The governor or her chief and other senior officials sit on one side of an open square table; agency directors sit across from them. Agency directors and managers from related agencies report on progress toward agreed-upon outcomes. For instance, a health care meeting will include the state's secretary of health; the secretary of the Department of Social and Health Services, along with her Medicaid director; and the director of the Health Care Authority (which insures state employees and runs the state's supplemental low-income health insurance plan). GMAP meetings are structured this way to ensure that everyone with responsibility for the GMAP priority under discussion is in the room at the same time.

The session begins with a look at the GMAP report for the responsible agencies. That report includes the action plan developed for these agencies as a result of their last GMAP meeting, as well as comments and data analysis from the GMAP staff.

The governor then typically asks two questions:

1. Did we do what we said we would do [based on the last session's action plan]?

2. Did it work?

> *The purpose of GMAP meetings is to learn in order to achieve outcomes, it's not about finding scapegoats.*

The group's discussion revolves around the GMAP report data and the agency directors' responses. The purpose is to learn—Did we try a strategy that didn't work? What might have worked better?—as well as to hold people accountable and recognize positive performance. Senior leaders drill down into the specific issues revealed by the report in an effort to learn what is driving improved performance and what lies behind any problems.

GMAP meetings end with a discussion of needed actions: how to maintain progress; how to address performance gaps. There is an agreement on next steps—on *who* will do *what* by *when*—all of which is captured by the GMAP team. That action plan is sent to the participants and creates the agenda when the same agencies meet again three months hence.

It All Focuses on the Governor's Priorities

I'm especially impressed by the way Governor Gregoire uses GMAP to emphasize her priorities to the 100,000+ Washington State employees. GMAP breaks each priority down into a few categories, with performance measures for each. For instance, the economic vitality priority includes these categories:

- Employment (one measure: number of new jobs created)
- Open for Business (one measure: export assistance to small and midsized firms)
- Foundation for Success (one measure: on-time completion of infrastructure construction projects)
- Workforce Skills (one measure: number of "high-demand" college degrees awarded)

Giving GMAP "Legs" and Depth

Early in 2005, just weeks after taking office, Gregoire introduced legislation to authorize the GMAP program; the legislature passed it that May. It also passed statutes institutionalizing results-based budgeting and citizen input to help establish government priorities. This early legislative support helped to give GMAP bipartisan support, making it more likely to receive support from future governors.

That first year the governor also issued an executive order directing agency heads to replicate the GMAP process with their own managers and division directors. This has helped to drive the key priorities and measures well into the ranks.

An Important Example: Reducing Child Abuse

Governor Gregoire was concerned about child abuse when she took office, and she soon identified prevention of child abuse as a top priority. She learned that a state statute required Child Protective Services to respond to reports of abuse within ten working days. That seemed far too slow. The governor gave Child Protective Services a new goal: social workers would respond within twenty-four hours to the highest risk reports of abuse. When she convened the first GMAP meeting in June 2005, the topic was child abuse.

The June GMAP discussion revealed that social workers in one region of the state weren't meeting the new twenty-four-hour response time target for reporting child abuse. The leaders analyzed the problem and discovered that social workers in this region were frequently called to juvenile court, where they could sit for hours—sometimes up to two entire days—waiting for a required hearing. It was a huge waste of time. By the end of the GMAP meeting the governor decided to call on the court system and the state attorney general's office to come together and collaborate with the social workers on a solution.

The state hired consultant Stewart Henderson to facilitate a collaborative solution among the various players. He got senior-level sponsorship from the governor, the head of the state's social and health services agency, the chief judge of the juvenile court (an elected official), and a representative of the attorney general's office. Henderson and GMAP's first director, Larisa Benson, identified the team members and team leader; the governor formally invited the identified individuals to join the team.

At its first meeting the team developed a game plan to reduce court wait times. A key element in the solution was that social workers would be given an appointment for each court hearing time; no longer would they wait in court for hours. Team members sold the solution to their own agencies, and within a few weeks the agencies began implementing it.

Significant Results

Barely three months after the first team meeting, the solution was demonstrating results. Social workers in the pilot offices were spending 25 percent less time in court. The court also got stricter about insisting that social workers submit their reports on time. By the end of 2006, social workers were responding to abuse reports within twenty-four hours 90 percent of the time or more. More important, the percentage of children being revictimized after a first report went down. Table 12.1 shows the specific numbers. Larisa Benson notes that this reduction in the revictimization rate translates into more than 200 kids who didn't suffer a recurrence of abuse.

Table 12.1. Social Worker Response Times to Child Abuse Reports.

	% of Time Social Workers Respond Within 24 Hours	
Before GMAP intervention (1/05)	73.5%	
After GMAP intervention (1/08–12/08)	96%	
	% of Children Revictimized Within 6 Months	% of Children Revictimized Within 12 Months
Before GMAP intervention (1/05–6/05)	11.6%	14.4%
After GMAP intervention (1/07–6/07)	7.9%	9.0%

Reflecting on this experience, Stewart Henderson says that the initial buy-in from senior leaders "made a huge difference. When we hit obstacles, the sponsors handled them for us. The process allowed us to tell the various stakeholders, 'Hey, the governor is paying close attention to this.'"

This case demonstrates one of GMAP's greatest strengths: its ability to focus two or more agency leaders on a shared goal. Two of the key agencies involved in child abuse prevention are not under the governor's direct control. The juvenile court's chief judge and the attorney general are elected officials with their own legal authority.

> GMAP gives state leaders the ability to say, "The governor is paying close attention to this."

Henderson, Benson, and the governor were in a position of asking for, not requiring, these officials' participation. They got that participation in part because of their interpersonal skills, in part because the governor made this a priority, and in part because GMAP shines a light on important problems and emphasizes fact-based analysis.

The GMAP Logic Model

Part of the GMAP method is to create a logic model that demonstrates cause-and-effect relationships between agency activities and the ultimate desired outcome (safe children, for example). Detecting change in the ultimate outcome often takes years; the logic model gives Washington State employees and leaders a way to *continually* check the pulse of their efforts. If the logic model is accurate (a big "if"—these models need to be reviewed and validated or altered periodically), then leaders can monitor employees' ongoing activities and outputs to determine if a long-term strategy is being implemented effectively.

Harvard's Bob Behn, an expert on performance leadership who has studied GMAP and other Stat methods, points out another reason for using logic models (Behn, 2008). Agencies are more likely to collaborate around common goals when they agree on a cause-and-effect theory for connecting their outputs to the desired outcomes.

GMAP Logic Model

Figure 12.1 is a GMAP logic model. Notice the arrow on the lower-right side of the figure. A manager's influence is greatest at the activity or output level, and it gradually lessens as the effort moves toward the ultimate outcome. Bob Behn argues that employees are more motivated to work on outputs and activities under their control than on broader outcomes. This model shows employees what is within their control, and it demonstrates how their actions contribute toward the desired outcomes. Of course many things affect the ultimate outcome; logic models simplify reality and don't capture the complexities of achieving

Where do measures come from?

Goal: Ensuring vulnerable children are safe

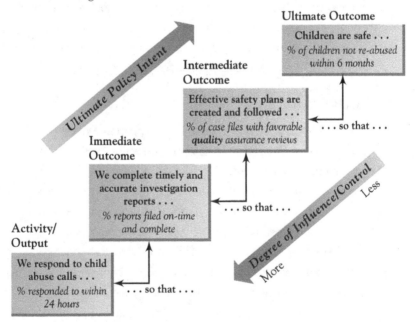

Figure 12.1. GMAP Logic Model for Ensuring Vulnerable Children Are Safe.

Source: Permission received from the Children's Administration, Washington State Dept. of Social and Health Services.

important outcomes. But logic models do try to identify the critical cause-and-effect relationships, showing employees how their *actions* make a difference.

Figure 12.2 displays the same logic model shown in Figure 12.1 for ensuring vulnerable children are safe, with the addition of performance data through 2008.

As the data show, between 2005 and January 2008, state social workers improved their track record of responding to reported child abuse within twenty-four hours, from 73.5 percent to 95 percent of the time. And the number of children being revictimized by abusive parents or caregivers is being reduced by several hundred each year.

Engaging Citizens in Setting Priorities and Performance Measures

Another GMAP feature is its emphasis on citizen engagement. In 2006, Washington State began involving citizens in GMAP, through a three-step process:

1. *Citizen workshops.* During 2006 and 2007, a professional opinion research firm facilitated a series of interactive citizen workshops for about fifty people at each of twelve locations around the state. The governor's chief of staff and the GMAP director attended each session. Participants ranked their top priorities for state government and also identified measures to use for each priority area. Their input informed the final performance measures used by GMAP.

2. *Community leader roundtables.* Members of the governor's cabinet met in roundtable discussions with community leaders around Washington who were interested in specific policy areas. Cabinet members used these discussions to hear directly from key stakeholders in their policy area.

3. *Town hall meetings.* Up to 500 people came to each of six town hall sessions. The governor attended each and answered

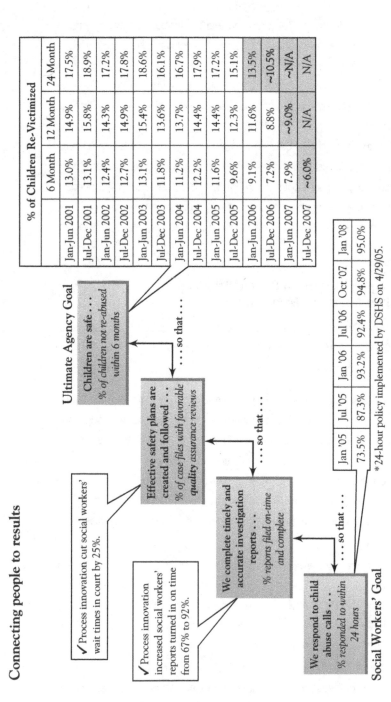

Connecting people to results

Social Workers' Goal

Figure 12.2. GMAP Logic Model for Ensuring Vulnerable Children Are Safe, Including Performance Data.

*Shaded numbers for more recent cohorts are estimates that will be revised later with more complete data.

*24-hour policy implemented by DSHS on 4/29/05.

Source: Permission received from the Children's Administration, Washington State Dept. of Social and Health Services.

questions for about ninety minutes. Several of these sessions were broadcast on public access TV and local news media.

The meetings captured the force and tenor of people's feelings. Stuart Elway, who led the citizen workshops, notes that "the governor sometimes tells agency directors, 'We heard from hundreds of citizens, and this is what they said. . . . This is how people hold me accountable, and it's how I'll hold you accountable.'"

GMAP and Collaboration

GMAP meetings are organized around results, not individual agency activities and outputs. Because these results reflect the governor's priorities, because state residents had input into these results, and because the entire GMAP process is made transparent to the public, the process generates impressive interagency collaboration.

GMAP creates important conversations among the state managers and leaders about shared goals and how to achieve them.

The governor also uses GMAP to generate ongoing conversations among middle and senior managers and with her about the managers' shared goals, progress, and problems. This gives middle and senior managers an unusual amount of face time with the governor. And smart managers quickly learn that their interest is the same as their colleagues' and the governor's: focus agency energies on improving performance and meeting stated goals. The more their agency cooperates with sister agencies in that enterprise, the better the results (and the more they'll shine).

Yes, but . . . Questions About GMAP and Other Stat Programs

At this point you might be thinking that this all sounds too easy, too perfect. GMAP and other Stat methods do raise several important issues.

*What About Fear? Won't Managers and Leaders Game
the System?*

When senior leaders emphasize "making the numbers," it often
tempts some managers to game the numbers. Some people may
alter the performance numbers; others may shoot for very easy-to-
achieve performance targets.

Stat leaders need to emulate Governor Gregoire's approach:
she sets a positive tone that reduces fear and game playing. She
likes to tell GMAP participants
that "no one gets in trouble at
GMAP for bringing forth data
that shows we're not achieving
our goals. You get in trouble if
you don't have an action plan
for what you're going to do
about it" (Benson, 2006, p. 4). GMAP also addresses potential
game playing by actively engaging agency directors in selecting
performance measures. GMAP staff attempt to find measures that
are compelling and relevant to the directors' interests.

> Gregoire emphasizes that you don't
> get in trouble for not achieving the
> goals; you get in trouble if you have
> no plan to address the shortfall.

The most effective way I've found to reduce fear and game
playing in any performance measurement system is to emphasize the L-word—*learning*. The best way to be accountable is to
learn from the data and revise strategies based on past results and
emerging insights. Stat methods will work only if the leaders focus
on learning.

*When Many Agencies or Units Are Collaborating
on a Shared Goal, Who's Ultimately Accountable?*

Good question. Many managers hold that when everyone's responsible, nobody's responsible. GMAP deals with this, in part, through
its detailed action plans. Recall that these action plans list who will
do what and by when. If the goal is to reduce prison recidivism, and
the head of the state prison system says he needs help in recruiting
and retaining good personnel, then the state's human resource

leaders will have a specific role in dealing with recruitment and retention targets for the prisons. That role will be spelled out in the action plan, and the HR leaders will appear at GMAP meetings to report on their follow-up.

In addition, GMAP's structure shines a light on key problems and on the governor's priorities. It's simply not in an agency director's interest to dodge responsibility when the state's leaders are regularly asking tough questions about performance. Quite the opposite: GMAP gives managers a chance to demonstrate competence. And that requires accepting responsibility.

Do You Need to Be in a Crisis for GMAP and Other Stat Programs to Work?

The short answer is no. Some people associate Stat programs with crises, given that the governments of New York City and Baltimore both faced enormous problems when they instituted a Stat system. But many organizations have instituted Stat programs when things were going well. Indeed, Washington State government was well regarded when Gregoire was elected. She instituted GMAP to take that government to the next level.

So What? Some Results . . .

Exhibit 12.3 lists some of GMAP's results through 2008, as reported by state officials.

Exhibit 12.3. Some GMAP Results in Washington State.

- A one-third decline in repeat instances of child abuse

- A savings of over $85 million (since 2005) for prescription drugs

- Restrained growth in state health care costs, coming in well below national benchmarks for both the private and public sectors

- Safer state highways; in 2007, fatalities per vehicle mile traveled had come down to an all-time low of 1 per 100 million

---

. . . And Some Important Recognition

When *Governing* magazine graded the fifty states in 2008 on four aspects of performance, it gave Washington State an overall grade of A–, the highest grade awarded to any state. The *Governing* editors noted that "no state in the nation is better at developing and sharing information than Washington" ("A– Washington," 2008).

GMAP also won the 2007 Council of State Governments' Innovations Award, and in 2008 the Council of State Governments gave GMAP its Governance Transformation Award. This award is given to a state program that excels at improving a state's capacity to govern effectively in the twenty-first century.

Analysis: Why Do Stat Programs Work?

In addition to the factors noted earlier, GMAP and other Stat programs seem to be producing important results for several reasons:

- *Openness and transparency.* Mark Twain once remarked, "When in doubt, tell the truth." Transparency is a huge plus with the public. Of course, openness can become a political problem if the numbers go south. Thus far, Stat programs have been politically beneficial. Gregoire was reelected by a comfortable margin after instituting GMAP, as were mayors O'Malley in Baltimore and Giuliani in New York City.

- *Clear benefits for key stakeholders.* Agency directors and managers who are motivated by results do very well in Stat programs. They gain real access to senior policymakers so priority issues and program strategies can be hammered out. And senior leaders benefit because these methods align agency priorities and behaviors with the leaders' top priorities. Most important, when Stat programs include community input as GMAP does, citizens see their priorities addressed and their trust in government can increase.

- *Ground truth and situational awareness.* As mentioned, the U.S. military sometimes uses the phrase *ground truth* to describe the reality of a situation on the ground as opposed to what various individuals purport it to be. *Situational awareness* (or *situation awareness*) is a term originating in the aviation world. It refers to the individual's ability to form a coherent mental picture of a dynamic external environment and an understanding of its meaning, based on input from a variety of sources. Stat programs give leaders and managers ground truth and situational awareness through the aggressive pursuit of data from all sources. Decisions aren't made on intuition or personal preference, they're made on hard data. Managers and leaders are all looking at the same facts and are focused on the same goals. For leaders who have long sought a way to get everyone on the same page, Stat methods have all the right elements.

- *Stat programs meet the two fundamental human needs.* Individuals can stand out through their participation in Stat meetings and by improving performance on goals (thus meeting the mastery need). Just as important, the method meets the belonging need through its emphasis on collaboration around broad outcomes.

A Cautionary and Hopeful Note

For all of the Stat strengths, this method won't work without committed leadership. When Larisa Benson (2006) describes GMAP's key principles, the first one is "leaders(s) at the top of the organization must be engaged" (p. 2). There's a reason she starts with that principle; everything else flows from it.

That said, if you're in the middle of an organization with leaders who aren't committed to the Stat methodology, you're not helpless. You can create your own Stat program. True, without senior leader involvement you may not get participation from other units. But your own unit will benefit, as will your customers and stakeholders.

THE BOTTOM LINE

Earlier in this book I mentioned a complaint voiced by many organizational leaders: Why don't our people see the big picture? Here's an equally frequent complaint heard at the staff level: Why don't our leaders tell us what direction we're going? The latter is often followed with something like this: "it doesn't matter to me what direction we take, just commit to one and communicate it!"

Stat programs like GMAP are an excellent method for answering leaders' and staff members' questions. Moreover, this method is one of the most powerful ways to overcome the mega-challenge of agency fragmentation because it gives managers shared goals that support senior leaders' priorities and it fosters collaboration to achieve those priorities. As Washington State is showing, this method is about far more than efficiency; it can lead to major improvements in people's lives.

Stat programs, when led well, also provide powerful and positive answers to the four questions that determine whether employees move from a *me* to a *we* mentality:

1. Do I have something to contribute that is needed, recognized, and used by the team?

2. Are we working on a project that is important to me and my own organization (important in terms of mission, priorities, values)?

3. Are we making progress; do we have a reasonable chance for success?

4. How will this project support or threaten any of my core needs or interests (and those of my home organization)?

Stat programs use and recognize employees' positive contributions. These programs focus on leaders' priorities. The relentless emphasis on tracking data demonstrates whether progress is occurring. And when leaders follow Governor Gregoire's example and emphasize learning and accountability, but not blame, the only employees threatened are those who won't work hard toward shared goals.

In addition to structural changes like co-location, and Stat methods like GMAP, managers and leaders can shape collaborative cultures through use of the new media available from the Internet. The Web is providing fascinating ways to help agencies share information and ideas and even form a sense of community. In Chapter Thirteen, I'll analyze how some agencies are transforming their cultures through the use of emerging tools on the Web.

13

Using the New Web to Help Stakeholders Collaborate in Value Creation

The power of this phenomenon [Web 2.0] does not reside in the technology itself, but in its potential as a tool for leaders grappling with industrial-era hierarchies.
—Frank DiGiammarino and Lena Trudeau

This chapter isn't about information technology (IT). Rather, it's about the ways that some organizations are using emerging IT tools to engage employees, customers, and other stakeholders to create value for themselves and their communities. Here I'll discuss how these tools can be used to increase collaboration within and across agencies, and some implications for collaborative leaders. First, we'll look at some examples of what is being called Web 2.0 and the fascinating opportunities it offers us.

The Urge to Engage Through the Web

Self-Organizing Communities

At 7:15 A.M. on April 16, 2007, a mentally unbalanced student at Virginia Tech shot two students. Within three hours he had killed a total of thirty-two people and wounded many others, finally killing himself. At 10:16 that morning, the university sent out an e-mail advisory, telling all students to stay inside because of a crisis on campus. At 10:23 A.M., a Tech student received a post on her Facebook page, asking if she was OK. By 11:34 A.M. that morning, an entire Facebook group, called "I'm ok at VT," had been created. The site invited students to report about their safety (see Figure 13.1).

Between the Facebook group, a few other self-organized sites, and postings on Wikipedia the information compiled was an accurate listing of the thirty-two victims. It was compiled before the university released names to the public. It was all created by volunteers, people who weren't hired to do this work but who spent hours on the task because they cared about the victims. And . . . nobody was in charge (also see Cohen, 2007; Palen and others, 2007).

The News

Tired of having the media tell you what news is important? Check out digg.com. Digg is a social news Web site whose readers have

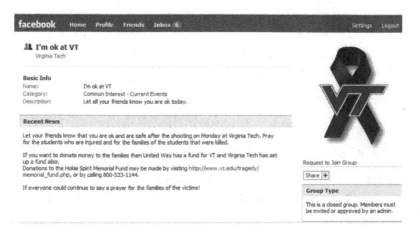

Figure 13.1. "I'm ok at VT" Facebook Page.

final say on the contents. Readers submit stories and links to digg
.com, which posts them online. Digg's readers vote stories up or
down. The most "dugg" stories appear on the front page. Digg has
registered over 100 million visits to its site per month, from as
many as 35 million different people.

Science

OpenWetWare, a Web site used by over one hundred research labs at
more than forty institutions around the world, helps biologists share
information, knowledge, and new discoveries. Scientists use this site
to organize their information and collaborate with others on shared
research interests. According to biology professor Otto Friesen, this
kind of site is extraordinarily helpful "because of the ease of use,
and the speed. It's so easy, and quick, we can read many papers we
otherwise might not see, and that adds to the quality of our work."

The Environment

The Great Lakes Wiki (http://www.greatlakeswiki.org/index
.php/Main_Page) is a site containing resources, information,
stories, and best practices relating to the Great Lakes. It supports
a network of sportsmen and -women, scientists, policymakers,
property owners, environmentalists, businesspeople, and others
who not only share information and ideas on their shared
passion—the Great Lakes—but also do virtual work together on
water quality projects.

R & D

InnoCentive is, as my Jewish mother would have said, a *shadchen*
(Yiddish for "matchmaker"). Companies that have technical
problems anonymously post them at innocentive.com. Engineers,
scientists, inventors, and others who don't work for the company
can submit their solutions. Most organizations pay $5,000 or more
for solutions they like. InnoCentive is a marketplace of ideas.
Those that use the site—including government, nonprofit, and

academic institutions as well as companies—can greatly expand their research capacity at very low cost.

Politics

Barack Obama's 2008 presidential campaign used the new Web in revolutionary ways (see Miller, 2008, for a good analysis). This was the first election campaign to effectively engage people through sites like Facebook, YouTube, and the candidate's own social networking site (my.barackobama.com). Unlike past campaigns, Obama's 2008 campaign gave people the tools to create a bottom-up and horizontal playing field, helping voters connect with him and with many others they'd never met.

And the Obama administration continued using these tools once in the White House. One example (among several): on March 26, 2009, the president hosted an electronic town hall meeting, answering questions that were sent in over the Internet. The White House received 104,000 questions (including several videos that were sent via YouTube). Then the administration asked Americans to vote online for their favorite questions, and 3.5 million people did so. The town hall was broadcast over the Web as well as cable stations (Fletcher and Vargas, 2009).

General Knowledge

One of the more intriguing examples of the desire for active involvement via the Web is the online encyclopedia Wikipedia. Founded in 2001, it is the largest encyclopedia in the world, available free to anyone, anytime. And the contents are provided by people like you and me, not by paid staff. That's right. Those who earn the designation of registered user can post new content, and anyone can edit an existing article (just click on "edit this page" at the top of an article). By 2009, Wikipedia was the most popular site on the Web.

The content of Wikipedia, the largest encyclopedia in the world, is created and edited by volunteers.

Over 100,000 people have contributed ten or more entries to Wikipedia. Through the power of a *wiki* (software that allows anyone to post and edit the content of a Web site), Wikipedia is produced in over 260 languages. Co-founder Jimmy Wales's vision for Wikipedia is to create a free, high-quality encyclopedia for everyone on the planet, in his or her own language (Wales, 2005). A lofty goal.

But can an encyclopedia be accurate when anyone and everyone can edit the contents? In fact, there are hundreds of hard-core users who seem to be addicted to the site and committed to ensuring its accuracy. The December 15, 2005, issue of *Nature* reported a study showing that Wikipedia's accuracy is almost as high as that of the *Encyclopedia Britannica*: Wikipedia averages four mistakes per article, the *Britannica* averages three (Giles, 2005). Although the Wikipedia concept may seem absurdly chaotic, it does have a structure. Volunteers who have earned the designation of administrator have the authority to delete pages (some of which are targets of obscenities) and to lock articles from being edited once disputes on their topics have been settled.

Engaging Through Web 2.0

The term *Web 2.0* has come into frequent use since 2004. The first generation Web was primarily a one-way conveyer of information, images, documents, and the like. But, as Michael Byrne, senior vice president of ICF International, has noted, the new Web is fundamentally different from the earlier version (see Exhibit 13.1).

The new Web is characterized by interaction, participation, and engagement. In fact, some sites, like YouTube and Wikipedia, are created entirely by their consumers. As noted by the authors of *Wikinomics*, an excellent book on the new Web, this sea change in the Web has a generational component: "While their parents were passive consumers of media, youth today are active creators of media content and hungry for interaction" (Tapscott and Williams, 2006, p. 47).

Exhibit 13.1. Web 2.0 Characteristics.

- It's social: it enables personal and professional networking.

- It's participatory: more than information exchange, the value comes from the interactions of the users. And users actively engage as "co-creators" of content.

- It offers a rich user experience: it includes virtual worlds, video like YouTube, interactive maps, and "mashups"—Web applications that combine data from two or more different kinds of sources (such as a Google map combined with crime or real estate data).

- It extends beyond single Web sites, including email, podcasts, mobile devices and others.

- It's a "perpetual beta," meaning it constantly evolves.

- It's organized from the bottom up: though often messy, no top-down model can generate the creativity of YouTube, Facebook, and similar sites.

Source: Byrne, 2008.

Using Web 2.0 to Support Collaboration: Four Approaches

At the beginning of this chapter I noted that my focus isn't on technology per se. Creative leaders are using the new Web tools to help people cut through information silos and bureaucratic barriers to talk directly with colleagues and stakeholders. There are many ways we can use Web 2.0 to foster collaboration. In this chapter I'll detail four of them:

- Crossing boundaries between employees

- Crossing boundaries between agencies

- Crossing boundaries between agencies and their customers or stakeholders

- Crossing boundaries among customers or stakeholders to form communities

Crossing Boundaries Between Employees

TSA's IdeaFactory

The Transportation Security Administration (TSA) launched the IdeaFactory in April 2007. This intranet site invites the agency's 43,000 frontline employees to exchange ideas and information on job-related issues and to offer suggestions on ways to improve agency operations. Based on a similar approach developed by Dell Computers, the IdeaFactory encourages employees to communicate laterally. All employees can view colleagues' suggestions, give constructive criticism, and vote on the ideas they like. Unlike the way some blogs operate, a response on IdeaFactory is attributable to the employee sending it.

The ideas submitted are voted on by TSA security officers. The TSA Innovation Council then decides which ones to implement. One year into site usage, TSA employees had submitted over 4,500 ideas and offered more than 39,000 comments on those ideas. Most important, approximately twenty proposals submitted to the IdeaFactory were implemented agency-wide in the first year (Bain, 2008).

Twenty employee-submitted proposals were implemented agency-wide in the first year of the IdeaFactory.

What kinds of controls does TSA put on the site? The Idea-Factory is hosted on a secure intranet site. Beyond that, the controls are "darn few," according to Kip Hawley, the TSA director who championed the IdeaFactory. "It became self policing . . . the lighter the touch on editing . . . we found, the better the quality of the ideas" (The Collaboration Project, 2008).

Intranet sites like the IdeaFactory offer many benefits. First of all, everyone can (and should) see the ideas posted on the site. Second, these sites are interactive, inviting other employees to comment on the posted ideas. Yes, that raises the possibility of malicious comments, but requiring employees to use their real names when posting comments leads to accountability, and employees who offer offensive comments can be excluded from the site, which is what the IdeaFactory does.

Perhaps the greatest benefits are the creativity and lateral communications unleashed by the IdeaFactory. Prior to its inception, there was no easy way to manage lateral communications in this large agency. The IdeaFactory is changing that.

Crossing Boundaries Between Agencies

Intellipedia

Information sharing across agencies is difficult in many communities: competition for resources and recognition and cultures that reward control-oriented behavior are just two of the factors limiting interagency communications. The U.S. intelligence community (IC), long famous for its poor information sharing, is slowly changing that. And Intellipedia is one of its most creative tools for doing so.

Formally launched in April 2006, Intellipedia's goal is to bypass the long-standing information silos in the IC by making it far easier for analysts to exchange knowledge and ideas. Modeled after Wikipedia, the site operates on a classified network and allows employees in the sixteen IC agencies with appropriate clearances to post ideas and information on areas of interest and to comment on each other's postings. Like the IdeaFactory, Intellipedia shows the contributors' identities. And the emphasis is on peer-to-peer interaction. Nobody needs her boss's OK to post an idea or comment on another's article.

The site quickly gained many analysts' attention. It contains over 900,000 pages and averages more than 15,000 edits per day. And it is helping to break down barriers between agencies. Analysts and managers can gain quick access to knowledge across the entire IC. Analysts get prompt feedback on their articles. And like so much of the new Web, it cuts across stovepipes and rigid hierarchies, generating speed, flexibility, and interaction. The site has been used to provide current, peer-driven analysis on North Korean missile tests, instability in Nigeria, and threats to the security of Iraq, among other issues (Vogel, 2009).

Crossing Boundaries Between Agencies and Their Customers or Stakeholders

Many of the most powerful and exciting Web 2.0 breakthroughs relate to agency-stakeholder relationships. The early Web made it possible for customers and others to access agency information. The new Web invites us to become partners with the agencies that affect us. Here are two examples of this creative partnering.

Crowdsourcing to Select a Symphony Orchestra

Michael Tilson Thomas, artistic director of the San Francisco Symphony, used social networking tools to assemble "the world's first collaborative online orchestra." Responding to Thomas's invitation, 3,000 musicians posted YouTube videos of themselves playing two pieces, and 96 were selected as finalists through online voting. Professional musicians winnowed this list of performers down further, and those invited to perform in the orchestra were selected (*crowdsourced* in Web 2.0 jargon) by YouTube users via online voting. Over 15 million YouTube fans watched the audition videos. The orchestra played a full concert at Carnegie Hall on April 15, 2009, to positive reviews ("YouTube Symphony Orchestra @ Carnegie Hall," April 15, 2009).

Using Twitter to Keep in Touch in Emergencies

Twitter is a Web 2.0 tool that allows users to post short notes (140 characters, max) to each other. The Los Angeles Fire Department quickly saw Twitter's potential power to give it situational awareness during fires and other emergencies. The LAFD tweets its Twitter subscribers when it is fighting a fire or spots a car accident blocking the roads, and it also uses Twitter to get information and feedback from its subscribers. For instance, the LAFD has received tweets from people reporting an overcrowded nightclub, and quickly sent inspectors who closed down the dangerous venue. Residents who spot fires also tweet the fire department, giving the agency hundreds of extra eyes and ears.

Brian Humphrey, who maintains the department's Web 2.0 tools, notes two critical advantages: speed and increased two-way communication. "We have responsibilities to the public to move the information as quickly as possible . . . [and] it is all about getting much more feedback" (Havenstein, 2007).

Crossing Boundaries Among Customers or Stakeholders to Form Communities

Web 2.0 goes beyond connecting employees with each other and with their customers and stakeholders. As Tapscott and Williams (2006) write, the Web now helps "create platforms for people to co-create their own products, services, experiences" (p. 38). In other words, today's Web helps people create *community*. Think about it: craigslist, Facebook and MySpace, eBay, and similar sites are far more than information repositories. Many people use such sites because they invite users to engage directly with other users. And some of these loosely connected communities are experiences in self-organization that no top-down organization could ever achieve. Consider these examples.

The March of Dimes and Share Your Story

The March of Dimes uses social media to empower its supporters and others concerned about birth defects. A page on its Web site invites people to do just that—share a story of their joys, frustrations, and needs for information and support (http://www.shareyourstory .org). Many people send in their stories and requests and others respond. And none of this is managed by March of Dimes staff or volunteers (except for supporting the Web site). The organization is helping people create community by communicating laterally among themselves.

Hurricane Katrina and PeopleFinder

When Hurricane Katrina hit the Gulf Coast in 2005, thousands of people frantically tried to find the whereabouts of loved ones. Government organizations were unable to respond, so a young man named David Geilhufe decided to act. He worked with three non-profits to create the PeopleFinder project, providing an easy way for people to locate and stay in touch with loved ones on the Gulf Coast. All they had to do was enter a name, zip code, or address into a search tool on the Web. Over 600,000 people did so in the weeks to come (Social Source, 2005).

The new Web helps people work with others they don't know, often helping people they've never met . . . and nobody's in charge.

PeopleFinder, Share Your Story, the Facebook pages created after the shootings at Virginia Tech, and myriad other examples reflect a fascinating trend in our society: individuals, acting out of concern for others they may not even know, take action and collaborate with people whom they've never met. And nobody is in charge.

Few government and nonprofits have explored the rich potential of using the Web to help an agency's stakeholders and others interact and form a community outside the agency. The possibilities are intriguing. What if

- Parks and recreation departments had a page on their Web sites that invited users to chat with each other about their experiences in their local parks? It might spur the development of a Parks Partners group that works to maintain the parks.

- Libraries created a blog on their Web sites for a virtual book club where readers could post comments on books they're currently reading? Patrons could agree to read and discuss a given book, use a voting tool to rate books (as Amazon .com does), and library staff could learn which books are of special interest. In fact, some libraries do this now.

- Human service and health agencies had computer terminals in their waiting rooms and invited clients to log on and ask questions and take an online quiz that provides feedback on health factors, offers useful tips on healthy life styles, and also makes it easy to join user groups that share common interests?

There are many other creative ways to use the Web to help stakeholders connect outside the confines of the formal agency. The details here aren't the point. Rather, what's important is how you *think* about the Web. Rather than viewing it as an extension of your organization, imagine it as a multidimensional network that can help your clients and stakeholders meet some of their own needs. Once you make that shift in thinking, the possibilities are endless.

Understanding the New Rules of the New Web

When any user can post content on a site and anyone can respond to and edit that content, it changes the rules in many ways. Leaders who understand this changing landscape are using the new Web to help people connect and collaborate in powerful ways. Those who don't get it are being bypassed. According to Gary Hamel (2009), one of our country's most influential business thinkers, the new Web reflects "post-bureaucratic realities" that leaders must understand if they want to attract and retain the Web-savvy generation now entering the workplace. Exhibit 13.2 captures some of these new realities.

On the new Web we gain power by sharing, not hoarding, information.

Some of these rules probably seem utterly chaotic to those who don't spend time on interactive Web sites. In fact, many Web 2.0 sites are messy, and there are more than a few that I hope my two

Exhibit 13.2. Web 2.0 Realities.

- All ideas compete on an equal footing. Every idea on the Web has the chance to gain a following . . . or not.

- Contribution counts more than credentials. It's not your résumé that counts, but what you can contribute.

- No one has the power to command; on the Web, leaders serve rather than preside.

- Groups are self-defining and self-organizing. People choose the communities they'll join and which people within a community they'll share with, or not.

- Power comes from sharing information, not hoarding it. You gain status and influence by giving away your expertise and content.

- *Intrinsic rewards* matter most. The new Web is demonstrating the power of recognition and of accomplishment.

Source: Adapted from Hamel, 2009 (see the Web site for this article for his complete list).

Millennial Generation kids will never discover. But consider this: If these Web 2.0 rules are the essence of chaos, how was it that Wikipedia and a few Facebook pages had the quickest and most accurate listing of the Virginia Tech victims on the day of the massacre? How can we account for the fact that the PeopleFinder project on the Web, created less than a week after Katrina hit the Gulf Coast, helped hundreds of thousands of desperate people trying to find their loved ones (at a time when agencies at all levels of government weren't able to do so)?

> *Web 2.0 is chaotic, messy, and makes little sense*
> *to those who need top-down control. These tools*
> *don't work in theory, only in practice!*

None of this makes sense given our traditional, top-down thinking. (The joke among Wikipedia contributors is that Wikipedia cannot work in theory, only in practice.) And that's just the point. The new Web challenges us to think in profoundly different ways. And it's important to note that this is a set of tools that can be used for great good but also for profound evil; the terrorists who set off the bombs in Mumbai, India, on November 26, 2008, killing at least 173 people, used the Web to coordinate their attacks. But leaders are foolish to ignore the new Web's power and potential. Our real choice is to decide when and how to use Web 2.0 tools, not whether. Here are some thoughts for moving forward.

Identifying Web 2.0 Collaborative Opportunities

How can government and nonprofit leaders harness the new Web to actively engage staff, customers, and other stakeholders? First, leaders need to know what they're getting into. If you're going to use the new Web effectively, it's important to reflect on the implications of the norms that govern its use. For instance, given that contribution counts for more than credentials on the new Web, it's expertise, information sharing, and selfless behavior that attracts support, not formal power and degrees. That will be a challenge to both managers and technical experts who are used to calling the shots. Related to that, some organizational values will be tested. When one's formal authority means far less than one's ideas and willingness to share information, some people are going to be upset.

And then there's the issue of people's expectation of active involvement on the Web. Because the new Web makes peer review so easy and powerful, its active users expect to have the opportunity to comment on others' ideas and contributions. Managers will have to balance the need for some policing with the benefits of peer review. And managers will lose some control in a Web 2.0 environment. That seems to be inevitable. In exchange, they'll gain enormous amounts of information, enthusiasm, involvement, and commitment, if they use these tools intelligently.

If you're still reading, I'll assume you haven't thrown up your arms in total disbelief and given this book to your least favorite work associate. As I've already noted, the new Web rules and norms are as challenging to most experienced managers as they are natural to twenty- and thirty-somethings. Exhibit 13.3 offers several strategies for making the new Web an effective tool for collaboration.

The first strategy—don't fight the new Web—should look familiar. In Chapter Nine, on dealing with difficult people and behaviors, I emphasized Buckminster Fuller's wise advice: "Don't fight forces, use them." Web 2.0 is only going to become more prominent in our lives. As young adults move into roles of larger responsibilities, their passion for the new Web will be felt throughout our agencies. It's our responsibility, and opportunity, to use the power of the new Web now.

The third strategy, creating a blog, is being done by many leaders today. Some of these blogs invite comments from employees, a good

---

Exhibit 13.3. Strategies for Tapping the Power of Web 2.0 to Promote Collaboration.

- Don't fight the new Web. Look for the opportunities in it. You don't have to fall in love with Web 2.0 to think carefully about its potential.

- Become a user. Check some of the interactive sites (it doesn't matter whether they're work related or not; just find one you like) and try out the tools.

- Consider starting your own blog. If you're nervous about it, try out blogging first with a community you're very comfortable in—a club, religious or civic group, or network of sports fans.

- Don't create what's already out there. Use and adapt the existing tools.

- Ask employees who make considerable use of the Web which sites they find useful, and how they use them.

- Ask your active Web users to help in soliciting responses from employees to this question: How can we use the Web to increase the exchange of information and ideas among employees and with our customers or stakeholders in order to provide better service?

- As you receive responses to this question, post them on an interactive site and invite employees to vote on their favorite responses. Form a team to review the vote and take action as appropriate.

Note: Thanks to Michael Byrne for several of these suggestions.

way to keep a finger on your organization's pulse and foster an open culture. Blogs can be effective tools for leaders for several reasons. They're timely; you can send them when you have something important to discuss (no need to wait for a quarterly or annual report to the staff). They're most effective when kept short and limited to one topic. They encourage the writer to be informal, which fits well with the generation moving into the workplace today. And they can be made interactive, which gives leaders a way to get quick feedback.

Soon after being named secretary of the Department of Homeland Security in 2009, Janet Napolitano began a blog on the DHS Web site, seeking an easy way to interact with employees (see http://www.dhs.gov/journal/leadership). DHS employees can respond to their leaders' blogs; they can (and often do) disagree strongly; their responses can be anonymous. And the DHS blog also allows employees to respond to each other's postings, generating the engagement characteristic of Web 2.0. Coast Guard Commandant Thad Allen is another government leader using blogs for frequent communications and interaction.

> *It's all too easy to adopt new Web tools with no idea of how they'll improve service.*

Concerning the second-to-last strategy, it's important to emphasize the last four words in that sentence: "to provide better service." The easiest mistake to make with Web 2.0 tools is to latch onto what's hot, or cool (interesting that these words sometimes mean the same thing) and to adopt the tool with no concept of how it will help your agency fulfill its mission. The litmus test is always about service, about impact, about mission.

THE BOTTOM LINE

When viewed through the lens of the four big collaboration questions, the ones that determine whether employees will move from a *me* to a *we* identity, the new Web's power to foster collaboration becomes apparent.

1. *Can I use Web 2.0 to contribute something that will be needed, recognized, and used by the team?* Web users become extremely creative at using the interactive Web 2.0 tools, sharing knowledge with people they've never met, forming Facebook groups to support a favorite political candidate or cause, and writing posts on issues that others care about. And colleagues can quickly and easily recognize and respond to each other's posts.

2. *Are we working on something that's important to me and my organization?* Well, if you want to suggest an approach for better serving customers, an innovative way to share information on common interests, or work with others on issues you feel passionately about (like saving the Great Lakes), the answer is obvious.

3. *Are we making progress?* Web 2.0 has numerous tools that make it easy for members of a team or community to chart their course and mark progress against their plan. For instance, SurveyMonkey.com is a site that helps users design online, professional surveys, collect and analyze responses, and share the results. Many nonprofits, strapped for funds, use this site to create their own surveys in order to get feedback on their programs and services.

4. *Finally, does the collaborative work support or threaten me and my home organization?* The new Web may be used to support partners' interests (recognizing positive contributions and helping people share information) but may also be seen as a threat because it makes so much work transparent. Enlightened leaders who believe that the facts are our friends will see many more benefits than threats in using Web 2.0.

> *Technology won't make*
> *hoarders into collaborators.*

And here's the kicker: The new Web doesn't *do* anything, really. It helps us take collaborative action on shared interests, *if we want to*. Web 2.0 won't change people who are control artists, it won't transform information hoarders into open communicators, nor will it open up a closed culture where the prevailing attitude is that information equals power. Technology can't do any of those things. But people can use Web 2.0 to work toward such changes. And the people most likely to try are those with a passion for collaboration, especially the Millennial Generation now entering the workplace. And they are at the heart of our last chapter.

14

Developing the Leadership to Create Tomorrow's Collaborative Cultures

At Cisco, we want a culture where it is unacceptable not to share what you know.

—Mike Mitchell, *director of technology communications,*
Cisco Systems

Here's a pop quiz: What organization do the following characteristics bring to mind?

- Control of resources equals power.

- Strong organizational units compete for resources and power.

- A top-down leadership style means a few senior executives make all important decisions.

- A cowboy culture rewards strong personalities who try to outdo each other for the leader's attention.

- The focus is on individual units and functions, not on the needs of the entire enterprise.

Does this sound like an organization you've worked in?

Cisco Systems: From Hierarchy and Cowboys to Flat and Collaborative

These were the characteristics that Cisco Systems managers and employees saw in Cisco circa 2001. Called "the plumber of the technology world" by some, Cisco earns three-quarters of its revenues from selling the routers, switches, and other network technologies that help power the Internet. Until 2001, Cisco was run in a traditional, top-down fashion; all important decisions were made by CEO John Chambers, in consultation with about ten other senior execs.

Seven years later, the company was a model of collaboration and innovation, a decentralized organization where people freely shared ideas and information, and important decisions were made quickly by teams that didn't report to the CEO. In 2008 and again in '09, it was flush with cash, rated the sixth best U.S. company to work for by *Fortune* magazine.

Cisco is a large corporation, but its story is applicable to the public and nonprofit worlds. How did it make such a sea change to become a poster child for the networked age?

Cisco Emerges from the Dotcom Bust, Determined to Change

After Cisco went through what John Chambers calls a "life threatening experience in 2001," when the tech bubble burst, its leaders saw the need for fundamental changes in the DNA of the huge company. The concept for change grew from the leaders' realization that Cisco, with its slow, top-down hierarchical model, couldn't compete success-fully in a globally networked world. The company needed a culture marked by the active collaboration of thousands of employees. That led to a number of changes.

Today, Chambers and the other Cisco executives make clear their expectation that employees will collaborate and share ideas freely; they make collaboration an important element in annual appraisals.

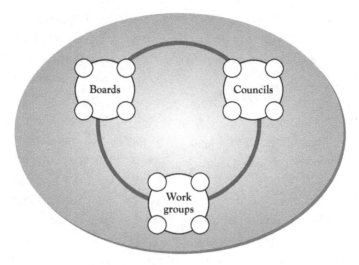

Figure 14.1. Cisco's Networked Structure.

Cisco also rewards executives on their demonstrated collaboration abilities and on the success of Cisco's portfolio of businesses, not on their own business unit's profits. And Cisco's leaders have created a network of 500 boards, councils, and work groups, spread across the corporation, which work on new products and processes (see Figure 14.1). In most cases they are free to make decisions and allocate resources without Chambers's OK.

At Cisco, ideas are generated formally and informally. The formal aspect involves the councils, boards, and work groups, which are cross-functional and interdepartmental, organizing around major initiatives and product lines. Each is authorized to make decisions up to a certain dollar amount. But there is also a thriving informal culture of innovation. Through the use of Web 2.0 tools, thousands of Cisco employees are regularly communicating with people outside their units to discuss ideas and generate interest in new ventures. As one Cisco exec puts it, "We are always looking for the applications that help people really have water-cooler talk, something that we thought was impossible in a global business" (McGirt, 2008, p. 3).

Cisco's new culture is also growing new leaders. Reflecting on his retirement, Chambers notes that he once had two potential successors; now he has five hundred—the people who lead the boards and councils. Chambers works hard (and successfully) to model what he wants from others. He writes his own blog, which is one of the most read at Cisco (but not *the* most read; that blog is written by one of the employees on the topic of collaboration). Mike Mitchell, another Cisco exec, says, "We want a culture where it is unacceptable not to share what you know" (McGirt, 2008, p. 3).

At Cisco, widespread use of Web 2.0 tools plus the decentralized structure empowering people to act at their level creates a rich exchange of ideas.

Many employees share ideas on their own blogs and vote on the most helpful blog posts. They also upload and watch each other's videos on a YouTube site within Cisco's firewalls, and describe their skills and knowledge areas on a Facebook-like company directory. This isn't technology for its own sake; all of these changes are meant to invite easy, informal idea sharing.

None of these changes were easy. Twenty percent of Cisco's execs left after the changes began, unable or unwilling to change their management style. Chambers notes that communicating the need for the changes was the biggest difficulty he faced. Cisco vice president Ron Ricci says, "The No. 1 item on the list of most CEOs . . . [is] to break down the barriers, between me and my customers, and me and my partners" (McGirt, 2008, p. 6). As those barriers started to fall, Cisco's fortunes rose.

The Fourth Lever: The People Best Positioned to Make Change

Thus far we've looked at three levers that leaders can use to create sustainable collaborative cultures: (1) a *structure*—co-location—that promotes collaboration and information sharing; (2) a *method*—the Stat approach—and the way Washington State has used this method in its GMAP process; and (3) a *system*—the new Web—and its set of tools that help employees engage internally, across agencies, with their stakeholders, and among stakeholders.

The Cisco story involves two of these levers: a structure—the company's boards, councils, and work groups—and a system—the use of Web 2.0 tools. But Cisco is also using another key collaboration lever, and it's the most important one: the *people* who can create sustainable collaboration. This is the focus of this last chapter. More specifically, we'll look at two sets of people: (1) tomorrow's leaders, the generation born between 1980 and 2000, and (2) today's leaders, those who can build collaborative structures and methods and can prepare tomorrow's leaders to lead.

The Millennial Generation: Tomorrow's Leaders Ready for Change

By all accounts, the twenty- and early thirty-something employees at Cisco are delighted with the firm's move toward a more collaborative environment. And that shouldn't surprise us. Everything we're learning about this generation predicts their embrace of such changes. In fact, it seems as though this generation was truly designed to move our organizations into the collaborative future we so clearly need.

Whenever you get discouraged by the many hurdles to collaboration, reflect on the characteristics of the generation born between 1980 and 2000. Sometimes called Generation Y, Gen Next, or more recently the Millennial Generation, this group of young people is wired differently from others now in the workplace. Their attitudes and talents seem perfectly suited to deal with society's biggest challenges. How can I make such an outlandish claim?

A variety of studies and books have come to the same conclusions about this new generation. The Millennials are consistently described as being

- Technologically savvy
- Eager to share information and ideas

- Hungry for change

- Respectful, comfortable working for change within the system

- Very comfortable working in teams, natural collaborators

- Optimistic

- Service oriented

- Eager for leadership roles

- Focused on making a big difference in the world

Sounds like a pretty wonderful set of characteristics, no? And in a world that's increasingly interconnected, this cohort seems to be the right group at the right time.

"Millennials are accustomed to collaborating; remember, these are the kids who even went to school dances in groups rather than one-on-one dates" ("Multitasking Millennials . . . ," 2008, p. 1).

Information sharing and networking is Millennials' default mode.

I must admit, my wife and I were delighted to see our kids do so much in groups rather than resorting to continual dating when they were adolescents. The Millennials were the first youngsters who grew up consistently doing group projects in school and being graded as a group (if you haven't visited an elementary school lately, you're in for a surprise; it's no longer a place where kids learn by age six to "do your own work"). Indeed, sharing information and working with others isn't an issue with this group; what puzzles most Millennials is why anyone would want to hoard information.

Yes, it can be difficult working with some Millennials. Many of them grew up with continual adult supervision (all helicopter parents, raise your hands!). Thus, as Zemke, Raines, and Filipczak (2000) point out, they have stronger needs for on-the-job supervision and structure than older workers. This is also the group that thought every soccer team was a winner because all of the teams got trophies at season's end. So their need for recognition is very high. And many Millennials have expectations for quick change, which will inevitably leave them disappointed in some organizations.

But think again about their other characteristics. They expect to make major change, care strongly about making the world a better place, and want to do so within existing systems. Many of them have a passion for service and believe there's far more to life than hefty salaries and individual perks (which turn them off).

And they're totally at home connecting laterally, through the Web: "While the government is still buying Rolodexes, the younger generations have 600 friends on Facebook and 250 professional colleagues on LinkedIn," according to Steve Ressler, a cofounder of the Young Government Leaders network. "We are used to working horizontal, are not afraid of authority, and want our ideas heard" (quoted in DiGiammarino and Trudeau, 2008, p. 6).

One more thing about the Millennials: they aren't unsettled by turbulence and sudden change. They experienced the trauma of the 9/11 attacks and the fears raised by the deep recession of 2008 and 2009 in their youth, and they seem more capable of bouncing back from major shocks than most. Zemke and others (2000) call them resilient, and that sounds right. In a world deeply shaped by the global economy, threatened by terrorism, pandemics, and global warming, the Millennial Generation seems amazingly well suited to take on the challenges. Table 14.1 outlines the major differences between Millennials and the other three generations currently in the workplace.

Won't These Characteristics Change as the Millennials Age?

That's a reasonable question. At first glance, the Millennials may seem like young adults of past generations—idealistic, eager to change the status quo, not focused on power . . . yet. But there's empirical evidence to suggest that today's Millennials will maintain their values and commitments over time. That evidence comes

Table 14.1. Millennials and the Three Previous Generations.

	Traditionalists	Boomers	Xers	Millennials
Outlook	Practical	Optimistic	Skeptical	Hopeful
Work ethic	Dedicated	Driven	Balanced	Determined
View of authority	Respectful	Love/hate	Unimpressed	Polite
Leadership by	Hierarchy	Consensus	Competence	Pulling together
Relationships	Personal sacrifice	Personal gratification	Reluctant to commit	Inclusive

Source: Adapted from and reprinted by permission of the publisher, from *Generations at Work*, by Zemke, Raines, and Filipczak. © 2000 Performance Research Associates, Inc., Claire Raines, Bob Filipczak, AMACOM books. New York, NY. All rights reserved. www.amacombooks.org

from two authors who have studied the history of generations in the United States from the sixteenth century to the present. From their research, William Strauss and Neil Howe (1991) have identified a succession of four generational types that have repeated themselves sequentially from Colonial times to today.

Four American Generational Types

Adaptives. Adaptives tend to be risk averse, like to conform to existing norms, and try to live up to the high standards of the powerful generation that preceded them. According to Strauss and Howe, the most recent Adaptive cohort consists of those born between 1925 and 1942. Adaptive leaders include William Howard Taft and Woodrow Wilson.

Idealists. Idealists often inspire a "spiritual awakening." Their strengths include visionary leadership; shortcomings can include a tendency toward narcissism. Recent Idealist cohorts consist of those born between 1860 and 1882 (as adults they helped lead the Progressive

Era changes), and the Baby Boom generation, born between 1943 and 1960. Abraham Lincoln and Franklin Roosevelt were members of Idealist generations.

Reactives. Reactives tend to be alienated, creative, and highly individualistic people who are skeptical of existing institutions and of the Idealists who preceded them. The most recent Reactive cohorts consist of those born between 1883 and 1900 (sometimes called the Lost Generation) and between 1961 and 1981 (Generation X). They don't usually lead major changes but often help manage the impact of such changes. Harry Truman and Dwight Eisenhower belonged to a Reactive generation.

Civics. Civics make up an "institution building" generation. Like the Idealists, they tend to set the social agenda for the country. They respect existing institutions, are very hard working, prefer to make change within the system, and set very high goals. The most recent Civic cohorts are made up of people born between 1901and 1924, which includes the group dubbed the "Greatest Generation" by Tom Brokaw, and the Millennials.

The Millennials, like other Civic Generations, are institution builders who want to make a big difference in the world.

Please go back and read the first sentence of the Civic generation description. In fact, reread the whole paragraph. The Millennials I've been discussing are a Civic generation. They are institution builders who want to make a big difference for the country. As Strauss and Howe point out, these generational types have repeated themselves, in the same sequence, since the 1580s (we've skipped a generation only once, during the Civil War). If these generalizations seem overly broad, consider these facts:

- The older Millennials are already proving to be highly civic, responsible for the first large increases in voting, volunteering, and other forms of civic participation in decades (see Putnam, 2008, for more on this).

- Most of the framers of the U.S. Constitution were members of a Civic generation and so were the members of the Greatest Generation.

As an old history major, I'm impressed by Strauss and Howe's research. And what they say about past Civic generations and the rising Millennial Generation should give all of us enormous hope for our country and our institutions. This group also inspires professor Robert Putnam, who has been chronicling the decline of civic life in the United States for years (see, for example, Putnam, 1995, 2000). He believes the Millennials may be a "new Greatest Generation" (Putnam, 2008, p. 2).

So What? Why This Emphasis on One Generation?

Why my emphasis on the Millennials? For this reason: if leaders give this generation of young workers access to current Web tools, give them easy ways to collaborate on important projects, and offer them appropriate leadership roles, they will produce extraordinary results. That's what Chambers demonstrated at Cisco. And that is what nonprofit and public-sector leaders around the country are learning. These Millennials can be a powerful lever for collaborative change.

The Other People Positioned to Create Cultures of Collaboration: Today's Leaders

Cisco Systems has clearly reconfigured itself to be a twenty-first-century organization, one that many others are using as a model. In leading the change at Cisco, John Chambers not only changed the company's structure, reward system, roles, and use of technology, he also adopted a different kind of *thinking*. Chambers says, "The future is about collaboration and teamwork. . . . Realize that the hardest one to change is the CEO, and yet this must start at the top . . . and that's hard. It took letting go. Watching the [new collaborative] groups over time . . . arrive at a better decision than I would had done, it really was exciting. It took training, and changing reward systems, and rewarding people who are collaborative and who focus on what was the overall benefit, as opposed to what's good for their individual function" (Burrows, 2009).

Chambers saw the wreckage of the dotcom bubble at the turn of the twenty-first century, and he asked his own version of the question Thad Allen asked when he was given responsibility for the Katrina rescue: *How can we form partnerships to deal with this crisis?* In their responses to the enormous challenges facing them, Allen and Chambers demonstrated a collaborative mindset.

When your default mode is to act through networks rather than through hierarchies and chains of command, you're thinking in a different way. And this may be the most powerful lever of all—changing the way we and others think. How can leaders adopt a collaborative mindset? How can they help those around them make the same change?

Developing a Collaborative Mindset in Yourself and Others

Exhibit 14.1 summarizes some approaches for developing a collaborative mindset suitable for a networked world.

Hire People Who Are Natural Collaborators

Perhaps this goes without saying: if we hire people who naturally think and act collaboratively, we don't have to go through months and years of training and coaching people to change their hierarchical or silo mindset. Well, if this should go without saying,

---

Exhibit 14.1. Strategies for Developing a Collaborative Mindset.

- Hire people who are natural collaborators.

- Help people reduce associative barriers.

- Identify important outcomes that can be met only through collaborative effort; hold all units accountable.

- Provide multiple opportunities to practice.

- Start with yourself.

---

how much time and effort does your agency invest in recruiting and interviewing applicants? Most agencies spend far too little time at this critical task.

One of the leader's most powerful tools is also one of the least appreciated: the screening and hiring process. Some agencies spend literally hundreds of staff hours learning about and interviewing applicants. Some use assessment centers, in which trained observers assess candidates' skills as they go through a series of in-basket tasks, group problem-solving exercises, and other activities. Of course, this takes a lot of time. But compare that investment of time with the time spent trying to change the behavior of employees who hoard information and build little empires. It's not even close.

Help People Reduce Associative Barriers

In his fascinating book *The Medici Effect*, Frans Johansson offers numerous methods for generating innovative ideas. To become more innovative, he notes, we must get past our "associative barriers"—the "chains of association" that take us down well-worn mental pathways and inhibit the creative process (Johansson, 2006, p. 40). For example, when you read the words "severe economic downturn," what comes to mind? Most people would reply "job loss," "recession," perhaps "fear." A highly innovative soul, with few associative barriers, might say things like "opportunity" or "change." Reducing associative barriers helps people learn to think in new and innovative ways.

Here are five ways to reduce associative barriers (some of these come from Johansson, 2006):

- *Expose yourself to different cultures* (national as well as organizational). Take a rotational assignment of several months (or more) in a different agency; this immerses you in a culture with different norms and assumptions. The Department of Defense and the U.S. intelligence agencies are among those now making rotations and joint duty assignments a requirement for promotion beyond a certain level.

- *Learn a new field.* As many aging Baby Boomers discover when they ask their doctors how to avoid dementia, it's good for the brain to study different disciplines. Creative right-brain types could learn accounting or economics. Left-brainers would benefit from picking up a musical instrument, trying yoga, or reading poetry. Both types might grow from tackling crossword puzzles (which rely both on pattern recognition and detail retrieval).

- *Work on a project with people from diverse disciplines.* Ask a young scientist where the most exciting discoveries are occurring today, and she'll probably tell you they are all at an intersection of two or more fields: biology, economics, and stock market analysis (discoveries on the behavior of the financial markets); geology, physics, meteorology, and other fields (discoveries on global warming). Working with teams of people from different disciplines stimulates creative thinking and helps reduce associative barriers.

- *Surface and challenge your assumptions or prevailing opinions.* Many assumptions are useful and save us time and worry. (I don't check the credentials of the engineer whose name appears on the certificates in elevators; do you?) But some get in the way. The biggest problem with assumptions is how invisible they can be. It's hard to "see" our own assumptions and equally difficult to discern those of a group, especially if you're a long-standing member. But study any disaster, and you'll find some unchallenged assumptions among the causes: the two NASA shuttle tragedies, the "failure of imagination" in the intelligence community prior to 9/11, the Bay of Pigs fiasco in the Kennedy administration. What widely held assumptions in your agency need to be surfaced and challenged?

---

*The problem with assumptions
is that they're invisible to us.*

ON THE

- *Get on the balcony.* In *Leadership on the Line,* authors Heifetz and Linsky (2002) offer a lovely metaphor to leaders: to gain a broader perspective, you need to get off the "dance floor" occasionally and move up to the "balcony." The dance floor is where operations take place, and that's where leaders can make their greatest impact. But you can't fully comprehend what's happening on the floor unless you occasionally remove yourself and get above it (picture the football coach sitting high up in the stadium press box). There are many ways to get on the balcony—listen to key stakeholders, conduct a retreat, experience your organization as a customer (which is what airline executives do when they fly, unannounced, in the coach section), bring in futurists to speculate about emerging trends. Getting away from daily operations helps you gain new perspectives, and can identify associative barriers that need to be removed.

One of the most fascinating examples of tossing off associative barriers occurred at Bletchley Park in England during WWII. An extraordinary group of code breakers cracked the vaunted German

Enigma code and helped turn the Battle of the Atlantic in 1941 and '42. Those working on Enigma included mathematicians, classics scholars, chess grand masters, finance experts, scientists, linguists, even bridge experts. These people used every one of the methods just listed to accomplish their remarkable breakthroughs. (For a wonderful account of this amazing group, read *The Code Book*, by Singh, 1999.)

Identify Important Outcomes That Can Be Met Only Through Collaborative Effort; Hold All Units Accountable

Holding people from different units accountable for an important outcome is one of the key features of the Stat methods described in Chapter Twelve. As Washington State and other users of Stat methods are demonstrating, it is one of the most powerful ways to generate collaboration and a collaborative mindset.

Provide Multiple Opportunities to Practice

There are good reasons why firefighters, SWAT teams, emergency managers, and crews of nuclear aircraft carriers place such a high premium on continual training. These units, sometimes called high-reliability organizations, share one key characteristic: failure in their business is not an option.

Leaders of high-reliability organizations understand that during emergencies our minds aren't necessarily at peak performance, so they ensure that employees have practiced certain thought processes and action steps over and over and over, under circumstances that simulate real-world circumstances. And such training helps build relationships, the key lesson from those who collaborated so beautifully at the Pentagon on 9/11.

Start with Yourself

That's one conclusion that John Chambers of Cisco System preaches. Change has to start at the top. It's also the conclusion of a variety of scholars who study organizational change. Yet most leaders I've worked with don't seem to truly grasp the power of their behavior during times of change.

The most effective way for a leader to prepare an organization for change and help employees develop a more collaborative mindset is to demonstrate that she's thinking and acting in a different way. It's not just about being a good role model. It's about demonstrating that you're absolutely serious about making change.

The bad news about starting with yourself? The more success you've had, the harder it can be to change. As Bill Gates has said, "Success is a lousy teacher. It seduces smart people into thinking they can't lose." You may need a trusted colleague or friend to coach and help you. People at work may push back at first, not letting themselves believe what they're seeing (I speak from firsthand experience!).

> *Success is often a poor teacher, leading bright people to think they can't fail.*

The good news is twofold: (1) you have total control over your own thought and behavior styles, and (2) this is one of the highest impact changes you can make. And the changes don't have to be enormous. If you normally brief your own leader(s) by yourself, start bringing a subordinate to share the briefing. If you're used to giving direction (all push), look for low-risk times to start using pull. If you're an idea person, the next time you're developing an idea, pull your team together and tell them, "Here's the skeleton of an idea; I'd like you to flesh it out and let's see if it has any merit."

THE BOTTOM LINE

President Kennedy once told a story about a French general who asked his gardener to plant a certain kind of tree. "But this tree grows very slowly," the gardener responded. "It won't mature for one hundred years." "Then there's no time to lose," the general replied. "Plant it today!"

Developing a collaborative mindset for an increasingly networked world requires practice, focus, and feedback. And like the general's tree, it takes a good deal of time.

But developing a collaborative mindset is supremely rewarding, in both our work and nonwork lives. It develops future leaders; it generates enormous innovation; it creates cultures that reward sharing of ideas and information. A collaborative mindset helps you look at the same challenges you've had before and see them differently. Cisco's CEO had an enormous emotional and intellectual investment in the way Cisco had developed during his many years at the helm. Yet he was able to stand back, look at the company and its competitive environment through a collaborative lens, and develop a truly different culture.

The Millennial Generation members moving into our agencies are hungry for leaders who use a collaborative mindset, both because that perspective and leadership style fits their values and because it helps people make a difference.

And isn't that, ultimately, the point of our work, to make a difference? To contribute to something larger than ourselves? To join with others who bring different skills and knowledge to a task that can enrich the lives of others, and in doing so to gain the deep satisfaction of devoting ourselves to shared purpose and shared effort?

I am convinced that a collaborative mindset is the leadership characteristic most critical for dealing with the networked world of the twenty-first century. And like the general's tree in President Kennedy's story, it has to be started today.

• • • • •

A Final Note to the Reader

In the Introduction I invited you to "make this book your own" by writing in it, filling out some exercises, using the worksheet in Resource A to plan your collaboration projects, and completing the self-assessment that follows the Introduction. I hope you'll revisit that self-assessment now. Reflect on the questions and your original answers. What's changed for you? What's been reinforced? Most important, how can you use the ideas in this book, and your own ideas, to pursue the critical work of collaboration?

Resource A

Create Your Own Game Plan

I. Briefly describe a situation or project that you're involved in that requires collaboration:

1. What is the goal?

2. Why does it matter?

3. Who are the stakeholders?

4. Use the stakeholder identification tool that follows to decide which stakeholders should be part of the collaborative team.

Tool for Identifying Stakeholders.

Influence or Expertise on Issue

Source: Adapted from Chrislip, 2002, p. 75.

II. Complete the following Skill and Experience Matrix for Collaborative Groups.

1. List the members of your collaborative group in the left-hand "Member" column of the matrix.

2. Decide what kinds of skills and expertise will be helpful for the team, then list them along the top row (columns 2 through 5). For instance, some teams find the following important:

> Subject matter expertise on the issue being addressed
>
> Technical skills
>
> Project management skills
>
> Facilitation skills
>
> Political skills
>
> Marketing skills
>
> Information technology skills

3. Ask each member of the team to list his or her major skills and areas of expertise in the matrix.

4. Discuss the results. How can you and the other team members tap each other's strengths in this project? Are there certain skills or knowledge areas that are missing?

Skill and Experience Matrix for Collaborative Groups.

MEMBER	SKILL AND EXPERIENCE AREAS				

III. Assess six key collaboration factors, using the following scale.

	Low				High
The parties have a shared interest, which they can't achieve on their own.	1	2	3	4	5
The parties want to work together now and are willing to contribute something to the effort.	1	2	3	4	5
The appropriate people are at the table.	1	2	3	4	5
An open, credible process exists.	1	2	3	4	5
There is a champion(s) for the initiative.	1	2	3	4	5
Trusting relationships are forming.	1	2	3	4	5

1. Which factors have a score of 3 or lower?

2. What can the team do to improve in these areas?

IV. Complete a force field analysis of your situation or project. (Note: you can use the length of the lines to indicate the strength of each force.)

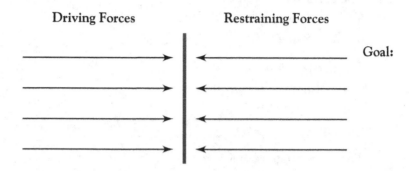

Driving Forces   Restraining Forces

                                                          Goal:

V. Identify the collaboration strategies that you might use. List the key restraining forces from the force field tool in the left-hand column below. List the strategies that might alleviate these forces in the right-hand column.

Restraining Force   *Strategy to Try*

VI. Complete the following collaborative leadership assessment, bearing in mind that effective collaborative leaders have these characteristics in common:

- They feel great resolve to achieve the goal; egos are in check.

- They listen carefully to understand others' perspectives.

- They look for win-win options.

- They use pull more than push.

- They think systemically; they connect the project to a larger purpose.

1. Thinking about yourself: Which of these qualities are your strengths?

2. Which of these qualities would you like to improve?

3. Which of these qualities would be most useful in your current project?

Resource B

Country Rankings on Five Cultural Factors Related to Collaboration

	Power Distance	Individualism	Uncertainty Avoidance	Masculinity	Long-Term Orientation
Arab countries	80	38	68	53	
Argentina	49	46	86	56	
Australia	36	90	51	61	31
Austria	11	55	70	79	
Belgium	65	75	94	54	
Brazil	69	38	76	49	65
Canada	39	80	48	52	23
Chile	63	23	86	28	
China, mainland					118
Colombia	67	13	80	64	
Costa Rica	35	15	86	21	
Denmark	18	74	23	16	
East Africa	64	27	52	41	
Ecuador	78	8	67	63	
Finland	33	63	59	26	

(Continued)

	Power Distance	Individualism	Uncertainty Avoidance	Masculinity	Long-Term Orientation
France	68	71	86	43	
Germany FR	35	67	65	66	31
Great Britain	35	89	35	66	25
Greece	60	35	112	57	
Guatemala	95	6	101	37	
Hong Kong	68	25	29	57	96
India	77	48	40	56	61
Indonesia	78	14	48	46	
Iran	58	41	59	43	
Ireland	28	70	35	68	
Israel	13	54	81	47	
Italy	50	76	75	70	
Jamaica	45	39	13	68	
Japan	54	46	92	95	80
Malaysia	104	26	36	50	
Mexico	81	30	82	69	
Netherlands	38	80	53	14	44
New Zealand	22	79	49	58	30
Norway	31	69	50	8	
Pakistan	55	14	70	50	
Panama	95	11	86	44	
Peru	64	16	87	42	
Philippines	94	32	44	64	19
Poland					32
Portugal	63	27	104	31	
Salvador	66	19	94	40	
Singapore	74	20	8	48	48
South Africa	49	65	49	63	
South Korea	60	18	85	39	75

	Power Distance	Individualism	Uncertainty Avoidance	Masculinity	Long-Term Orientation
Spain	57	51	86	42	
Sweden	31	71	29	5	33
Switzerland	34	68	58	70	
Taiwan	58	17	69	45	87
Thailand	64	20	64	34	56
Turkey	66	37	85	45	
Uruguay	61	36	100	38	
USA	40	91	46	62	29
Venezuela	81	12	76	73	
West Africa	77	20	54	46	16
Yugoslavia	76	27	88	21	

Source: http://spectrum.troy.edu/~vorism/hofscore.htm.

The *Power Distance Index* (PDI) indicates the extent to which power is distributed equally or unequally in a society. A high number represents greater power inequality. In more equal (low power) societies, there is less emphasis on status and formal power, relationships in organizations are more informal, children are expected to show initiative and speak up. In more unequal (high power) societies, power and status come from one's family or from tradition. Communications are hierarchical, change comes more slowly, children are expected to be obedient.

Individualism (IDV) and its opposite, collectivism, refer to the degree to which individuals are integrated into groups (a high number represents a very individualistic society). In individualistic cultures the ties between individuals are loose: everyone is expected to look after himself or herself and his or her immediate family. In more collectivist societies, people are integrated into strong, cohesive in-groups, often extended families, from birth onward, and these groups continue protecting them in exchange for unquestioning loyalty. (The word "collectivism" in this sense has no political meaning; it refers to the group, not to the state.)

The *Uncertainty Avoidance Index* (UAI) deals with a society's tolerance for uncertainty and ambiguity. It indicates to what extent a society's members feel either uncomfortable or comfortable in unstructured situations. The higher the score, the greater the desire to avoid uncertainty. Uncertainty-avoiding cultures try to minimize the possibility of unstructured situations through strict laws and rules and through safety and security measures. Those in uncertainty-accepting cultures are more tolerant of different opinions; they also try to have as few rules as possible (they have less need for formal structure).

Masculinity (MAS) versus its opposite, femininity, refers to the distribution of roles between the genders. A high score reflects a more masculine society. Masculine societies tend to be more competitive; assertiveness and toughness are valued, people are expected to speak up. In societies with higher femininity scores, there's a greater emphasis on modesty, and both men and women are expected to demonstrate a caring attitude toward others. In masculine societies, there is more of a division of gender roles; in feminine societies, men are expected to share the domestic tasks with women.

Long-term orientation (LTO) versus short-term orientation is the final index. A higher score is associated with a long-term orientation. Societies that value the long term emphasize financial savings; their firms emphasize market position (not quarterly returns). In societies with a short-term perspective people don't save as much, and their firms focus on the bottom line and near-term performance.

Bibliography

"A– Washington." *Governing.* http://governing.com/gpp/2008/wa.htm, 2008.

Abramson, M., Breul, J., and Kamensky, J. *Six Trends Transforming Government.* Washington, D.C.: IBM Center for The Business of Government, 2006.

American Association for the Advancement of Science. "Underrepresented Minorities Benefit from Program to Boost Participation in Science-Related Studies." News release. http://www.aaas.org/news/releases/2009/0401minority_phd.shtml, Apr. 1, 2009.

Arlington County, Virginia. *Arlington County After-Action Report on the Response to the September 11 Terrorist Attack on the Pentagon.* Prepared by Titan Systems Corp. Arlington County, Va.: Arlington County, 2002.

Armajani, B. "Dealing with Resistance." Management Insights. *Governing.* http://governing.com/mgmt_insight.aspx?id=6116, Dec. 3, 2008.

Austin, J. *The Collaboration Challenge: How Nonprofits and Businesses Succeed Through Strategic Alliances.* San Francisco: Jossey-Bass, 2000.

Bain, B. "4 Studies in Collaboration: TSA's IdeaFactory." *FederalComputerWeek.* http://fcw.com/articles/2008/02/29/4-studies-in-collaboration-151-case-2-tsa146s-ideafactory.aspx, Feb. 29, 2008.

Begley, S. "Anxious for Cures, Grant Givers Turn More Demanding." *Wall Street Journal.* http://www.myelinrepair.org/pdfs/WSJ_Article9.29.04.pdf, Sept. 29, 2004.

Behn, B. "What All Mayors Would Like to Know About Baltimore's CitiStat Performance Strategy." Washington, D.C.: IBM Center for The Business of Government, 2007.

Behn, B. "Collaborating for Performance: Or Can There Exist Such a Thing as CollaborationStat?" Paper presented at the 30th annual Research Conference of the Association for Public Policy Analysis and Management, Los Angeles, Nov. 2008.

Bellah, R., and others. *Habits of the Heart: Individualism and Commitment in American Life.* Berkeley: University of California Press, 1985.

Ben-Har, L., and Shiplett, M. "Smart Intelligence." *GovermentExecutive. com.* http://www.govexec.com/dailyfed/0109/012809mm.htm, Jan. 28, 2009.

Benson, L. "What Makes Washington State's GMAP Program Tick?" Paper delivered at the Research Conference of the Association for Public Policy Analysis and Management, Madison, Wis., Nov. 2–4, 2006.

Bolman, L., and Deal, T. *Reframing Organizations: Artistry, Choice and Leadership.* (2nd ed.) San Francisco: Jossey-Bass, 1997.

Brafman, O., and Beckstrom, R. *The Starfish and the Spider: The Unstoppable Power of Leaderless Organizations.* New York: Penguin Group, 2006.

Bramson, R. *Coping with Difficult People.* New York: Ballantine Books, 1981.

Burrows, P. "At Cisco, 'Downturn' Screams Long-Term Opportunity." *BusinessWeek.* Online Extra (video). http://www.businessweek.com/magazine/content/09_12/b4124030877661.htm, Mar. 12, 2009.

Byrne, M. "Homeland Security: A System of Systems." Presentation to the University of Connecticut Collaborative Leadership in Homeland Security program, Storrs, Conn., 2008.

Chrislip, D. "The New Civic Leadership." In B. Kellerman and L. R. Matusak (eds.), *Cutting Edge: Leadership 2000* (pp. 18–24). College Park, Md.: James McGregor Burns Academy of Leadership, 2000.

Chrislip, D. *The Collaborative Leadership Fieldbook.* San Francisco: Jossey-Bass, 2002.

Chrislip, D., and Larson, C. *Collaborative Leadership: How Citizens and Civic Leaders Can Make a Difference.* San Francisco: Jossey-Bass, 1994.

Cialdini, R. *Influence: The New Psychology of Modern Persuasion.* New York: Quill, 1984.

Cohen, N. "The Latest on Virginia Tech, from Wikipedia." *New York Times.* http://www.nytimes.com/2007/04/23/technology/23link.html, Apr. 23, 2007.

The Collaboration Project. "TSA's Kip Hawley Featured at Collaboration Project Inaugural Meeting." Audio highlights. http://www.collaborationproject .org/display/news/TSA%27s+Kip+Hawley+Featured+at+Collaboration+Project+ Inaugural+Meeting, 2008.

Collins, J. *Good to Great: Why Some Companies Make the Leap . . . and Others Don't.* New York: HarperCollins, 2001.

Collins, J. *Good to Great and the Social Sectors.* Boulder, Colo.: Jim Collins, 2005.

"A Conversation with Thad W. Allen." *Arizona Daily Star.* http://www.azstarnet .com/sn/mailstory-clickthru/157488.php, Nov. 26, 2006.

Covey, S. *The Seven Habits of Highly Effective People: Powerful Lessons in Personal Change.* New York: Simon & Schuster, 1989.

Covey, S.M.R. *The Speed of Trust.* New York: Free Press, 2006.

Deal, T., and Kennedy, A. *Corporate Cultures.* Reading, Mass.: Addison-Wesley, 1982.

Denning, S. *The Secret Language of Leadership.* San Francisco: Jossey-Bass, 2007.

DiGiammarino, F., and Trudeau, L. "Virtual Networks: An Opportunity for Government." *The Public Manager,* Spring 2008, pp. 5–11.

Dukes, E. F. "From Enemies, to Higher Ground, to Allies: The Unlikely Partnership Between the Tobacco Farm and Public Health Communities in the United

States." In W. Lovan, M. Murray, and R. Shaffer (eds.), *Participatory Governance* (pp. 165–187). Burlington, Vt.: Ashgate, 2004.

Dukes, E. F., and Firehock, K. *Collaboration: A Guide for Environmental Advocates.* Charlottesville: University of Virginia, The Wilderness Society, and National Audubon Society, 2001.

Fisher, R., and Ury, W. *Getting to Yes: Negotiating Agreement Without Giving In.* Boston: Houghton Mifflin, 1981.

Fletcher, M., and Vargas, J. "The White House, Open for Questions." *Washington Post,* Mar. 27, 2009, p. A2.

Foster, R. *Innovation: The Attacker's Advantage.* New York: Summit Books, 1986.

Frame, J. "Government in a Wiki World." *Government Executive,* Sept. 15, 2008, pp. 41–49.

Friedman, T. *The World Is Flat.* New York: Farrar, Straus & Giroux, 2005.

Friedman, T. *Hot, Flat, and Crowded.* New York: Farrar, Straus & Giroux, 2008.

Fukuyama, F. *Trust: The Social Virtues and the Creation of Prosperity.* New York: Free Press, 1995.

George, Y., and others. *AGEP Info Brief I: Increases in the Annual Number and Percent of New Underrepresented Minority Graduate Student Enrollees in STEM at AGEP Institutions.* http://www.nsfagep.org/infobriefs/AGEP_Info_Brief_I.pdf, Jan. 2007.

Giles, J. "Internet Encyclopedias Go Head to Head." *Nature,* Dec. 15, 2005, 438, pp. 900–901.

Gladwell, M. *Blink: The Power of Thinking Without Thinking.* New York: Little, Brown, 2005.

Goldsmith, S., and Eggers, W. *Governing by Network: The New Shape of the Public Sector.* Washington, D.C.: Brookings Institution Press, 2004.

Government Accountability Office. *Coast Guard: Observations on the Preparation, Response, and Recovery Missions Related to Hurricane Katrina.* GAO-06-903. http://www.gao.gov/new.items/d06903.pdf, 2006.

Green Suppliers Network. "Welcome to the Green Suppliers Network." http://www.greensuppliers.gov/gsn/home.gsn, 2009.

Hamel, G. "The Facebook Generation vs. the Fortune 500." Gary Hamel's Management 2.0. *Wall Street Journal.* http://blogs.wsj.com/management/2009/03/24/the-facebook-generation-vs-the-fortune-500, Mar. 24, 2009.

Havenstein, H. "LA Fire Department All 'aTwitter' over Web 2.0." *PCWorld.* http://www.pcworld.com/printable/article/id,135518/printable.html, Aug. 3, 2007.

Heifetz, R., and Linsky, M. *Leadership on the Line.* Boston: Harvard Business School Press, 2002.

Henderson, L. *The Baltimore CitiStat Program: Performance and Accountability.* Washington, DC: IBM Endowment for The Business of Government, 2003.

Hofstede, G., and Hofstede, G. J. *Cultures and Organizations: Software of the Mind.* New York: McGraw-Hill, 2005.

Jackson, J. "Intellipedia Suffers Midlife Crisis." *Government Computer News.* http://www.gcn.com/Articles/2009/02/18/Intellipedia.aspx?Page=1, Feb. 18, 2009.

Johansson, F. *The Medici Effect.* Boston: Harvard Business School Press, 2006.

Kanter, R. M. "Collaborative Advantage: The Art of Alliances." *Harvard Business Review,* July-Aug. 1994, pp. 96–108.

Kettl, D. *The Next Government of the United States: Why Our Institutions Fail Us and How to Fix Them.* New York: Norton, 2009.

Kitfield, J. "Coast Guard Official Fills Leadership Void in Katrina Relief Effort." *Government Executive.* http://www.govexec.com/story_page.cfm?filepath=/dailyfed/0905/092305nj1.htm, Sept. 23, 2005.

Kotter, J. "Developing a Change-Friendly Culture." *Leader To Leader*, Spring 2008, pp. 33–38.

Kraut, R., Egido, C., and Galegher, J. "Patterns of Contact and Communication in Scientific Research Collaboration." *Computer Supported Cooperative Work*. Conference Proceedings. New York: Association for Computing Machinery, 1988.

Leighty, B. *Linking Plans, Outcomes, and Performance: A Blueprint for Success at the Virginia Retirement System*. Richmond: Virginia Commonwealth University, Office of Public Policy Training, 2001.

Li, C., and Bernoff, J. *Groundswell: Winning in a World Transformed by Social Technologies*. Boston: Harvard Business School Press, 2008.

Linden, R. *Working Across Boundaries: Making Collaboration Work in Government and Nonprofit Organizations*. San Francisco: Jossey-Bass, 2002.

Linden, R. "The Discipline of Collaboration." *Leader To Leader*, Summer 2003, pp. 41–47.

Linden, R. *The Fine Art of Managing Relationships*. IQ Report E-Document, 2007, 39(2). Washington, D.C.: ICMA.

Lipnack, J., and Stamps, J. *The Age of the Network: Organizing Principles for the 21st Century*. Essex Junction, Vt.: Oliver Wight, 1994.

Lipnack, J., and Stamps, J. *Virtual Teams*. Hoboken, N.J.: Wiley, 1997.

Looking for the Lost Voice. Film. Distributed by Maya Films, 2005. (For more information, see Tribeca Films, http://www.tribecafilm.com/filmguide/archive/Looking_for_the_Lost_Voice.html.)

Lucy, W. *Close to Power: Setting Priorities with Elected Officials*. Chicago: American Planning Association, 1988.

Marek, A. "Always Ready for the Storm." *U.S. News and World Report*. http://www.usnews.com/usnews/news/articles/061022/30allen.htm, Oct. 22, 2006.

Markon, J. "FBI, ATF Battle for Control of Cases." *Washington Post*, May 10, 2008, pp. A1, A6.

Masse, T., O'Neil, S., and Rollins, J. *Fusion Centers: Issues and Options for Congress*. CRS Report for Congress: RL 34070. Washington, D.C.: Congressional Research Service, July 7, 2007.

McGirt, E. "How Cisco's CEO John Chambers Is Turning the Tech Giant Socialist." *Fast Company.com*, Nov. 25, 2008.

Miller, C. "How Obama's Internet Campaign Changed Politics." *New York Times*, Nov. 7, 2008.

Moynihan, D. *From Forest Fires to Hurricane Katrina: Case Studies of Incident Command Systems*. Washington, D.C.: IBM Center for The Business of Government, 2007.

"Multitasking Millennials Work Well in the Web 2.0 World." *Knowledge@W.P. Carey*. http://knowledge.wpcarey.asu.edu/article.cfm?articleid=1601#, May 7, 2008.

Mummolo, J. "Girl's Cries for Help 'Fell on Deaf Ears.'" *Washington Post*. http://www.washingtonpost.com/wp-dyn/content/story/2009/01/14/ST2009011402052.html, Mar. 9, 2009.

Naisbitt, J. *Megatrends: Ten New Directions Transforming Our Lives*. New York: Warner Books, 1982.

National Commission on Terrorist Attacks Upon the United States. *The 9/11 Commission Report: Final Report of the National Commission on Terrorist Attacks Upon the United States*. New York: Norton, 2004.

Neighbors for Joint Development in the Galilee. "Welcome." http://www.neighbors.org.il/index.php?sid=420&lang=en, 2009.

Newcomer, K. "The Certainty of Uncertainty." Address to the National Association of Schools of Public Affairs and Administration. http://www.naspaa.org/about_naspaa/about/presidential_address/Kathy_Newcomer.pdf, 2006.

Newell, T. *James Madison and "the Business of May Next."* Branchwater Leadership Resources, LLC, 2008.

Palen, L., and others. "Crisis Informatics: Studying Crisis in a Networked World." Paper presented at the Third International Conference on e-Social Science, Ann Arbor, Mich., Oct. 7–9, 2007.

Peters, K. "DHS-Supported Fusion Centers Raise Civil Liberties Concerns." *Government Executive.com*. http://www.govexec.com/story_page.cfm?articleid= 42635&dcn=e_gvet, Apr. 30, 2009.

Philadelphia Children's Alliance. "Co-Location Update: The Case for Co-Location in Cases of Child Sexual Abuse." http://www.philachildrensalliance .org/Partners/partners.htm, n.d.

Posner, R. "Time to Rethink the FBI." *Wall Street Journal*, Mar. 19, 2007, p. A13.

Putnam, R. "Bowling Alone: America's Declining Social Capital." *Journal of Democracy*, 1995, 6(1), 65–78.

Putnam, R. *Bowling Alone: The Collapse and Revival of American Community*. New York: Simon & Schuster, 2000.

Putnam, R. "The Rebirth of American Civic Life." *Boston Globe*. http://www .boston.com/bostonglobe/editorial_opinion/oped/articles/2008/03/02/the_ rebirth_of_american_civic_life, Mar. 2, 2008.

Schaper, D. "An E-Mail Vacation: Taking Fridays Off." *Morning Edition*. National Public Radio. http://www.npr.org/templates/story/story.php?storyId=91724075, June 20, 2008.

Schein, E. *Organizational Culture and Leadership*. San Francisco: Jossey-Bass, 1985.

Schorr, L. *Common Purpose: Strengthening Families and Neighborhoods to Rebuild America*. New York: Doubleday, 1997.

Schwarz, R. *The Skilled Facilitator: Practical Wisdom for Developing Effective Groups*. San Francisco: Jossey-Bass, 1994.

Seifter, H. *Leadership Ensemble: Lessons in Collaborative Management from the World's Only Conductorless Orchestra*. New York: Times Books, 2001.

Sheridan, M., and Hsu, S. "Localities Operate Intelligence Centers to Pool Terror Data." *Washington Post*, Dec. 31, 2006, pp. A3, A8.

Sherif, M., Harvey, O., and White, B. *Intergroup Conflict and Cooperation: The Robbers Cave Experiment*. Norman, Okla.: University Book Exchange, 1961.

Shrage, M. *Shared Minds: The New Technologies of Collaboration*. New York: Random House, 1990.

Singh, S. *The Code Book*. New York: Anchor Books, 1999.

Social Source. "Katrina PeopleFinder Project." http://socialsource.blogspot.com/2005/09/katrina-peoplefinder-project.html, 2005.

Stoler, M. *George C. Marshall: Soldier-Statesman of the American Century*. New York: Simon & Schuster, 1989.

Stone, D., Patton, B., and Heen, S. *Difficult Conversations: How to Discuss What Matters Most*. New York: Penguin Books, 1999.

Strauss, W., and Howe, N. *Generations: The History of America's Future, 1584–2069*. New York: Morrow, 1991.

Svara, J. *The Facilitative Leader in City Hall: Reexamining the Scope and Contributions*. Boca Raton, Fla.: CRC Press, 2008.

Tapscott, D., and Williams, A. *Wikinomics: How Mass Collaboration Changes Everything*. New York: Penguin Books, 2006.

Thomas, C. "Interagency Network of Enterprise Assistance Providers." *The Public Manager*. http://thepublicmanager.org/articles/docs/V37N1_InteragencyNetwork_Thomas.pdf, Spring 2008.

Thompson, C. "Open-Source Spying." *New York Times Magazine*, Dec. 3, 2006, pp. 54–61, 76–77, 100–104.

Tocqueville, A. de. *Democracy in America*. (R. Heffner, ed.) New York: Mentor Books, 1956. (Originally published 1835.)

Torrell, L. "Concentric Concerns: The Art of Administrative Collaboration." *CultureWork*, http://aad.uoregon.edu/culturework/culturework43.html, Jan. 2009.

Vernis, A., Kglesias, M., Sanz, B., and Saz-Carranza, A. *Nonprofit Organizations: Challenges and Collaboration*. New York: Palgrave Macmillan, 2006.

Virginia Tech Review Panel. *Mass Shootings at Virginia Tech: Report of the Virginia Tech Review Panel.* http://www.governor.virginia.gov/TempContent/techPanelReport-docs/FullReport.pdf, Apr. 16, 2007.

Vogel, S. "For Intelligence Officers, a Wiki Way to Connect Dots." *Washington Post,* Aug. 27, 2009.

Wales, J. "Wikipedia Is an Encyclopedia." http://lists.wikimedia.org/pipermail/wikipedia-l/2005-March/020469.html, Mar. 8, 2005.

Walters, J. "Christine O. Gregoire: Negotiator-in-Chief." *Governing.com.* http://governing.com/poy/2007/gregoire.htm, Nov. 2007a.

Walters, J. *Measuring Up 2.0.* Washington, D.C: Governing Books, 2007b.

Waters, D., and Lawrence, E. *Competence, Courage and Change: An Approach to Family Therapy.* New York: Norton, 1993.

Waugh, W. "Leveraging Networks to Meet National Goals: FEMA and the Safe Construction Networks." *Collaboration: Using Networks and Partnerships.* Washington, D.C.: IBM Center for The Business of Government, 2004.

Weisbord, M. *Productive Workplaces: Organizing and Managing for Dignity, Meaning, and Community.* San Francisco: Jossey-Bass, 1990.

Winer, M., and Ray, K. *Collaboration Handbook: Creating, Sustaining, and Enjoying the Journey.* Saint Paul, Minn.: Amherst H. Wilder Foundation, 1994.

"YouTube Symphony Orchestra @ Carnegie Hall—Act One (April 15, 2009)." Artforum. http://artforum.com/video/id=22549&mode=large.

Zemke, R., Raines, C., and Filipczak, B. *Generations at Work: Managing the Clash of Veterans, Boomers, Xers and Nexters in Your Workplace.* New York: AMACOM, 2000.

Zenger, J., and Folkman, J. "Ten Fatal Flaws That Derail Leaders." *Harvard Business Review.* http://hbdm.harvardbusiness.org/email/archive/dailystat.php?date=060409, June 2009.

Acknowledgments

This is one of the most significant parts of this book, because writing this work was a true act of collaboration (how else to write a book on this topic?). The cases and examples were contributed by practicing managers and leaders who have thought long and hard about collaboration's potential and pitfalls. Their insights and lessons learned are far more important than the theories that academics dream up. A large number of people read and critiqued parts or all of the manuscript. They offered everything from a better choice of words to a useful concept I hadn't considered. And they pointed out passages and sections that needed major overhauls.

So, to put it succinctly, I'm truly indebted to a number of people who showed their commitment to collaboration by contributing their collaboration examples, and by reading and improving earlier versions of this book. It is a far better product for their efforts. My great appreciation goes to Tovi Alfandari, Stu Armstrong, Bob Behn, Larisa Benson, Celeste Bernardo, Richard Bonnie, Jacki Bryant, Michael Byrne, Chris Cote, Naim Daoud, Kris Debye, Bill Delaney, Chris Demme, Frank Dukes, Harvey Eisenberg, Gretchen Ellis, Stuart Elway, Len Faulk, Otto Friesen, Amiram Goldin, Jay Gregorius, Allen Hard, Jennifer Harkness, Jack Harvey, Stewart Henderson, Bud Higgins, Lynard Ty Johnson, Roosevelt Johnson, Gail Johnstone, John Kamensky, Arlene Kaukus, John Kerwyn Keith, Katherine Knowles, Phil Kutzko, Steve Lambert, Bill

Leighty, Peter Loach, Tim Longo, Kevin Marshall, Tom Martin, Terry Newell, Lillian Ney, Eric Pugh, Chuck Rapp, Michael Rawlings, Kris Rietmann, Tammy Rubel, Myra Howze Shiplett, Chuck Short, Donna Shumate, John Springett, Rob Stalzer, Bob Stripling, Joe Szakos, Carroll Thomas, Laurie Dean Torrell, and Charles Werner.

My sincere thanks also go to Samuel Atkins, a true Renaissance man, whose fingerprints are all over this book and who has helped with everything from technology assistance to graphic design to editing.

I'm also indebted to Allison Brunner, Nina Kreiden, and Lindsay Morton at Jossey-Bass. Allison was a wonderful coach and colleague throughout, reading and commenting on the early concept and later drafts, offering candid critiques and helpful ideas without ever exceeding her role as editor (always a difficult but critical balancing act). Thanks to Lindsay for her help during the editing process, making herself available and offering sound guidance whenever needed. And I'm indebted to Nina for her guidance with a variety of editing and logistical needs, and her good humor.

A witty American author once noted that "one of the hardest things about being a writer is that you have to be willing to kill your 'darlings.'" I took him to mean that we need to fall out of love with parts of the text that don't serve the larger design, that are too wordy, or that make the same point for the fourth time. Some of the people who read this manuscript pointed out a few "darlings" that shouldn't survive. I made those cuts. Painful, but necessary and important advice. The book is better for such tough love.

Thank you all.

About the Author

Russell M. Linden is a management educator and author who specializes in organizational change methods. He teaches at the University of Virginia, Federal Executive Institute, and University of Connecticut. He writes a column on management innovations for *Management Insights*, an online column sponsored by Harvard's Kennedy School of Government and *Governing* magazine. He has written four previous books, including *Seamless Government* (Jossey-Bass, 1994) and *Working Across Boundaries* (Jossey-Bass, 2002), which was a finalist for the best book on nonprofit management in 2002 (awarded by the Alliance for Nonprofit Management). In 2003, he was the Williams Distinguished Visiting Scholar at the State University of New York (Fredonia) School of Business.

His clients have included a partnership of the U.S. Forest Service and Bureau of Land Management; numerous local and state government agencies; the National Institutes of Health; military and intelligence agencies; nonprofit agencies including the National Geographic Society, the Archdiocese of Washington, D.C., and nonprofits in Israel; the U.S. Departments of State, Treasury, Health and Human Services, Veterans Affairs, and Education; two state attorneys general; one governor; and one U.S. congressman.

His volunteer commitments include scholarship programs that help low-income youths afford college. Russ Linden's bachelor's and master's degrees are from the University of Michigan. His Ph.D. degree is from the University of Virginia. He and his wife have two adult children, and live in Charlottesville, Virginia.

Index

Page references followed by *fig* indicate an illustrated figure; followed by *t* indicate a table; followed by *e* indicate an exhibit.